Englishman
in the
Court
of the
TSAR

The Spiritual Journey
of Charles Sydney Gibbes

By Christine Benagh

Conciliar Press
Ben Lomond, California

An Englishman in the Court of -the Tsar

© Copyright 2000 by Christine Benagh

Published by   Conciliar Press / Conciliar Media Ministries
P.O. Box 76
Ben Lomond, California 95005-0076

Current paperback edition: ISBN 978-0-9822770-1-0
Previous hardcover edition: ISBN 978-1-888212-19-8

We gratefully acknowledge the following copyright holders for permission to reprint their material:

Charles Gibbes, owner of the papers and photographs of Fr. Nicholas (Charles Sydney) Gibbes

The Wernher Foundation, for the portrait of Tsarevich Alexei

The Yale University Press for use of material from *The Fall of the Romanovs: Political Dreams and Personal Struggles in a Time of Revolution*, copyright ©1995 Yale University Press

Library of Congress Cataloging-in-Publication Data

(from original paperback edition)

Benagh, Christine L.
     An Englishman in the court of the Tsar : the spiritual journey of Charles Sydney Gibbes / by Christine Benagh
          p.   cm.
     Includes bibliographical references and index.
     ISBN 1-888212-19-5
     1. Russia—History—Nicholas II, 1893–1917.   2. Gibbes, Charles Sydney, 1876–1963.   I. Title: Spiritual journey of Charles Sydney Gibbes. II. Title.

DK258.B39 2000
947.08' 3—dc21   00-035862
                                                            CIP

Contents

Photo Section *(located following page 152)*:

1. Grand Duchesses Tatiana and Olga.
2. Grand Duchesses Anastasia and Marie.
3. The Empress reading on the balcony at Tsarskoe Selo.
4. Alexei with his three tutors, Pierre Gilliard, P.V. Petrov, and Charles Sydney Gibbes.
5. A portrait of Tsarevich Alexei, by an unknown artist.
   (Courtesy Wernher Collection, Luton Hoo)
6. Alexei out for a drive with his tutor, Charles Sydney Gibbes.
7. The Empress, Olga, and Tatiana as Sisters of Mercy.
8. Charles Sydney Gibbes giving a lesson to Anastasia.
9. The imperial classroom at Tsarskoe Selo.
10. Marie and Anastasia in amateur dramatics (1912).
11. Guards at the gate of the palace. For a time, Charles Sydney Gibbes was not allowed to enter.
12. Tsar Nicholas and Pierre Gilliard sawing wood at the compound of the Governor's House, Tobolsk (1917).
13. Tsar Nicholas riding a bicycle during his time of captivity in Tobolsk (1917).
14. A revolutionary procession outside the Governor's House, where the Imperial Family was being held in Tobolsk.
15. Alexei and Olga on board the *Rus* at the beginning of their last journey.
16. The Ipatiev house in Ekaterinburg, where the Imperial Family was confined and murdered.
17 and 18. Investigation underway at the Four Brothers mine, where some human remains of the Imperial Family were found.
19. Box containing the human remains of the Imperial Family found at the Four Brothers mine area. (This box was in Charles Gibbes's charge for a time.)
20. St. Nicholas House, 4 Marston Street, Oxford; George Gibbes in doorway.
21. Chapel at St. Nicholas House, containing some of the treasures of the Imperial Family Charles Sydney Gibbes had collected.
22. Charles Sydney Gibbes in 1925.
23. Charles Sydney Gibbes, soon after his ordination to the priesthood (as Fr. Nicholas) in 1935.
24. Archimandrite Nicholas Gibbes with Archbishop Nestor in 1938.

Dedicated to the memory of my dear,
courageous mother,
Elva Fletcher Langseth

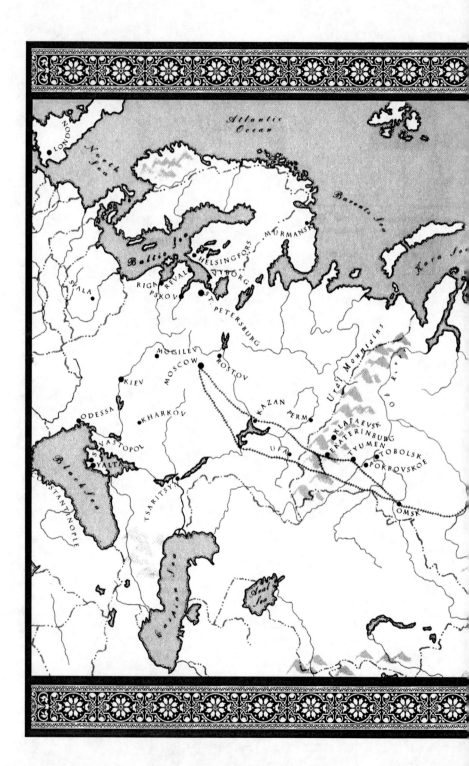

Acknowledgments

Nothing is accomplished alone, and I delight in recalling with love and gratitude the people and influences that shaped and encouraged this work. A little over a decade ago John Stoll Sanders first pricked my interest in the Russian Imperial Family, and as I delved into their story, I was intrigued by the career of Charles Sydney Gibbes, an Englishman who, after ten years as a tutor to the Tsar's household and his subsequent experiences in the Far East, adopted the Orthodox faith and became a priest in that ancient and venerable church. I decided to tell his story.

Once my family and friends knew of my interest, they lent wholehearted support to the effort. From the beginning Felicity (Peggy) Allen, whose wisdom, inspiration, and affection have been a light since our college days, assisted with pertinent articles, news clippings, and her own advice as I plodded along. My late husband, Henry Collier, always smoothed out my travel plans and patiently endured the inconvenience of my absences and preoccupation. Henry Jr. and his wife, Bernadette, provided headquarters at their homes in London and later in Miltown Malbay, Ireland, from which I ventured out to Oxford and Finmere to gather information. On the home front, daughter Mary and her husband Brian O'Neil kept the hearth warm and our pets—a dog and two cats—happy during our absence, and assisted in countless other ways. From Boston and Washington, D.C., daughters Barbara and Christine offered comments and tidbits of helpful information as I worked along. My sister, Elva, and her husband, Walton Corbitt, have offered steady shoulders on which to lean, as did my late brother Marcus and his wife, Lillian, who still helps her knowledge of Russian. Father Mark Arey spurred me with his genuine interest and enthusiasm when the project

3

was still incubating. George and Lee Ann Anderson read portions of the manuscript and made many helpful suggestions.

From 1985 until 1991, I paid almost yearly visits to George Gibbes at St. Nicholas House in Oxford, where he provided many interesting insights as we discussed the possibility of my doing a book on his adoptive father. Charles Gibbes, the adoptive grandson of Father Nicholas, received me at his charming thatched cottage in Finmere in the winter of 1997 and provided still more anecdotes into the family history. I am deeply indebted to him for permission to use material that is the backbone of this book: quotations from Fr. Nicholas's papers and many of his photographs.

Faraway assistance has come from unexpectedly helpful friends, some of whom I have never met, but who have supplied invaluable help with personal recollections and information: Bishop Kallistos of Diokleia, who graciously read the first proof and offered invaluable comment and suggestions; Nicholas Chapman of the Orthodox Christian Book Service; John Harwood, librarian/lecturer at The Missionary Institute of London; Ambassador David Beattie, also in London; Protodeacon Christopher Birchall, editor of *Canadian Orthodox Herald* in Vancouver, British Columbia; the Very Rev. Archimandrite David of the Skete Monastery of St. Seraphim of Sarov; the Rev. Edward Barnes, principal of St. Stephen's House in Oxford; and Doreen Gibbs, a cousin in Hampshire who had a store of interesting stories to share.

To all these and to any I may have overlooked due to a faulty memory, I acknowledge a debt I can repay only with my thanks.

Christine Benagh
Lent, 2000

Preface

An enormous divide seems to open up between the nineteenth century and our own day, and we are still surrounded by the visible evidence of how wide and how deep it is, of how different our lives seem to be from all that went before. We now dwell in a different world. To all appearances, Western man has undergone a sudden and dramatic transformation—social, economic, political, and spiritual. Centuries-old monarchies were consigned unceremoniously to the dustbin, and the scramble began to arrange governments in which "the people" would play the major part. Off came the constricting clothing, and with it the distinctions within the social structure for which it had provided the costumes. The arts burst the bonds of classical forms and restrictions and dashed into wild and ever more daring paths, each attracting its own set of initiates.

The revolution extended to faith and theology as well, for though the Christian vocabulary was retained, the concern for God was replaced by concern for humanity, its nature and welfare. All this realignment was reinforced by the alluring prospects for economic independence promised by growing industrialization. This new prosperity was expected to replace the ruptured traditional social bonds and loyalties with material well-being for the newly autonomous individual.

This great divide between our century and the nineteenth fascinated historian Barbara Tuchman, who set out "to discover the quality of the world from which the Great War came," for it was the war that ended the old world. She describes it as "the proud tower" from which "death looks gigantically down" on the doomed decades (1890–1914). Among the personalities whose careers she examined for signs and portents of the impending catastrophe, she looked for "some ordinary everyday shopkeeper or clerk representing the mute inglorious anonymous middle class" but did not find him.[1]

There was such a man, an Englishman, Charles Sydney Gibbes. Though far from ordinary, he was a clerk in the traditional sense and certainly of the middle class, and he might have remained anonymous but for the astonishing twists of fortune in his career—a career fraught with many of the very doubts and disillusionments, tensions and torments that frayed the social fabric of his era.

However, his experiences took him beyond the boundaries of the Anglo-American and West European tradition, the limits which Tuchman had set for herself. It was Gibbes's fate to find his life deeply entwined with that of the last Russian Tsar and his family. As tutor to the imperial children, Gibbes shared some of the happy times of their halcyon days, but even more intimately the hardships and sufferings of their final journey into captivity and death. Then, cast adrift in the vastness of Siberia after the seesawing battle between the White and Red forces was settled with the Bolsheviks triumphant, Gibbes made his way to Harbin,

---

[1] Barbara W. Tuchman, *The Proud Tower.* (New York: The Macmillan Company, 1966; Bantam edn., 1967), p. xvii.

Manchuria—a refuge for many tsarist sympathizers. With characteristic resourcefulness, Gibbes managed to make a new career for himself in that unlikely place.

During those years, 1901—1928, when he was in constant contact with the culture and institutions of Eastern Europe, so poorly regarded in the West, Gibbes learned a great deal, and at enormous personal cost. He then devoted the latter part of his eighty-seven years in a unique and unprecedented tribute to the devoutly Orthodox Imperial Family. He became a priest in their holy and venerable Church, and returned at last to England as Fr. Nicholas Gibbes to share with his own countrymen the wisdom gained in his pilgrimage. His story is told in this book.

❦ ❦

Fortunately, Charles Sydney Gibbes was a meticulous preserver of things, and throughout most of his long life he saved with care letters, journal and diary entries, playbills, lesson plans, photographs, receipts and accounts, and significant souvenirs that provide a record of the activities and developments in his unique career. These papers provide the factual foundation on which much of this story is built.

It comes as a surprise to find how few of these papers are reflective in nature. Despite his thorough education at St. John's, Cambridge, and a lifelong taste for the finest in literature and the arts, Gibbes was always more a man of action than of words. Unlike most other members of the imperial household who survived the Revolution, he never wrote an account of his experiences, though he had many lucrative offers that must have been tempting in times of economic difficulty. Even with his great treasure of memories, photographs, and records, he wrote nothing. This brings us to the most striking feature of Gibbes's character: his disposition to take decisive, courageous, even dangerous, action when faced with a challenge. This complicates the work of a biographer, for he never tried to explain or justify his decisions; he just acted and let the deeds speak for themselves. In consequence, I have had to weigh the evidence he did leave in light of the steps he took, in order to supply the rationale for his intriguing career.

There are many, many sources covering the history of Russia during the reign of Nicholas II, its fate in the Great War, the fall of the monarchy, the Revolution, and the ruin that followed; and a selection of these has been consulted to provide perspective and understanding of those tumultuous times. However, this book is not intended to be a history of those events, but rather the story of a man who lived through them. Still, the gravity and continuing consequences of that tragedy have made it a constant struggle to maintain focus on an interesting but minor character, to provide enough background without letting Gibbes be engulfed by the tides that swirled around him.

In recent years, the prevailing tone of criticism of the last Tsar and Tsaritsa has softened in the face of developments subsequent to the Revolution—the horrors and collapse of the great communist experiment. While trying to be truthful and objective, I have taken advantage of this new sympathy in many instances because it was the attitude of Charles Sydney Gibbes.

For some years George Gibbes, Charles's adopted son, kept the papers and other mementos at St. Nicholas House in Oxford, an Orthodox chapel established by Fr. Nicholas Gibbes in memory of Tsar Nicholas. From 1987 through 1991, I had frequent correspondence with George and paid almost yearly visits to talk with him about Fr. Nicholas and his life. In 1989 most of the papers and other valuable items most directly relating to the Imperial Family were sold, some to the Wernher Collection at Luton Hoo and some to the general public through the famous auction houses, Sotheby's and Christie's. Copies of many of the papers are now deposited in the Bodleian Library (shelfmarked MSS Facs. C.100–7 and e.51), where I went carefully through them, and most of the comments and observations attributed to Charles Sydney Gibbes, his family members and colleagues are from these papers. Direct quotations from these sources are given without footnote citation.

In 1997 the Foundation vacated its lease at Luton Hoo, and at present the collection is stored in London, where arrangements are being made for its display.

1

Beginning at the End of an Era

When Charles Sydney Gibbes stepped out through the doors of St. John's College, Cambridge, he immediately found himself standing on another threshold. The year was 1899, and the new twentieth century loomed just ahead. The nineteenth century had experienced perhaps more rapid and life-altering changes than any previous century in history. The astonishing discoveries of the scientists, the rapid industrialization of the cities, the increased speed of transportation and communication, the empowerment of the middle class, all offered great promise. Already the air was charged with anticipation, but there was also apprehension, a nervous expectation that momentous—even catastrophic—things were about to happen.

Charles Sydney, known within his family as Syd, was born January 19, 1876, at Bank House, High Street, Rotheram—a sizable town on the river Don, situated almost in the center of England. Though quite early he lost all trace of the distinctive Yorkshire accent, he took pride for the rest of his life in being a

Yorkshireman, with all the name implies of rugged endurance and self-reliance.

Syd was the ninth child of John and Mary Ann Elizabeth Fisher Gibbs, and the youngest of the four surviving sons. There were two sisters. The older, Nettie, had married the Rev. Gwyn Llewellyn Davies of Aberystwyth and was no longer at home. The second sister, Winifred Adeline, was younger than Syd, and these two would remain the best of chums for the rest of their lives, even after she too married a clergyman.

Their father was the respected manager of the Rotherham branch of the Sheffield and Rotherham Bank, and the older sons had followed him into banking—John, the eldest, in Argentina, Arthur in India, and Percy in Gloucester. So they might well have become known as John Gibbs and Sons, Bankers, but for Syd.

By temperament studious and introspective, displaying strong religious sensibilities, Syd seemed much more suited for the church than for banking, and was fortunate indeed to have a father who was sympathetic and offered every encouragement to this exception from the pattern. Since the family was comfortably affluent, John Gibbs saw to it that Syd received a thorough education, with early schooling in Broadstairs and Hornsea, followed by two terms at University College Aberystwyth in Wales. Syd was attracted there by the fascinating stories told by his older sister about that wonderful college by the sea. He was a quick, diligent student, and the records show that his tutors invariably noted these qualities as well as his "high character, good sense, and agreeable manners."

From Aberystwyth Syd proceeded to St. John's College,

Cambridge, and was admitted to the degree of Bachelor of Arts in 1899, having achieved honors on his examination in the Moral Sciences Tripos. This was a comprehensive testing in those branches of philosophy considered necessary to fit a nineteenth-century Englishman for public life either in government or in the church. During his Cambridge years, Syd began to spell the family name "Gibbes," concluding on the basis of some information he had happened upon that the added "e" was more historically accurate, and we will follow his preference.

His early student years had been tranquil and happy, the arduous periods of study punctuated by holidays at home in Rotherham or in the more relaxed setting of the family's country house at Normanton-upon-Trent. In either place, he and Winifred always enjoyed each other's company and found plenty to amuse them. They loved to go shopping together and specialized in browsing through curio shops. They read to each other, and they also dabbled in photography about which Syd was particularly keen.

The Gibbeses were a quietly pious Anglican family—two sisters married clergymen, and Syd's father's fondest hopes were for him to make the church his life. In going up to university in 1895, Sydney Gibbes had gone from this tranquil setting into an atmosphere unsettled and unsettling. For the serious student, higher education is almost always an eye-opening, mind-expanding experience, but Gibbes was fated to arrive in Cambridge at a time when the currents of philosophical and scientific thought rushing into the intellectual brew there had produced a heady atmosphere.

For more than half the century, conflict between science and religion had engaged the attention of the English reading public as thoughtful churchmen, journalists, scientists, and scholars filled newspapers, periodicals, and books with their deeply serious, and often heated, debates on grave new issues. These new ideas seemed, on the one hand, to threaten the very foundations of the Christian faith and of civilization itself; but on the other, they seemed to offer a brave, new, and almost limitless world of which a liberated mankind could take control. The vigor and confidence of the scientists and their supporters had put the churchmen and social conservatives decidedly on the defensive. This brought about deep confusion and unease in Victorian Christianity, a gnawing fear that some vital and valuable element of life was threatened combined with a tentative but stubborn hope that the promises of a bright new age just might prove true and sufficient.

More has been written about the impact of the industrial revolution, the rise of the middle class, and the scientific advances of the period than about the collision of these forces with religious faith and the erosion of belief that ensued. That impact, however, is crucial, for it made possible the total secularization of society, providing an atmosphere in which unbelief became, not only a respectable option, but in the eyes of many then and now, a mark of intellectual superiority.[1] Society in general was left without a compass by which to focus its efforts, whether spiritual, social,

---

[1] In *Without God, Without Creed: The Origins of Unbelief in America* (Baltimore & London: Johns Hopkins University Press, 1985), James Turner, using detailed documentary evidence, has traced with clarity and balance the development of unbelief in America, and his conclusions are applicable to the same phenomenon in England, which had begun earlier. That history is told in some detail by Bernard M. Reardon, *Religious Thought in the Victorian Age: A Survey from Coleridge to Gore* (London & New York: Longman, 1971, 1980, 1995). I have relied heavily on both these books.

political, economic, or domestic—a bewilderment with which we still struggle.

These tensions were naturally concentrated to a high degree in the universities, with Cambridge running an especially high fever. It is interesting to note that before 1850 physical science was called natural philosophy, because until then it had shared the same metaphysical concerns as all philosophy. Cambridge took special pride in the scientists it had nurtured—Newton, Sedgwick, and Darwin among them—and their enthusiasm for the concept of empirical, verifiable data as the only basis for true knowledge can be seen in the subsequent designation of all branches of philosophy as "moral sciences."

Gibbes entered St. John's with his Christian belief intact, and he was not immediately undone because his roots in the faith were strong. He was, however, constantly exposed to what Bernard Reardon calls "dissolvent literature," and this reading, perhaps unconsciously, began to chip away at the foundations on which his faith and aspirations had been built. As he prepared for his Moral Science Tripos, his attention was focused on political economy, ethics, and psychology. An entire third of this three-part exam was devoted to the relatively new study of psychology. This field had been slow to gain recognition because mental processes could not be measured and weighed in the same way as the material of other scientific investigations. However, it gradually won respectability, and even prominence, as it generated wide discussion and speculation about the nature of the mind. One central problem was whether the mind of man—which most scientists of the time viewed as the product of purely natural development: evolution, objective experience, social conditioning, and the like—could know anything about the being of God, who is outside nature.

Most of the books being read by serious students were skeptical. Herbert Spencer's *Principles of Psychology* (1855) treated mind as the end product of an animal nervous system. Lester Ward conjectured in his *Dynamic Sociology* (1883) that the nucleus of the highest nervous system is contained in the lump of protoplasm. G. Henry Lewes argued in *The Physical Basis of the Mind* (1877) that mental processes were only another aspect of physical processes, while the "soul" was the subjective experience of objective bodily phenomena. William Carpenter stated the hard question in his *Principles of Mental Physiology* (1874): "How can a solely physical mind achieve knowledge of the extraphysical?" Darwin, whose reputation was by this time tremendous, put it even more pointedly in his *Autobiography*: "Can the mind of a man, which has, as I fully believe, been developed from a mind as low as that possessed by the lowest animal, be trusted when it draws such grand conclusions [about God and supernatural phenomena]?" [2]

These blows, aimed at what had up until then been considered a settled, though admittedly limited, conception of God, took their toll. The arguments sounded so reasonable, and few stopped to consider that Darwin and his colleagues were themselves drawing some pretty lofty conclusions about the nature of things with minds developed from the same lowly origins. But the haunting question remained: Can we know anything at all about God? Have all past perceptions been wishful fancies? The two psychological topics, "The Formation of Belief" and "The

---

[2] Quoted in Turner, *Without God*, p. 178.

Psychology of the Reasoning Process," on which Gibbes was to write formal essays as part of his Moral Sciences examination, indicate that he had received a heavy dose of the deleterious influences we have been considering.[3]

But worse was still to come. Gibbes proceeded from St. John's to the theological courses at Cambridge and Salisbury. Within the seminary setting, confusion and uncertainty had given way to near panic, a situation that the theologians had unwittingly done much to bring on themselves. Once empirical science had become the dominant spirit of the day, they were unwilling to let God remain incomprehensible in divine mystery and confidently led Him into the laboratory for rational analysis. However, their valiant attempts to bring God up to date and delineate His role in nature—after all, the design of the natural world presupposed a Designer—received a nasty knock as Darwin and company proceeded to demonstrate in embarrassing detail that the design or pattern of nature was cruel, wasteful, and without compassion. In addition, the religious authorities themselves had pretty thoroughly humanized God as they struggled to make Him relevant and keep pace with this era of social and intellectual progress. He was now expected to behave toward the world in an understandable and sympathetic manner, like a high-minded Victorian gentleman. But He didn't. The Designer of nature as presented by the scientists was either not good or not God.

To make matters worse still, the ultimate religious authority, the Holy Scriptures, had been brought into question by the

----

[3] Turner, *Without God*, pp. 177-78. Information on the Moral Sciences Tripos on which Gibbes's B.A. was based was provided by the courtesy of Dr. Elizabeth S. Leedham-Green, Deputy Keeper of Manuscripts, Cambridge University Library.

onslaught of historical and textual criticism that had begun in Germany but was now thriving in England. Here also, the theologians were not blameless. Since the Reformation, tradition had been jettisoned and everything staked on the absolute integrity and sufficiency of the letter of the Holy Word as written. Now, however, serious doubt was cast on this bedrock by geologists and archaeologists who demonstrated the implausibility of the chronology in the Bible as it had been interpreted. Just as damaging, historical criticism of the biblical text itself was undermining confidence in the authenticity of the scriptural authors and consequently in their veracity.

But the real problem was much deeper and largely undetected. In the West, as James Turner points out, there no longer existed "a vocabulary in which to argue for some kind of 'poetic' cognition of reality."[4] There was nothing comparable to the apophatic hymnic theology of the Eastern Church, which glories in singing of God as incomprehensible, ineffable, inconceivable, which celebrates without trying to explain.

A few terms of study in such an atmosphere sent shock waves through Gibbes's religious consciousness, and his reaction was allergic. He could not, would not, find his vocation in this stifling air from which it seemed to him all spirituality had been expelled. He decided to bolt rather than face the possibility of spiritual collapse.

He was not alone in his distress; many of his countrymen were suffering similar agonies as their faith crumbled. An especially poignant example is G. F. Romanes, who had been a devout evangelical until he became convinced that Darwin had

---

[4] Turner, *Without God*, p. 197.

disproved Christianity. But even in the face of this reverse conversion, he confessed that "with the virtual negation of the divine the universe for him had 'lost its soul of loveliness. When at times I think, as think at times I must, of the appalling contrast between the hallowed glory of that creed which once was mine, and the lonely mystery of existence as now I find it—at such times I shall ever feel it impossible to avoid the sharpest pang of which my nature is susceptible.'" [5]

Gibbes's feeling of desolation was equally painful, and it convinced him that this was not the profession in which his spirit could live and thrive. His distaste for academic theology remained with him to the end of his life and was something he never hesitated to declare.

But man's spirit abhors a vacuum. As belief in Christianity weakened, exotic varieties of spiritualism flourished everywhere. Gibbes dabbled in some of these while trying to shore up what remained of his spiritual resources. He began to keep a book recording and examining his dreams and took a great interest in the occult. He visited clairvoyants and even investigated the popular spiritualism movement with its table-tipping and séances, all miserably shallow attempts to demonstrate "scientifically" that there actually were extranatural existences that adepts could communicate with and summon at will so as to put others in contact. Even such intellectual lights as Elizabeth Barrett Browning and William Butler Yeats were attracted to these possibilities. The ridicule heaped on the followers each time one of the popular mediums was exposed as a charlatan only added to the malaise.

---

[5] Romanes's *A Candid Examination of Theism,* as quoted by Reardon, *Religious Thought,* p. 219.

Syd's decision to withdraw from his course of study was a bitter one, for his revolt, while certainly not against his family, was obviously against the church, and he was acutely aware of the hurt and disappointment this would bring, particularly to his father. To his surprise and relief, his family continued to offer loving understanding, but this did little to lessen his pain during the following months as he searched in vain for some suitable employment. All the years of study contributed nothing to his qualifications for a secular profession, and he often said that he had become "a drug on the market."

His uncle Will Fisher, prominent as editor of the *Sheffield Daily Chronicle,* wrote on Syd's behalf to the Rev. William Chawner, Vice-Chancellor, Cambridge University, in December of 1900, asking the Syndics to consider his "well read, studious, industrious, and entirely trustworthy" nephew for a place at the university press.

> Mr. Gibbs, as I happen to know, has since his undergraduate days taken great interest in literary and art matters, particularly recent developments in book publication, and as his temperament is essentially artistic, I feel convinced that he could safely be relied upon in all matters in which judgment and taste are required.

This earnest recommendation brought no results, and there were other efforts from family members to obtain consideration for various posts, but all to no avail.

As he searched through the newspapers vainly seeking job prospects, Gibbes must have been pleasantly diverted by the lively reviews of the arts then flourishing in St. Petersburg, Russia, in what was its silver age. There were plays, ballets, operas, art exhibitions, all things he had a deep interest in. There were also numerous attractive ads seeking English tutors willing to come to Russia. Now that was something he could do: he had a talent for language, though as yet he knew no Russian. The pay was good, often as much as £150 per annum, plus expenses for travel, board, and lodging. It did not take long for him to make his next critical decision to give Russia a try.

This was another disappointing blow to the doting family, who were expecting greater things of their star. Most of them considered such a move frivolous and a waste of talent, yet they remained affectionate and supportive. A former tutor at St. John's was more blunt: "You'll just be a governess."

Syd's own disillusionment and the disappointment of his family may have obscured from all of them the moral strength that lay behind his decision. It took courage and determination to strike out like a pioneer into unknown territory, instead of hanging on as one more limp, dispirited clergyman fearful of the economic consequences of acknowledging the doubt that had struck him and undermined his effectiveness.

Despite the criticism, in the spring of 1901 Gibbes sailed for the romantic capital of that remote and strange land, one considered by most Englishmen (when they thought about it at all) to be benighted, icebound, and locked in the past by its naive, superstitious religion and archaic system of government. But Russia is the set for the next stage of Gibbes's unique pilgrimage.

2

St. Petersburg, a Magical City

As he stepped out onto the quay in St. Petersburg, Charles Sydney Gibbes presented an appearance impressive enough to stand out in the throng of private tutors lured, like himself, to this great city. He was tall and slim with a straight, confident carriage, impeccably tailored and groomed. His nose was too prominent for him to be considered actually handsome, but beneath the medium brown hair, his exceptionally clear, smooth face was lit by intelligent eyes set under a high forehead.

Syd's decision to come to St. Petersburg may not have been entirely a happy one, but his first view of the city, now freed from its winter shackles as the thick sheet of ice on the Neva River began to break up, may have encouraged him somewhat. St. Petersburg was new in comparison with most important European cities, and it stood as a bright and glistening tribute to the steely will of one man, Peter the Great, who in the eighteenth century had defied the river to build his premier city in this particular spot. But the city was built at a terrible human cost: the buildings—their façades now shining blue and white, yellow and white, red and yellow, many with golden spires and cupolas—stood also as monuments to the sacrifice of tens of thousands of workmen who went to their death dragging logs and stones and earth to fill the treacherous marshes. Inch by costly inch they built the platform on which Peter could stage his grand production, a city many said was "built on bones."

But this was a city Gibbes was prepared to relish. He loved drama and there was plenty to see and savor, especially along Theatre Street. He was also interested in dance, and the ballet was reaching its pinnacle in Russia at the time. These and other arts as well were subsidized by the Emperor himself from his private purse. In fact, Gibbes may even have had an early glimpse of him and other members of the Imperial Family, for they often attended the theaters.

Gibbes had always been an enthusiastic though careful shopper, and along the broad avenues and in the parks and courtyards of this bustling, cosmopolitan city there were shops, bazaars, even a flea market in which he could browse. The *Angliiskii Magazin* (the English department store) must have been a special delight, for that wonderful store was located in the most fashionable part of town and on the most important thoroughfare, Nevsky Prospekt. An Englishman had established it in the eighteenth century, and though it now had Russian proprietors, it still stocked things that Gibbes would have considered indispensable: English soaps, hose, gloves. It probably even smelled English. Nevertheless, over the years he continued to order his shirts and collars from home, engaging Winnie as his personal shopper. "I have the collars," she wrote in one of her letters, "and I hope to get over to Sheffield soon to find the shirts."

St. Petersburg was a pleasure just to walk through with its wide streets, carefully planned parks, the beautiful buildings that had much more color than those in the rest of Europe—colors that glowed against the snow in winter and highlighted the green groves of summer. All of these were ranged along the wide Neva or beside the many canals and smaller tributaries of that great river. Acting on the instincts that so far had served him well, Gibbes took residence at No. 88 on the important Nevsky Prospekt in one of the many surprisingly comfortable and well-equipped apartments available there, thus establishing himself near the throbbing center of the city's bustling life.

> Even in the early nineteenth century these large apart-ments incorporated many modern ideas—an open plan, central heating, smokeless fires, a combination sitting room-bedroom, hanging plants and a separate entrance hall. Rents included water, light in the hall and on the streets, and the fuel for heating and cooking. Water was brought in great vats and there were always wooden steam baths in the courtyards; to wallow in one's own dirty bath water, as Europeans did, seemed unspeakably unclean to Russians. [1]

Such features were especially attractive to someone with Gibbes's exceedingly fastidious nature.

Gibbes had been engaged by the Soukanoff family, wealthy

---

[1] Suzanne Massie, *The Land of the Firebird* (New York: Simon & Schuster, 1980), pp. 251-52.

landowners who had paid his transport and were now providing
salary and an ample housing allowance for him to tutor their son
and teach him English. Private tutoring in Russia at this time
was nothing like that in England. Far from being "just a governess," Gibbes found himself engaged in a highly respected,
well-paid profession, one that offered many opportunities for
advancement. There was so much enthusiasm for private instruction that the imperial government in 1834 had provided special
status for tutors and teachers, including an official rank and badge
of office and generous pension provisions.

The first year went smoothly enough, and Gibbes tutored
himself intensely in Russian while teaching his pupil English.
When the time came for his paid leave the following summer, he
took young Soukanoff along to England, where his education
was enriched by actual experience of life in that country, contact
with the Gibbes family, and an exceptional opportunity to practice English conversation. After enjoying the moderate English
summer, tutor and pupil returned to Russia in September laden
with presents for all.

After what had seemed a satisfactory year, Gibbes was surprised and disappointed, and perhaps somewhat alarmed, when
the Soukanoffs did not reappoint him, particularly as he was now
all but locked in by the winter that comes so early in those parts.
Letters kept coming from England expressing the concern of
the whole family for his welfare. They were still looking and
hoping for an employment opportunity that would bring him
home again. One of Uncle Will's letters enclosed a light-hearted
cartoon clipped by Winnie and an advertisement for employment, along with the information that his uncle had already

contacted the prospective employer, who would like to hear from
Syd himself.

Gibbes continued to receive encouragement from sympathetic
friends. He had written to one acquaintance describing his latest
disappointment and commenting that the Soukanoffs were "not
very nice people" and "the boy was very slow." "Don't despond,"
replied the friend, "be sure all is for the best & remember *our*
disappointments are God's appointments." This letter is among
those saved from his earliest days in Russia, so Gibbes may have
come later to appreciate its prophetic truth.

Despite this setback, the year just past had not been wasted.
It had provided the opportunity for him to learn the Russian
language; he had begun giving private English lessons to other
interested pupils in the city and had also accepted a number of
occasional tutoring assignments. As long as these lessons held
out, he was confident he could hang on, at least until the following summer, when something better might yet turn up on his
return to England. The lessons did keep coming, for everything English was much in vogue just then in the capital, and
many students and their parents were eager to have such a well-
qualified Englishman as teacher.

With his easy and natural sociability enhanced by genteel,
cultivated manners, Syd acquired a number of personal friends in
the sizable English colony that had established itself in the Russian capital. He joined in the active social life of the enclave and
soon found himself receiving invitations to "come for the evening,"
where there would be an informal supper, discussion of news from
home and in St. Petersburg, and impromptu entertainment with
music or readings furnished by the guests.

By 1903 Gibbes had come to love this city with its rich and
bustling life, its crisp, sparkling winter so different from the soggy,
slushy ones of England. The pageantry of the winter celebrations
and amusements the hardy Russians had devised to make the
most of this harsh, challenging season intrigued him. After the
first deep frost the entire population began to appear wrapped
in furs, and the life of the city shifted into winter mode. The
sledge drivers dashed through the streets in their special dress;
the vendors of tea and sweets wrapped their boiling samovars in
skins; elaborate ice slides appeared in the parks and squares and
were enjoyed by young and old alike. Fantastic villages were con-
structed on the frozen river to accommodate the winter bazaars
and carnival entertainments. Every player on this frosty stage, it
seemed, had a part to play and a costume to wear. This quality so
impressed Gibbes that he often remarked on the innate theatrical sense in the Russian people, an instinct "so deeply engrained
in the Russian nature that one often feels that Russians act their
lives rather than live them."

He took notice of the same dramatic quality in their worship,
though he viewed it with the cool detachment of one whose own
faith was in a state of suspension. Russia had remained staunchly
Christian long after most other countries in Europe had come to
regard religious faith as a secondary factor at best in public and
political life. But to be in Russia was to be caught up by the measured rhythm in which the Orthodox faithful reenacted, relived,
in vivid detail the events in the life of Christ. These events were
celebrated through the year by their Church with great beauty—
liturgical splendor in language, music, iconography, vestments,
gestures. And this actively lived devotion spilled over into every

facet of life. The entire population, rich and poor, peasant and aristocrat, were drawn together into the rhythm of the feasts and fasts.

By now Gibbes had confidence enough in his business prospects to make a decisive move and ship the bulk of his belongings to St. Petersburg. His professional reputation was firmly established when he received the impressive appointment to a teaching post in the Imperial School of Law, a special preparatory school for sons of the hereditary nobility—one of the two institutions sponsored by the Tsar and designed to train young men for government service. Gibbes made a name for himself there by departing from the usual practice of encouraging the pupils to inform on one another. This practice was quite offensive to his English schoolboy's code of honor. Gibbes not only turned a deaf ear to the pupils' tales, he reprimanded the informers.

He had also become very much involved in the St. Petersburg Guild of English Teachers. This was an officially authorized association designed to aid teachers in organizing reading circles for professional improvement, keeping in touch with new educational movements, presenting papers and lectures dealing with educational matters, establishing a library of appropriate resources, and also by offering occasional social entertainments for mutual enjoyment. The guild's prestige was sufficient to attract such patrons as Sir Arthur Nicolson, His Britannic Majesty's Ambassador, and the Honorable John W. Riddle, United States Ambassador.

Gibbes served several terms as a member of various committees, then went on to become secretary and later vice president of the organization. The entertainments sponsored by the guild often included plays of a light nature, ones that could be produced with minimal preparation and setting. The rehearsals and stage management were great fun, and everyone took part either as a character in the play or as a stagehand. Syd appeared in several, billed as C. S. Gibbes, B.A. Cantab. He also directed several productions, winning accolades for his work.

Though he had been a student of political economy at Cambridge, Gibbes had never been deeply engrossed in politics; neither were his close friends, nor his students and their parents. The English colony in St. Petersburg was insulated by its provincial attitude that measured everything by British standards—their monarchy, their parliament, their church, their industries, their institutions of learning, were the criteria. Gibbes walked out every morning to purchase not only the Russian newspapers, but also those from England on sale along the Prospekt; he was, of course, aware of the political and social tensions erupting, often violently, in St. Petersburg. But he and his English circle of friends viewed these as the spasmodic symptoms of a primitive and clumsy system suffering the growing pains attendant on bringing itself into the enlightened twentieth century.

Still, it may have come as something of a surprise to Gibbes to have his sedate routine disturbed one memorable Sunday in January, 1905—a day known afterwards as Bloody Sunday—when turmoil exploded into what was actually a warning tremor of the coming cataclysm. The event was headlined in gory detail by the Western press as the brutal suppression of a workers' protest by an obsolete, cruel, and oppressive régime. Actually, the situation was considerably more complicated.

Tsar Nicholas II and the autocratic system itself were already under heavy pressure: from without, by the rising tide throughout Europe of sympathy for government representative of the people; and from within Russia, by the students, educated élite, and radical activists who had embraced these intoxicating ideas. As often happens, it was the students who were first indoctrinated and then activated to become the leaders in rebellion—not because of their own political vision, but because in their youthful impatience and aspiration, they were easily incited to violent acts by the fiery rhetoric of an aggressive and radical socialist minority dedicated to total destruction of the autocracy.

The politicization of the universities had begun barely six years earlier, as the result of an incident that in itself should have had only minor political implications. When Alexander II was assassinated in 1881, the nation was shocked. He had been the Tsar Liberator, the man who freed the serfs, and yet he was killed by the very people who should have been pleased with his policies. In response, the government of Alexander III instituted stringent security measures in its efforts to combat the increasing number of terrorist assaults. Tight restrictions were placed on public demonstrations and political gatherings.

In this tense climate, students at the University of St. Petersburg were forbidden to hold their annual Founders' Day celebration in February of 1899. They protested rowdily, and many were arrested. However, after a few days the authorities were convinced that the students were no threat, and they began to go back to their classes.

The ever-vigilant socialists—who, we should note, received considerable monetary and ideological support from abroad, especially from Germany—saw an opportunity and seized it. They organized small committees to infiltrate student groups, fan their grievances, and direct them onto a new level. They hammered home the message that reforms should not be confined to liberalizing university regulations, but had to be expanded to include the entire system of government. Elimination of the autocracy was the revolutionaries' aim; they wormed in to set up a kind of "boot camp" in the universities, training students for combat in the coming struggle, in which they expected to change the entire world for the better.

Nicholas II and his Council of Ministers were acutely aware of the revolutionary threat, and plans were in place for trying to cope with the unrest of students and industrial workers in the city, though the current situation seemed to require no more than police monitoring. However, before being blown to bits by the revolutionaries in 1904, Vyacheslav Plehve, the Minister of Internal Affairs, had organized a network of state-sponsored labor unions to provide educational and recreational activities for workers in the cities, designed to counter and defuse the aggressively hostile forces agitating among them. The revolutionary activists had early inserted themselves into this movement, sowing discontent, urging the workers to demand far broader economic and social benefits than their employers could provide.

In an attempt to counter these antigovernment elements, undercover agents were also strategically placed inside the unions. One of the most influential of these was Father Georgi Gapon, a young and charismatic Orthodox priest who, according to Dominic Lieven, was able to build a remarkable rapport with the workers for whom he was providing Christian counsel and support. However, all the while he himself was being converted to socialism, and so thoroughly that in January 1905 he set about organizing a surprise industrial strike in St. Petersburg, resorting to massive and illegal protest as the only effective way to obtain satisfaction of the workers' demands.

"Suddenly in January 1905, the government was faced with Gapon's plan to lead a huge demonstration to the Winter Palace and demand a string of very radical political and economic reforms, including the convocation of a constituent assembly."[2] These political stipulations had little to do with the demands of the workers on their employers and clearly indicate the socialist influence. To the outside world, it seemed that only an autocratic monster would fail to honor the earnest pleas of this army of the people, honest and hard-working men; but it was inconceivable for the Tsar to accept personally what amounted to an ultimatum presented by a mob on issues that had not been previously examined or weighed.

Unfortunately, the marching workers had mistakenly, or perhaps intentionally, been informed that the Tsar was at the Winter Palace, which he was not. In fact he seldom was there, since the Imperial Family's primary residence was the Alexander Palace at Tsarkoe Selo—a matter of common knowledge to anyone informed on public affairs.

The government had never before been confronted by such a demonstration—they were banned—and its forces were neither trained nor equipped to control the enormous crowd, estimated by some at 150,000, now facing them. Of the available forces— the Cossacks, the cavalry, and the infantry—the infantry was

---

[2] Dominic Lieven, *Nicholas II: Twilight of the Empire* (New York: St. Martin's Griffin, 1993), p. 139.

chosen because it was most readily available, but they found themselves greatly outnumbered. With nothing to use but their rifles, they did indeed use them, with results that were "clumsy and cruel."[3] (Few accounts record the fact that many of the marchers actually anticipated violence and carried farewell notes in their pockets.)

The Tsar's response to the tragedy illumines his sense of personal responsibility in matters of state and the terrible burden it imposes. The course advised by his ministers—to announce publicly that the army had fired without orders—seemed to Nicholas dishonorable. As autocrat, he must himself shoulder the blame. He invited a delegation of the workers to meet with him and took the opportunity to assure them of his deep concern for their welfare and of his government's plan to address their grievances; in return, he asked for their loyalty and support.

This measure had negative repercussions, and the delegates were derided and abused by their colleagues. A wave of industrial strikes spread through the country, resulting in many clashes with police and general disruption. Plehve's successor, Sviatopolk-Mirskii, took up a much softer line with the dissidents. The labor unions were left alone to follow their radical leaders, who raised resentment and violent protest to the status of virtue. Universities were liberalized, with the consequence that all sorts of nonstudents, workers and political activists, were allowed to participate in student activities, changing them into protest groups. At the same time censorship of the press was relaxed, providing an open pipeline for adversarial propaganda.

From his residence on Nevsky Prospekt, Gibbes had watched

[3] Lieven, *Nicholas II*, p. 139.

the army of workers parade past that Sunday in January with banners and icons, and in the days that followed he observed the police patrols and the frequent, sometimes ugly, demonstrations in the streets. He mentioned the disturbances in his letters home, but never sounded truly alarmed. They had little or no effect on his pupils or his teaching routine, reason enough to conclude that the situation was under control. Those unpleasant skirmishes seemed to be taking place in a different world, one in which he had no part—yet.

⋙ ⋘

By 1906 Gibbes's reputation was such that he could establish a "season," a regular weekly schedule of public readings from January through May, usually on Thursday or Friday evenings. Looking at his programs filled with selections from Shakespeare, Spenser, Tennyson, Dickens, and Shelley, one might wonder how he managed to acquire an audience for such fare. But St. Petersburg was a cosmopolitan city. Books and newspapers in English were easy to come by and very popular. Gibbes's fine, cultivated voice and tasteful selection of pieces made his programs a modest success right up until 1914, when the Great War cast its pall over all entertainments. He also used his season to include, on certain occasions, recitations by his pupils, and though their recitations were of a much lighter nature, they increased the programs' popularity.

Gibbes's records give the flavor of these evenings. "Mr. Gibbes begs to announce that he will resume his Readings from English and American Literature . . ." He himself gave the serious readings, and he must have especially enjoyed reading Shakespeare, as selections from *Julius Caesar, King Lear, Richard II, Richard III,*

Henry IV, and *Henry V* are a regular feature. Tennyson and Dickens were also favorites: "In Memoriam," "Locksley Hall," "Morte d'Arthur," "Enoch Arden," excerpts from *Pickwick Papers, Oliver Twist,* and *David Copperfield.* Works by George Bernard Shaw and Oscar Wilde also appear, though less frequently. On one occasion Gibbes presented Wilde's sparkling comedy, *The Importance of Being Earnest,* in its entirety. From American literature he liked to read Edgar Allan Poe, Bret Harte, and Mark Twain, all writers whose words delight the ear.

The pupils recited lighter pieces with titles reminiscent of then-popular elocution lessons: "Punch Brothers Punch," "A Restless Night," "Mr. Piper's Mittens," "Nothing to Wear." These were gleaned from such anthologies as *The Golden Collection of Humourous Readings, Pearson's American Readings, Modern Readings and Recitations, and Albion Humourous Readings,* all available in the library of the Guild of English Teachers or local English-language bookstores. Gibbes accumulated quite a library; he had the resources for instructing his students in grammar and syntax with exercises taken from such texts as *Paraphrasing & Analysis & Correction of Sentences* by D. M. J. James, M.A., and *Exercises in Correcting Grammatical Lessons* by Alex. Mackie, M.A.

Even in this security and success, Syd thought as often of his family back in England as they did of him, and when he returned to Russia from his summer vacation in 1907 he brought his sister Winnie back with him to stay until the following spring. He took great delight in showing her around the marvelous city he had been writing home about, introducing her to the plays and ballets and art museums, acquainting her with his friends and pupils, taking her to the tea shops and cafés. Syd and Winnie had always enjoyed shopping together—at home she would go out to look for and send special items he wanted—and here in St. Petersburg was the most expansive emporium of international goods they had ever encountered. They reveled in it, and her visit was their most exciting adventure so far.

They had spent many a happy hour reading to each other during their growing up, and Syd found a place for Winnie in his formal reading programs that season. It must have been great fun to listen as they clowned their way through "A Pair of Lunatics."

A reading and recital will be given at Sbovrinovinef 5, Kt 52 on Friday, April 25, 1908 at 8:30 P.M.

This will be the last reading at which Miss Gibbes will assist before her departure from Russia. *The Programme* among other items will include the following:

"The Obstructive Hat"	F. Austey	Miss Gibbes
"A Pair of Lunatics"	W. K. Walker	
	He	C. S. Gibbes
	She	Miss Gibbes
"A Lesson with a Fan"	Anonymous	Miss Gibbes
"A Broken Heart"	Anonymous	Miss Gibbes

Since Winnie could not depart until the river Neva thawed, she had an opportunity to witness the spectacular ceremony staged every year as the Tsar, accompanied by the church hierarchy, met the city officials to celebrate as the ice began to break up in April.

As soon as the ice broke, the cannons of Peter and Paul Fortress were fired to announce the happy event. The commander of the fortress, wearing the insignia of his rank and accompanied by his officers, would board a splendidly decorated barge and cross to the Winter Palace directly opposite to carry to the Emperor some of the clear Neva water in a handsome crystal goblet. He would present it to the Emperor in the name of spring, informing him that the power of winter was broken and the river once more free. The Emperor drank the water to the health of his capital and returned the goblet, filled with gold pieces, to the commander.[4]

Now ships could enter the harbor once more, and soon afterward Syd escorted Winnie back to England. The family must have rejoiced in her reports of how well he was doing and the prestige he enjoyed. By autumn of that year an even greater opportunity came, one that would shape the rest of his life.

In June 1908, King Edward VII and his Queen Alexandra had cruised into the Finnish port of Reval aboard the royal yacht *Victoria and Albert* to meet Tsar Nicholas II and the Empress Alexandra on their yacht *The Standart,* exchanging visits for several days between the two vessels. This event was of considerable diplomatic significance to Russia, which was still smarting after its humiliating defeat in the Russo-Japanese War, when its entire Baltic fleet had been destroyed.

The Tsar's goal of establishing a more significant presence on the Pacific rim of the empire and securing an ice-free port there made a good deal of sense, since Russia was blocked on the west by European nations and had no real control over the vital Black

---

[4] S. Massie, *Firebird,* p. 249.

Sea exit through the Dardanelles. The eastward thrust was reasonable, but the logistical problems were not. Such a campaign involved sailing almost around the world and transporting land troops across the expanse of Siberia in winter. When the navy and the army had struggled more or less into position, they were confronted by Japanese forces much more formidable and clever than anyone in the West had imagined. The Russians suffered a costly and bitter defeat.

There had been cheers in London, for the British were very much interested in establishing a port of their own in the Japanese straits and rejoiced when the Russian efforts failed. For a time relations between the two countries had been severely strained, so the ceremonial pomp, the dinners and cordial toasts to "the friendly feelings between two great peoples" that took place during this state visit were very important.

But for all the earlier tensions, the official attitudes, and the present protocol, this meeting was also a warm family affair. The Russian Empress Alexandra Fyodorovna was the granddaughter of Queen Victoria, and her relationship with the Queen had been especially close because of the early death of Alexandra's mother, Princess Alice of Hesse. The English Queen had supervised the upbringing of young Alix and her siblings. King Edward was the Empress's uncle, and Uncle Bertie he was called by the imperial children—the four Grand Duchesses, Olga, Tatiana, Marie, and Anastasia, and the young Tsarevich Alexei.

The Tsarevich had his own, tragic inheritance from his sovereign British grandmother: hemophilia, the terrible plague Victoria unknowingly bestowed upon several of her male descendants as the royal houses of Europe intermarried. It is a disease carried without symptom by the mother and transmitted haphazardly to some of her male offspring. Hemophilia prevents the blood from clotting normally. There was no effective treatment for it at that time. Uncontrollable bleeding was a constant danger with even the slightest wound, and internal hemorrhaging caused excruciating pain and disfigurement.

During one casual conversation at a family luncheon, Uncle Bertie commented to Alexandra that her daughters spoke poor English and with terrible accents. Alexandra's native language was German; she had to work hard to learn Russian and was never able to speak it without an accent. She was at ease with English; it was the language of many of those she loved best, including her mother and grandmother, and she spoke it every day with her husband. However, she realized that her command of the language was far from perfect and had actually grown somewhat eccentric, as her letters attest. She determined at once to find a proper teacher for the girls.

The Empress's search for such a man led to Charles Sydney Gibbes. He was undoubtedly recommended because of his fine work at the Imperial School of Law, where many officials of the imperial court sent their sons for instruction. However, Gibbes was in England while these matters were being considered and so had no inkling of the honor about to be offered him. It came as an enormous surprise when he was summoned in the early autumn of 1908 to appear at the imperial court for consideration as a tutor in English, an appointment of such distinction that it threw him into a state of highly agitated nerves.

Though full of excitement and anticipation, when he donned the required evening dress and took his seat beside State

Councillor Peter Vassilievich Petrov in a court carriage for the drive to Tsarskoe Selo, Gibbes looked the very picture of the cool, composed English gentleman. Here the next stage, a critical one, in Gibbes's journey begins.

3

༄

Tsarskoe Selo, Provincial Retreat

The fifteen-mile drive gave Gibbes time to compose himself, though he was still tense and apprehensive as he entered this completely new and fascinating world. They rode past the bustling railway station, the fashionable Vauxhall Restaurant, and turned into the long tree-lined boulevard leading from the station to the Alexander Palace. Tsarskoe Selo, "the Tsar's Village," was not a village at all, but rather the intentional blending of rural charm and sophisticated urban life into quite a large town, arranged around two imperial palaces that far surpassed any royal establishment in England. The town had its own town hall and a large military installation of five thousand carefully chosen soldiers, with the accompanying barracks, mess halls, armories, and parade grounds.

Riding along the main boulevard, Gibbes and Petrov could see the elaborately landscaped lawns and gardens surrounding the smaller, but still imposing palaces and mansions of the aristocratic families who had stationed themselves to tap into a main artery of the empire. On they drove through the vast, velvet green of the great public Imperial Park, set about with classical statues, synthetic ruins, monuments, artificial lakes, and even a series of unconnected canal segments—part of an unfinished project begun early in the eighteenth century by the Empress Elizabeth, who had cherished the idea of being able to glide noiselessly from St. Petersburg to Tsarskoe Selo. The project turned out to be a boon for the park, because these sizable pools were wonderful, not only for bathing, but for boating. Gibbes described them as artificial expanses of water, "all of which have now in the course of time assumed to themselves the natural air of one born to the place rather than that of adopted beings which is their rightful condition."

Finally, the carriage reached the great iron fence patrolled on every side by Cossacks, its gates opening into the private grounds of the Imperial Family. Their smaller Alexander Park was still extensive enough to contain the two imperial palaces, set about a quarter of a mile apart, along with acres of groves and gardens threaded through by riding paths and promenades and studded with exotic pavilions, mini-palaces, and elaborate ornamentation.

The first "rustic" retreat had been established here by Catherine I, second wife of Peter the Great, who wanted an escape from the harsh stone city her husband had erected along the Neva River. Her chosen spot was at some distance southwest of the city, where the marshes were softer and more friendly to vegetation. Even in the time of Tsar Nicholas II, the country surrounding Tsarskoe Selo remained "in its pristine savagery of barren swamp," according to Gibbes.

The first, rather modest two-story wooden building was later encased in a lavish palace built by her daughter, the Empress Elizabeth, in Catherine's memory. Elizabeth had commissioned the architect Rastrelli to outshine Versailles, and he did. The imposing blue-and-white structure had two hundred rooms, the hall of mirrors had reflecting glass not on only one side but two, and the chapel wing was topped by five golden cupolas surmounted by crosses. In front of the palace huge, baroque caryatids, their muscular arms shrouding their faces, supported the balconies above. The great central halls of the Catherine Palace and the expansive front square provided the setting for official banquets and receptions, military reviews, and great balls. Along the labyrinthine corridors in the side wings were apartments for many of the ladies and gentlemen of the imperial suite and for numerous government officials and their families.

The graceful and more classic Alexander Palace was smaller, but it was still every inch a palace, containing one hundred rooms. The splendid reception halls in the center of the building were reserved for state dinners, audiences, and official gatherings; one wing contained apartments for the ladies- and gentlemen-in-waiting, and the other wing was set aside as the residence of the Imperial Family.

Their apartments housed a world all their own. Because Nicholas and Alexandra had been forced to hurry their wedding after the unexpected death of his father, Alexander III, at first they had to accept temporary housing in six not very large rooms in Anichkov Palace with the Dowager Empress Marie, where the situation was trying, to say the very least. They had no appropriate reception rooms, and though she was now the empress, Alexandra had to ask her mother-in-law's permission to use an official state room whenever she gave an audience. When the Emperor received his ministers in their own small drawing room, she had to withdraw to the bedroom. Since they had no dining room, they took their meals at the table of the Dowager Empress, where they had no say about what was served and certainly could not complain.[1]

So it must have come as an enormous relief when at last the imperial couple were able to move to Tsarskoe Selo. Here they chose one wing of the smaller Alexander Palace, and the Empress set about decorating their new quarters herself with furniture and bright chintzes brought from England. These rooms had a cozy, homey atmosphere quite unlike that of the rest of the palace. Given the conditions in which they had been living, we can read a bit between the lines that Nicholas wrote ecstatically to his mother when he first saw their apartments in 1895:

> Our mood . . . changed to utter delight when we settled ourselves into these marvellous rooms: sometimes we simply sit in silence wherever we happen to be and admire the walls, the fireplaces, the furniture . . . the rooms are remarkably airy, light and cosy.[2]

These rooms became the domain of one of the happiest families in all of Russia, and, as many of their defenders have pointed out, it is unfortunate that the light from this delightful, affectionate household did not have more opportunity to shine out

    [1] E. M. Almedingen, *The Empress Alexandra, 1872-1918: A Study* (London: Hutchison & Co., 1961), p. 41.
    [2] Lieven quoting the Tsar's letter to his mother in *Nicholas II,* p. 59.

into the jaded, decadent society of St. Petersburg and beyond.

The extraordinary haste of the imperial wedding occasioned other and great difficulties for Alexandra. Ominously it labeled her a "coffin bride," since she first appeared in public shrouded in black and following the funeral cortege of Tsar Alexander III. She was forced to mix and mingle with her new subjects before she had mastered their language and before she was thoroughly familiar with the intricate rites and ceremonies of the Orthodox faith she had devoutly embraced.

The subdued wedding followed one week after the funeral without any celebration. There was no reception to give friends and relations an opportunity to meet and rejoice with the couple, and consequently none of the spontaneous bonding with the people created in the impromptu street celebrations sparked by such a grand event. There was no honeymoon, because the young Tsar had to plunge immediately into a heavy load of duties for which he had never been properly prepared. After all, his father was only forty-six and had appeared to be healthy and robust. For the bride this meant that she saw very little of her bridegroom and was often quite lonely.

At this point in its history, Russia had the most elaborately formal court in Europe. In and around Moscow as well as St. Petersburg there were not just one or two, but numerous palaces, each with an army of servants that could be mobilized to attend when the Imperial Family was in residence. They hurried about their duties in colorful, even exotic, liveries as they opened doors or bowed in and out with trays and messages. Many of them performed specialized duties as dressers, secretaries, maids, valets, governesses, coachmen, couriers, gardeners, guards, cooks, and on and on. The imperial household resembled nothing so much as a huge and marvelous mechanical toy, in which the varied attendants, each in the proper costume, moved through their precise, unchanging routines like parts of an intricate machine. The machine had been wound up and set going long ago, and it continued to run on stored momentum, without regard or adjustment for the particular Imperial Family it was currently serving.

Count Vladimir Fredericks, as Minister of the Imperial Court, presided over the vast network of routines and protocol, many of them quite bewildering. There was, for example, a special team of servants assigned to the duty of smashing the imperial china and glassware as it was retired to prevent its being put to an unworthy use. Grand Duke Alexander Mikhailovich, known in the family as Sandro, was astounded on the eve of his marriage to the Grand Duchess Xenia, sister of the Tsar, to find a vast wardrobe laid out for him with four dozens of every item: day shirts, dress shirts, nightshirts, dressing gowns, tunics, hose, shoes, boots. The massive display was crowned by a pair of fifteen-pound dressing gowns of metallic silver with matching silver slippers. These were traditionally prescribed for the bridal couple on their wedding night, though they resembled much more the panoply of a medieval knight.[3]

Count Fredericks also supervised the presentation of awards and gifts in the name of the Tsar, though the Tsar himself often knew nothing about it and was surprised when he was thanked

---

[3] Ian Vorres, *The Last Grand Duchess: Her Imperial Highness Grand Duchess Olga Alexandrovna* (New York: Charles Scribner's Sons, 1964, 1965), p. 47.

by the recipient. Anna Vyrubova, intimate friend of the Empress, recalled that Alexandra seemed unable to change any details in the established palace routines, even in such a matter as their daily tea. "Tea" was precisely defined in the rules of the household, and when tea was ordered, the same bread and biscuits appeared each time, served in the same manner. Gibbes referred to the imperial court as a kaleidoscope in which he had to struggle to find a space for tutoring his charges.

Alexander Palace had its own large share of this imposed grandeur; there were servants everywhere. Perhaps the most spectacular attendants were the four giant "Ethiopians." (One of these was actually an African-American, Jim Hercules, who journeyed home to Florida each year but just as loyally returned with little gifts for the children.[4]) These impressive men were dressed like characters from the Arabian Nights in scarlet trousers, jackets embroidered in gold, white turbans, and noiseless oriental slippers curving at the toes; their sole function was to tend the doors leading to the Imperial Family quarters, opening and closing them as visitors arrived and departed.

But this elaborate ritual, which had been in place since the time of Catherine the Great, stopped at those doors and seemed to have no effect on the simple tastes and habits of the close-knit family of Nicholas and Alexandra. Gibbes relates that the imperial children "lived on the floor above their parents, where they had their own sitting rooms, dining room, bed-rooms and bathrooms. They could easily join them at any time by means of a little private stairway communicating direct." And in those

---

[4] Robert K. Massie, *Nicholas and Alexandra* (New York: Atheneum Publishers, 1967; Dell edn.), p. 123.

quarters, "The little grand-duchesses were being brought up hard: they slept on camp-beds, washed in cold water, and had very plain food. Cake seldom appeared at tea."[5]

But of course, Gibbes was unaware of these family habits as he rode past the grand houses and the Cossack patrol, being challenged and queried by numerous guards and police inspectors before entering the palace, having the massive doors opened by liveried attendants as others rushed to take his hat. So he must have been astonished when he was ushered into a very plain wainscoted schoolroom containing one large square table, a number of straight-backed chairs, a blackboard, a storage cabinet, and a jumbled selection of pictures and icons on the walls. In these unpretentious surroundings he was formally introduced by Mlle Sophia Tutcheva to his future pupils, the Grand Duchesses Olga and Tatiana, at that time thirteen and eleven years old. In the somewhat daunting presence of their chaperone, he now had to give a first lesson to these royal pupils whom he had never before met.

Whether it was the simplicity of the surroundings, the warmth and responsiveness of the two young girls, or his own experience and careful preparation that enabled Gibbes to overcome his nervousness and conduct a creditable lesson we cannot be certain, but the preparation must have been a big factor. He knew their ages and wisely decided to use his excellent speaking voice to read aloud something that would interest the Grand Duchesses, who already knew a good deal of English. After the reading, Gibbes asked them pertinent questions in order to assess their comprehension level and to hear for himself the offending accent

---

[5] Almedingen, *Empress Alexandra*, p. 68.

they had acquired from Mr. Epps, the Scotsman who had preceded him.

We do not know exactly what he read, but we do know that he had by this time quite a lot of experience in teaching English to young Russian ladies and perhaps had got a sense of their taste. From his lists, we also know most of the books he had on hand and which ones he liked to use with his students. We can safely assume that at this critical hearing he would not have chosen an American author, as much as he liked them; an English author would be much more appropriate. He often read publicly from his volumes of Charles Dickens, whose themes and sentiments were both proper and popular at the time and would have been suitable for these young ladies. He may well have read a chapter from *Oliver Twist* or *David Copperfield*, or even more likely, a touching story of one or another of Dickens's tragic girls, Little Nell, Little Dorrit, Polly, Frances Dombey, all of them so lovely, so good, and so pathetic in undeserved adversities. If one of these was his choice, it might be viewed in retrospect as a sad foreshadowing of the fate of the lovely, innocent girls before him, though none of their dark future was suspected in those bright days. Gibbes's manner and presentation won the approval of Mlle Tutcheva and the pupils as well.

Syd did not know this immediately, because the Empress had to review the report and give her consent; but that evening he wrote to Winnie telling of his adventure and of his almost incredible new prospects and the awesome surroundings in which they might be realized. Shortly after this, he received formal notification of his appointment as English tutor to the Grand Duchesses. When he sent this word home, his father was

greatly pleased, his earlier disappointment completely overcome to see what a splendid career Syd was making for himself—actually attached to the imperial household! "If only your
dear Mother had lived to see it." Mary Fisher Gibbs had died
in 1906.

On his next visit to Alexander Palace, the nine-year-old Grand
Duchess Marie had been added to his pupils. "The Grand Duchesses were good-looking, high-spirited girls, simple in their tastes
and very pleasant to deal with. They were quite clever, and quick
when they gave their mind to it." However, each had her unique
personality and gifts.

Olga, the eldest, was the most like her father. She had light
brown hair and bright blue eyes, a slightly snubbed nose that she
herself made fun of, and a beautiful smile. She danced and rode
with grace and was the most talented musician among the girls.
She had near-perfect pitch and could play anything she heard.
She also possessed considerable intellectual depth, always interested in scientific developments and in abstract ideas. She might
have become a very distinguished and influential woman had she
lived to fulfill her potential.

Tatiana was the most striking in a family of beauties. She was
tall and slim like the Empress, though her darker hair, fair
complexion, and wide-spaced eyes gave her a poetic look, which
Baroness Buxhoeveden says was "not quite in keeping with her
character," which was more practical.[6] She wore her clothes with
flair, and even when all four girls were in the same costume,

---

[6] Sophie Buxhoeveden, *The Life and Tragedy of Alexandra Feodorovna,
Empress of Russia* (London, New York, Toronto: Longmans, Green, 1930), p.
153.

Tatiana's was the most becoming and hung the best. Her siblings called her the Governess because she was so good at managing the little ones and at giving help to the household staff. She was also the nominee to petition their parents when some special privilege was being requested.

Marie was also a beauty, but of a more conventional type; it might be more accurate to say she was pretty. She had the wide Russian face and in coloring was very like Olga. Enormous deep blue eyes were her outstanding feature. "Marie's saucers," her friends and cousins called them. She was the artist in the family, with a fine talent for drawing. But she was also unfailingly energetic, kind, and helpful, especially when her mother was nursing one or another of the children through the dangerous childhood diseases—diphtheria, typhoid, scarlet fever, chicken pox—for which there were as yet no vaccines. The Empress always insisted on doing this nursing herself. "Marie is my legs," she used to say.

Even before this prestigious appointment, Sydney Gibbes was a very busy man. He was now director of several of the higher courses in modern languages at the Imperial School of Law. He had a full roster of private students, his own public readings, and activities in the Guild of English Teachers. His new appointment, while it overshadowed the others, had to be fitted into this already full schedule.

Gibbes maintained his residence in St. Petersburg to keep an eye on his other interests; he was much too careful in such matters to let them be half-heartedly tended by someone else. Consequently, two or three times a week he had to ride the train to Tsarskoe Selo, take a drozhky from there to the Alexander Palace, and give at least two lessons, often four, each time. His usual routine was to go in midmorning and read aloud whatever selections he had chosen for his pupils that day. Then on the blackboard, he wrote sentences from the reading to illustrate certain points in grammar and usage, and his pupils had to identify parts of speech, parse and diagram sentences, master the spellings, and write sentences of their own. After the first session, there was time for an informal luncheon with other members of the household staff.

In the afternoon, often quite late, there would be a second session, in which a new reading was given as dictation so that the Grand Duchesses could write down what they heard; then they were queried on the content. Gibbes took special care to make these readings instructive as well as enjoyable, choosing articles with information about such things as the phases of the moon and its changing appearance over the course of a month, modern inventions such as the camera, telegraph, telephone, chronometer, and so forth. For these he would give an elementary explanation of the machine's workings and list some of its benefits to society. He introduced terms relating to government: autocracy, monarchy, anarchy, tyrant, republic, democracy, oligarchy, aristocracy, parliament. He compiled a list of facts relating to the Bible with appropriate readings from Scripture to illustrate.

The copybooks he lovingly preserved for fifty years reveal some of the difficulties a foreign ear has with the English language: "pales" for "palace," "skreaming" for "screaming," "werds" for "words." They also reveal his love for and understanding of children, a quality that would later be given full throttle, though up until this time he may not even have been aware of it. He still felt that his permanent interests lay in St. Petersburg, and he looked on his imperial assignment as an extraordinary piece of good fortune which would last only until the girls grew up.

The following fall, the Empress asked Gibbes to teach Anastasia, who was now eight years old. This was Gibbes's first encounter with the Empress herself, and he described the meeting as a happy one. "In 1909 she still looked very young, had a fresh complexion and beautiful hair and eyes. In her dress and manners she was extremely simple. She gave you her hand with dignity mingled with shyness, which gave her a truly gracious air, very pleasurable to see and feel."

The youngest of the girls, Anastasia seems to have made a special impression on Gibbes, for he speaks of her in quite a different tone.

> . . . She was then but a tiny child slightly built and frail looking. Her movements were quick and keen and her eyes sparkled with life and intelligence. Of exquisite colouring, fragile and dainty, she yet possessed the physical strength so characteristic of the family and which belied her delicate appearance. She was, moreover, a little lady of great self-possession, always bright and happy. Ever bent on inventing some new oddity of speech or manner, her perfect command of her features was remarkable. I have never seen anything quite equal to it in any other child.
>
> The little Duchess was not always an easy child to instruct, especially by lessons which had to be given

in the "traditional" manner. As I had taken the Moral
Sciences and my Tripos and later on a special course in
Child Psychology, I introduced as much innovation as I
felt I dare. We had, as a rule, charming lessons, but sometimes there were storms.

Her classroom antics were memorable, and he records some
rocky sessions. There was a particularly trying one in which he
did not give her the usual, and expected, five marks for a satisfactory lesson. They sat for a time in silence, and then without
saying a word Anastasia left the room and returned very shortly
carrying a large bouquet of flowers. With a winning smile she
said, "Mr. Gibbes, are you going to change the marks?" He shook
his head, and the young lady marched out of the room and went
directly to the Russian professor. "Peter Vassilievich, allow me to
present you with these flowers." Of course, he should have refused them, but as Gibbes commented, "Professors are human."
The storm passed and their relations returned to normal, but
Gibbes was very careful in his marking, and Anastasia brought
him bouquets after every lesson.

On another occasion, following a children's fancy-dress ball,
she darted into the classroom with her face blackened like a
chimney-sweep and carrying a small ladder, symbol of the trade.
Gibbes decided to act as if this were nothing unusual, but just as
they were beginning the lesson, the sisters burst laughing into
the room bringing the Empress with them. "Anastasia," she cried
aghast, "go and change at once." The child returned shortly, glowing red from her scrubbing, and took her place with great aplomb.
Their lesson continued as usual with the Empress sitting through

the session, and everyone pretended not to notice the ladder still lying on the table.

The Grand Duchesses also had lessons in Russian, French, religious knowledge, history, and music; and the various instructors had to adjust their schedules, not only to one another, but also to the midmorning walk the children took with the Tsar when weather and his schedule permitted, and to the church services the family unfailingly attended on holy days, birthdays, and the feast days of the saints for whom each of them was named. The Feast of St. Nicholas, of course, was a national holiday. They also attended services of thanksgiving offered for significant national events and those of supplication in times of trouble.

Until now Gibbes had associated chiefly with the English colony in the capital, where most of his friends were either indifferent to religion or in a state of confusion and disillusionment similar to his own; they felt no interest in what they considered the antiquated Russian Church. The spiritual crisis we have previously noted in England was also acute in sophisticated circles in St. Petersburg. According to Prince Zhevakov:

Religious Petersburg began to look for answers to its doubts and spiritual questions in new ways and entered the realm of "popular" religion, that has no theological problems or contradictions, and was not committed to any body of dogma. It was all the easier to do so since there was no shortage of representatives of this kind of faith. And soon such representatives who had hitherto frequented the poorer parts of the city, . . . began to find their way into the drawing rooms and salons of high society.[7]

This spiritual malaise provided the atmosphere in which Gregory Rasputin, and others like him, were able to establish themselves in high circles of St. Petersburg society. Gibbes and several of his friends were infected by the same unease. These well-educated worldly-wise were making regular visits to a back-street fortune-teller, Dyadya Misha, and dabbling in theosophy and similar fads until well after World War I had begun.

Russia had remained officially and culturally Christian longer than the Western nations; visible and audible reminders of its ancient and deep-rooted Orthodoxy were everywhere. The melodious pealing of many-toned bells from hundreds of churches and monastery towers filled the air. They called the faithful to worship, proclaimed holy days, festivals, funerals, weddings, baptisms. They rang alarms for fire or other disasters. These peals had a language of their own, and the faithful understood it. The bells and glowing domes of the churches also filled remote villages and sounded through the fields of the peasants. They were a constant reminder of another, eternal world, a world in which even the lowliest could participate through the sacred mysteries of the Church.

Everywhere, everywhere, there were icons. Each Russian shop had its own; they were in the many small shrines along the streets where people stopped to pray, on coaches and sleds, over doorways and bridges. Even the exterior walls of the churches were

---

[7] Quoted by Alex de Jonge in *The Life and Times of Rasputin* (New York: Coward, McCann and Geoghegan, 1982), p. 92.

adorned with them, and every house had its *krasnyi ugol,* its "bright" or "beautiful" corner where the family icons were kept and venerated. This unique religious art form, so rich in color and with its special artistic line, spoke with great meaning to even the simplest among the faithful. But icons and their veneration would have been contemptuously dismissed as superstitious idolatry by most of the Englishmen and the intelligentsia of the capital.

For all his own disillusionment, Gibbes could not long ignore the role of the Orthodox faith in the life of the Imperial Family. The ancient rites and ceremonies were, of course, deeply woven into formal court ritual, but they were even more deeply woven into the daily routine of this devout family. They didn't just go through the motions; they lived the teachings of the Church, and their piety was the foundation stone of the happiness and mutual affection that so distinguished them. Gibbes could sense that this faith, which he had heretofore thought so alien and strange and which was generally discredited as naive in the West, provided them with illumination and sustenance he never expected to experience. He was far from ready to embrace Orthodoxy, but his prejudices were being challenged by the contrast between this atmosphere and that of blasé and decadent St. Petersburg.

4

Tutor to the Tsarevich

Three years passed before the Empress asked Gibbes to become a preceptor to the Tsarevich Alexei and to instruct him in English, something she had tried and failed to do herself. The child, who was now eight, was no stranger to the tutor, for as soon as the boy could walk he often wandered into the classrooms,

a tiny little chap in wee, wee white knickerbockers and a Russian shirt trimmed with Ukrainian embroidery of blue and silver. He used to toddle into my class room at 11 o'clock, look around and then gravely shake hands. In this period scarcely a word ever passed between us on these occasions as he undoubtedly felt the difficulty of his position in that I didn't (or wasn't supposed to) know a word of Russian, and he was the only one of the family that hadn't had an English nurse from birth and couldn't speak a word of English. Under these circumstances silence was the most dignified proceeding and in silence he shook hands and he toddled off.

Being appointed as a governor to assist in the training and education of the Sovereign Heir to the throne of all the Russias was an awesome responsibility, one that Gibbes accepted as a sacred duty, with the deep commitment of an English monarchist born and bred. Though his own country's monarchy was a constitutional one, his appreciation of the autocratic principle was probably keener than that of Pierre Gilliard, the other very excellent governor, who was a French Swiss with more democratic sympathies. Venerable Russian State Councillor Peter Vassilievich Petrov was the chief of the team.

The life of this beautiful child, so anxiously awaited by his parents to secure the succession of the dynasty, was destined to reflect poignantly the woeful fortune of the empire he was intended to preserve. His handsome little masculine body and his bright spirit appeared to be all that anyone could wish; yet an insidious disease tainted his blood, making it all but impossible for him to survive in the rough-and-tumble world of everyday. He had emerged from his mother's perilous womb just as Russia was suffering humiliating defeat at the hands of Japan—a defeat that severely damaged the prestige of the monarchy and was one of the first in an intensifying succession of misfortunes that led on to the nation's fatal catastrophe.

The empire waiting to welcome the Heir was also a rare and interesting sociopolitical body with its own exotic beauty, but a deadly bacillus, as Winston Churchill would later call it, was already burrowing. This disease was so deforming and disabling the empire that there was little hope for its survival in an unsympathetic world which had turned its back on many of the institutions and traditions still dear to most Russians.

A vigorous Christian faith had somehow survived in their land, even as a diluted version of the same faith was receding steadily in the West. Simple and unsophisticated it may often have seemed to Western observers, but its grandeur enriched all classes, lifting even the life of the poorest peasant above the sordid and providing a rhythmic order for the year and meaning for his hardest days. The ancient Russian autocratic political system, so derided and despised by twentieth-century political thinkers, still presented a shared vision of sovereign splendor which that mass of very diverse people could appreciate and revere. The autocracy was their link to one another and to their Orthodox Father Tsar—through him to the worldly benefits he could dispense, and beyond him to the otherworldly and to God Himself. Theirs was a strange and courageous beauty, but that world was brought near to ruin by the strikes and uprisings of 1905–1907, and completely demolished by WWI and the Bolshevik Revolution.[1]

After the assassination of Vyacheslav Plehve in 1904, as we have noted, the imperial government lost control of the labor movement in which it had been working hard to establish stability and harmonious relations. The workers, who were usually peasants coming into the cities from the countryside, came under the influence of the radical socialists, who cozened them into

[1] The liveliest English account of the old Russia is Suzanne Massie's in *Land of the Firebird.*

expecting from the Tsar concessions and benefits he could not grant, a delusion that led to the disaster of Bloody Sunday. A torrent of strikes and uprisings followed in many of the major industrial cities, where resentment against factory owners and government officials now ran high. Then came a general strike by the union of railroad workers that crippled the country for a time. Government ministers and other officials, even the Tsar himself, could not get from one place to another in the capital except by motorcar or boat. More critical was the constant threat of further obstruction posed by this militant railway union.

On October 30, 1905, Nicholas yielded at long last to the enormous pressures of the strikes and the continuing terrorism of the revolutionaries. He issued an Imperial Manifesto committing to a semiconstitutional form of government with an elected parliament, the Duma, and promising freedom of speech, conscience, association, and assembly. Sergius Witte, the first Prime Minister and also the first person ever to be placed in charge of all internal affairs, had been the mover behind the framing of the document, and though Nicholas agreed to the terms, it was only after deep and painful soul-searching, because he earnestly believed they violated his coronation oath.

Nicholas was also convinced that the Russian people were not ready for representative government and that too-rapid liberal reforms would destroy all order and be the ruin of the country. He had taken to heart the observation of his grandfather, Alexander II, that history offered no example in which liberal reforms were stopped before they had gone too far, and his own tragic fate was a grim confirmation of this. Alexander's freeing of the serfs in 1865 had earned him the title of Tsar Liberator, but it also earned the enmity of the revolutionaries: they set out to assassinate him, and finally succeeded in their third attempt on March 13, 1881. When the bomb from their second try exploded harmlessly not far from Alexander's carriage, he got out and walked over to speak with the terrorists—only to be blown to bits by another missile. He was carrying in his pocket at the time the draft for a constitution.

Tsar Nicholas became more doubtful still when unrest and terrorist activity continued despite his concessions. The casualty figures give some idea of the frightening atmosphere in which these events were unfolding. Between 1905 and 1909 the total number of victims of terrorist attacks numbered 5,913, of whom 2,691 were killed.

The revolutionaries had actually been spreading their terror for a long time. Two ministers of the interior with plans for land reform had been killed earlier, D. S. Sipyagin in 1902 and V. K. Plehve in 1904. Peter Stolypin, whose reforms were the most comprehensive and promising, was shot dead in 1911. Grand Duke Sergei Alexandrovich, Governor General of Moscow, whose wife Elizabeth was sister to the Empress, was a prominent victim in 1905, less than a month after Bloody Sunday. The revolutionaries were determined that nothing, not even enactment of the very reforms for which they were relentlessly agitating, should rob them of the worldwide socialist transformation they envisioned. The Tsar himself remained, of course, the primary target of these attacks, with the Heir a close second, and their every move had to be planned and coordinated with prodigious security measures.

While these political whirlwinds swirled through the land, the Tsarevich and his family were fighting a difficult private battle against the spells of incredible pain from the hemorrhage and swelling often brought on by the most ordinary boyhood activities. Many people in and around the capital and those connected with the court realized that some mysterious malady plagued the Heir, but no one outside the tight family circle knew the truth, and the wildest rumors circulated about what it might be. The family's decision to keep silence was in keeping with the etiquette of the court and of the age—it would be improper to announce as fact that the life of this significant boy was so tenuous. The entire family prayed and hoped for a miracle, the Empress with particular fervor. Not even his tutors were informed about the true nature of these baffling spells of illness that occurred suddenly and lasted for days, causing such a dense gloom to descend on the palace that it could be felt by everyone. Gibbes and Gilliard must have pondered and discussed this riddle when they were first appointed in 1912, for it was well into 1913 before they could begin any serious instruction with the boy.

Alexei had suffered by far the worst episode of hemophilia in his life. In the autumn of 1912 the family vacationed at their rustic lodge in eastern Poland to enjoy the luxuriant forests and fresh running streams. The Tsar and his daughters rode on horseback through the woods, but the boy was not permitted to ride and had to be content with boating. It was in Bialowieza that he slipped while jumping into a boat and an oarlock dug into his groin. At first there was a blood-filled swelling, but after a few days it subsided, and the family proceeded to Spala, the Tsar's favorite hunting spot.

The lodge there was a relatively primitive building with very poor lighting and ventilation. One day while most of the imperial suite were out hunting and riding, the Empress decided to take her son for a ride in the fresh country air. But the rough jostling of their carriage on the country roads set off intense bleeding in the groin and sent the boy into such agony that he was almost unconscious by the time they made it back to the lodge. There followed eleven days of sheer torture for all: the anguished patient, his fearful parents and sisters, the worried and helpless doctors. So critical was the situation that several cautious bulletins were issued, indicating that the life of the Heir was in danger.

Just when things were looking blackest and the doctors had said there was nothing more they could do, Alexandra in desperation telegraphed to ask Gregory Rasputin to pray for the boy. At that time Rasputin was in Siberia, having been ordered by the Tsar to return to his home after a particularly disgraceful public display in a St. Petersburg night spot. His response was immediate. "God has seen your tears and heard your prayers. Do not grieve. The Little One will not die. Do not allow the doctors to bother him too much."[2]

The prayers and presence of Rasputin had helped the ailing child on other occasions, occasions so numerous that Grand Duchess Olga Alexandrovna said she could not even count the times. This episode, however, had particularly fateful consequences—the boy was obviously dying, Gregory Rasputin was hundreds of miles away, and still he appeared to save the child. The miracle firmly established this Siberian peasant with the

---

[2] R. Massie, quoting Vyrubova in *Nicholas and Alexandra*, p. 186.

Empress as a true "man of God," the one, the only one, she could look to for real help with her ailing son.

Alexandra's trust would have disastrous consequences for the dynasty she was spending herself to preserve. Hereafter she would ignore all accusations made against Rasputin—they were many and shocking—and would go to any lengths to protect the single person who seemed able to relieve the Heir's torture and restore his health. Only someone who has kept vigil at the bedside of a child moaning in pain which cannot be relieved, wracked with fever that cannot be controlled, whose only relief comes when he sinks at last into unconsciousness, can possibly comprehend the desperation with which Alexandra clung to this strange, uncouth peasant who had lumbered out of Siberia and into their lives.

A man like Rasputin would have been a familiar figure in Orthodox Russia. They had a long tradition of so-called holy fools and wandering pilgrims who made their way on foot throughout the land—a land vast, harsh, and rugged. These religious vagabonds made their way living on prayer, berries, roots, and nuts, sleeping under the sky when in the wilderness; but in towns and villages the people were always ready to give them shelter and food.

Gregory Rasputin had been a dissolute youth, a hard drinker and a notorious seducer of women. When he was caught stealing wood in his village of Pokrovskoe, he was sentenced to a severe public beating. Soon afterwards he went to spend several months in Verkhoturye Monastery, where he fell under the influence of a hermit, Makary. The experience transformed him: he gave up his scandalous ways, renouncing tobacco and meat totally, and vodka for many years. He had also learned to read and even write a little, and had memorized many passages of Holy Scripture which he recited to his acquaintances as he engaged them in spiritual conversation.

Many who knew Rasputin thought the beating had damaged his mind, a possibility some historians take seriously, and it might shed some light on the troubling oscillation between states of religious fervor and wild debauchery that characterized his later years.[3] For his debaucheries he was always repentant, and in spite of his lapses he never lost his sense of having a unique spiritual vocation, though he was neither priest nor monk. He was twenty-eight when he set out on his wanderings, which took him to many of Russia's most famous holy places and brought him into contact with influential church officials. These were initially impressed with this peasant, so full of ardor and simple faith which he could express in a strikingly direct way. Bishop Hermogen was an early sponsor, and though he later denounced Rasputin for his scandalous conduct, it was the bishop who opened to Rasputin the door of St. Petersburg society—a door that ultimately led him to the Alexander Palace.

Once there, Gregory did much good, but the other side of his personality supplied enough sordid gossip to energize the enemies of the Tsar and Tsaritsa. They publicized his every lapse, supplying highly colored details, and went even farther beyond truth to insinuate that the Imperial Family, particularly the Tsaritsa, was totally under Rasputin's spell and took part in his orgies. The political effect was cataclysmic; the public was led to believe that a devil was running the country.

---

[3] de Jonge, *Rasputin*, pp. 42–43.

Alexei was unable to walk for more than a year after this terrible episode, and was still pale, nervous, and weak when Gibbes began at last to work with him. It was not surprising to find that he had been spoiled and was used to having his own way, though the indulgence often seemed excessive even for a prince. On one occasion the child rang for his attendant during an English lesson and requested a chocolate. It was duly brought by his sailor guard Derevenko in a crystal goblet, and the boy gobbled it down. "The habit has begun and ought to be stopped. It is piggish to eat like that in company," noted Gibbes. According to Pierre Gilliard, "He [Alexei] had never been under any regular discipline. . . . I had to struggle against the servile flattery of the servants and silly adulation of some of the people around him."[4]

Getting the Heir to settle down to lessons and establish an orderly routine was a long and often trying job. Gibbes spent many of their early sessions experimenting with ways to establish a relationship with this boy who could not speak English, and to whom he was to speak no Russian. His Cambridge courses in child psychology had stressed the importance of making learning enjoyable, a philosophy that he put into practice here. But it is one thing to know the theory and another to put it into effective use.

However, Gibbes soon came to appreciate the value of children's games, of pretending to be grown up, to be a soldier, a sailor, an investigator of deep mysteries, an adventurer exploring strange lands, a hero dealing with some terrible danger. By

---

[4] Gilliard, Pierre, *Thirteen Years at the Russian Court: A Personal Record of the Last Years and Death of Czar Nicholas II and His Family* (New York: Doran, 1921), p. 89.

playing and pretending together the teacher and pupil created an imaginary world of their own, a special place to be filled with characters and events of their own conceiving. Still it took several months of hard work to achieve an atmosphere of trust and mutual understanding in which they could begin serious instruction. Gibbes gives details of some of their early sessions.

The beginning material was very elementary: *Mother Goose Book* and *Golliwog's Circus Book*. There were also picture books, and Gibbes talked with Alexei about what was in the pictures. The experimental sessions were enlivened by making paper hats and boxes, paper flags with flagpoles rolled from paper, and then playing out a situation in which they could be used. Once when Alexei had brought in some wire, Gibbes took command of the situation by cutting off two lengths to make sending and receiving cables, so the two could telegraph to each other holding one wire to their ears and another between their teeth. "He seemed very surprised to hear with his teeth. Then I continued the story of the 'Fish and the Ring', and when I repeated it, he seemed to remember it and certainly replied better when I asked him questions."

The holy days and Lenten observances took much time from lessons in February and March, but by Easter a true friendship and rapport had been established. Alexei seemed much more at ease, trying to speak more English and seeming to understand more. Even so, the boy still occasionally gave Gibbes a bad time of it. At one memorable session it was well into the evening before they had a chance to begin their lesson, and by then the Tsarevich was tired and hungry but still full of nervous excitement.

First, he cut up bread with his scissors, then it had to be thrown to the birds, the casement opened for him to get up and down, and afterwards shut, rather nervous work. Then he would twist wire round his teeth and wanted to do the same to mine, but naturally I was afraid. Worst of all, he got the scissors again and would insist on cutting or pretending to cut everything. The more I tried to prevent him, the more he shrieked with delight. He doesn't look handsome then: a most curious expression. He wanted to cut my hair, and afterwards his own, and when I tried to prevent him, he went behind the curtain and held it round him. When I opened it he had actually cut some off, and he was rather disconcerted when I told him he had made a bald place. He then tried to clip the wall with the scissors and to cut the curtains; and eventually he set to work to take out the lead weights from the curtains. When he had done that, he invited me to go with him to the playroom, but I told him it was almost six. He went off downstairs, shouting how he had got the lead out of the curtains.

No lesson that day, but the episode, though "more exciting than pleasant," did demonstrate that the boy was learning more English.

By the time Gibbes left in the late spring of 1914 for his summer vacation in England, he was well satisfied with the progress his pupil was making and with the good relations they were enjoying.

5

Night Comes On

All reports agree that the weather in the spring and summer of 1914 was brilliant. A confident, optimistic Syd sailed home in May under warm, sunny skies across a sparkling sea to spend a tranquil summer with his father, who had now retired and was living in the family home in Normanton, having given over the Bank House to his successor. The elder Gibbs took great pleasure in his son's company and his accounts of life at the Russian Imperial Court, and had long ago forgotten any disappointment at Syd's choice of vocation. During those mild days, they took long walks together and enjoyed the good table spread by Aunt Hattie, who had come to live in the house and take care of John Gibbs.

Syd had taken many photographs of his imperial pupils and of the surroundings in which he worked, and he shared them with members of the family who came to see their émigré while he was home and to hear of his adventures. This happy summer together would be Syd's last with his father, though neither had an inkling of it at the time. The world spreading out beyond the Gibbs family circle appeared as serene and firmly established in its splendid order as Winston Churchill has poignantly described it.

> The world on the verge of its catastrophe was very brilliant. Nations and Empires crowned with princes and potentates rose majestically on every side, lapped in the accumulated treasures of the long peace. All were fitted and fastened—it seemed securely—into an immense cantilever. The two mighty European systems faced each other glittering and clanking in the panoply, but with a tranquil gaze. . . . Were we after all to achieve world security and universal peace by a marvellous system of combinations in equipoise and of armaments in equation, of checks and counter-checks on violent action ever more complex and more delicate? Would Europe thus marshalled, thus grouped, thus related, unite into one universal and glorious organism capable of receiving and enjoying in undreamed abundance the bounty which nature and science stood hand in hand to give? The old world in its sunset was fair to see.[1]

That old world indeed appeared so fair, so calm, that hardly anyone envisioned the ruin that lay just ahead. In June there were spectacular naval displays when Admiral David Beatty led the British flotilla to Kronstadt, near St. Petersburg, to salute the

---

[1] Winston S. Churchill, *The World Crisis* (New York: Charles Scribner's Sons, 1931), pp. 97–98.

Russian Navy and the Tsar aboard the *Standart* with his family. This dashing officer, the youngest flag officer in the fleet, was fresh-faced and beardless, quite unlike the conventional naval commander. But his brilliant actions had moved Admiral Packenham to whisper in awe, "Nelson has come again."[2] After Kronstadt the flotilla proceeded to Kiel for a ceremonial visit to the German Navy. This too was a grand spectacle that seemed to confirm an atmosphere of harmony and friendship despite the display of Germany's awesome military might.

But this calm vision of a peaceful future was suddenly ruptured by the assassination of the Austrian Archduke Franz Ferdinand and his wife by a Serbian nationalist in Sarajevo on June 28, 1914. Gibbes had, of course, become much more politically alert since joining the staff of the Imperial School of Law, where political matters were routinely discussed, and as a part of the imperial household he heard many rumors, substantial and otherwise, about the dangers of Austria's threat to Serbia. St. Petersburg itself was a swirling cauldron of political gossip. In 1908, the very year Gibbes joined the staff at Alexandra Palace, there had been a humiliating incident involving Austria's scheme to legitimize annexation of Bosnia-Herzegovina.

This problem was part of an untidy residue left from the Russo-Turkish war of 1875, in which Russia had come to the aid of her fellow Orthodox Christians in the Balkans, who had risen to challenge the Muslim-Turkish yoke they had endured since the fifteenth century. Their success alarmed Britain, France, and Germany, who were unwilling to have the Balkan Peninsula under Russian control. Using the Bosporus and the Dardanelles as

---

[2] Churchill, *World Crisis*, p. 61.

leverage, they called a conference at Berlin in 1878 to revise Russia's Treaty of San Stephano. The Treaty of Berlin divided Bulgaria into three parts and declared Serbia, Montenegro, and Rumania independent. The Island of Cyprus went to Britain, and Austria-Hungary was allowed to "occupy and administer" Bosnia-Herzegovina, but not to annex it until some agreed-upon future date.[3]

In 1908 the Ottoman Empire appeared on the verge of collapse, and Austria decided to exploit the situation and establish her claim to Bosnia-Herzegovina. The Austrian and Russian ambassadors met and arrived at an agreement under which Russia would formally acknowledge Austria's sovereignty in that region in exchange for Austria's support of the Russian request for unrestricted use of the important Black Sea straits. The embarrassment came when the Austrian ambassador made public announcement of the first part of the agreement without mentioning the essential second half.

Nicholas had been ten years old when the Treaty of Berlin was made, and knew nothing about it until confronted by the Kaiser, who brought it forth now with threats of serious and unpredictable results if the pact were not honored. In fact, it was believed that Germany was poised to mobilize to protect the interests of its ally, Austria. The takeover became an accomplished fact, while Russia could do nothing to secure the strategically important access to the straits, particularly since Britain and France were unwilling to lend their support—a policy they would sorely regret when the Great War was upon them.

---

[3] *Rand McNally Atlas of World History*, R. R. Palmer, ed. (New York, Chicago, San Francisco: Rand McNally & Company, 1965), p. 173.

The spark of Sarajevo detonated charges all along a tangled network strung long since by decades of conflict between the European powers competing for influence in this strategically important region. These conflicts had often been settled by unpalatable peace treaties imposed on the sullen Balkan states, Turkey, and the Caucasian region. The Austrian response to the assassination was a deliberately designed insult rejecting all expressions of regret and accusing the Serbian government itself of complicity in the nefarious deed. They insisted that Austrian officials be permitted to supervise the Serbian investigation.

At that point Serbia made a plea for Russia's assistance. The Tsar was exceedingly anxious to avoid war, for Russia was not adequately prepared; yet it was unthinkable to allow their traditional friend to be swallowed up and Russia to lose all influence in the Balkan area. Nicholas suggested submitting the dispute to the Hague Tribunal; he appealed to the ties of family loyalty between himself and the Kaiser, to the historic friendship between their countries; but Wilhelm was adamant in support of Austria and threatened direst consequences if Russia made a move to aid Serbia. In fact, he demanded that Russian mobilization along the Serbian border be immediately stopped and confirmation of this telegraphed to him, while the Austrian military activity continued.

Everyone understood that Germany was the real menace; Austria provided the excuse. Despite the appearance of general peace, there had long been a certain uneasiness in the air. Many observers believed that Germany would not risk upsetting its spectacular economic and social progress or even its magnificent military organization by actually going to war, no matter how loudly it roared and waved its fist. But there were some who understood that these very achievements made the nation restive: it wanted room in which to flex its muscle and display its energy and enterprise.

After the departure of Bismarck in 1890, Emperor Wilhelm had launched his nation on a new course toward becoming a world power. Wresting Serbia from Russian influence would be a big step in that direction, giving Germany unimpeded influence in the Balkans and beyond into Turkey and the Near East. The Germans had a dual strategy in place for the present situation. They were gambling on Russia's backing down because of military unreadiness and the threat of internal revolution; but should the first calculation be mistaken and fighting become necessary, that same unreadiness would make it possible to defeat Russia promptly and with ease. "It's now or never," the Kaiser penned in the margin of a dispatch to Austrian Emperor Franz Joseph, for he realized that in two or three years Russia's rapid modernization would negate such a possibility.

Gibbes of course understood that the Sarajevo murders had serious international implications, but he was among those who did not expect war. Then on June 28, Austria declared war on Serbia, and on June 29 shelled Belgrade. When the news reached St. Petersburg on June 30, the Tsar bowed his head in silence, and then, with great reluctance, ordered full mobilization. As Serge Sazonov observed, "This would mean sending hundreds of thousands of Russian people to their death. How can one help hesitating to take such a step." [4] Germany had already issued its

---

[4] Serge Sazonov, quoted by Bernard Pares in *The Fall of the Russian Monarchy* (London: Cassell Publishers, 1939), p. 185.

declaration of war, but the document was withheld by Ambassador Pourtalés until the visiting French delegation led by Count Poincaré had sailed away from St. Petersburg for home. The declaration was delivered on August 1.

On August 2, the Tsar and Tsaritsa appeared on the balcony of the Winter Palace to inform the Russian people that they were at war. The response was a tremendous outpouring of patriotism from the vast crowd who filled the square. The Tsar repeated the oath made by Alexander I on learning of Napoleon's invasion: he would never make peace until the last enemy soldier had been driven from Russian territory. At that the people, who represented every class, ethnicity, and political persuasion, went down as one on their knees, singing "God Save the Tsar" and the stirring hymn, "Lord, save Thy people and bless Thine inheritance." All political rancor and protest of previous days was thrown aside, and hearts united to defeat the German enemy. By August 4, France and Britain had also declared war, forming the Entente against Germany.

By mid-August Gibbes had received a telegram from the Tsaritsa requesting that he return to Tsarskoe Selo. Already it was impossible to go by way of the Baltic Sea, so he had to embark from Hull far to the north, and then take an overland route through Scandinavia, sail across the Gulf of Bothnia, then proceed through Finland to St. Petersburg. It was a hazardous route, with floating mines a real possibility in every stretch of water.

As chance would have it, the exiled Grand Duke Michael was making his way home on the same train. Michael had consummated a defiant, secret marriage to the alluring, twice-divorced commoner, Natalia Cheremetevskaya, even though he

had given the Tsar his word that he would not do so. His un-
seemly waywardness had been punished by exile in England, but
now that war had been declared, the exiles were permitted to
return. The Grand Duke, his wife, now Countess Brassova, and
the son born before their marriage were stepping out onto the
platform of Finland Station at the same time as Gibbes. Michael
was sent immediately to the front to command a division in the
Caucasian region.

When Gibbes reported for duty he found Tsarskoe Selo bustling. The Tsar was constantly busy receiving reports and visits from his own and foreign ministers and from the war front,
which he visited frequently. The Empress had thrown herself
into hospital work, for which she had a true gift. She, Olga, and
Tatiana had taken a Red Cross course in nursing to qualify as
Sisters of Mercy, and in those uniforms they reported daily for
work, hard work, in the hospitals they sponsored. They assisted
with operations, ministered to the dying, and often dressed appalling wounds. Even Marie and Anastasia visited the hospitals
with flowers and cheery greetings. Over and above this, all the
women of the household spent their spare time knitting or hand-
stringing icons to give the soldiers in token of their Emperor's
gratitude.

To the tutor's great delight, Alexei, now wearing the khaki
uniform of a private soldier, had made remarkable development
both physically and mentally. He was much more serious, willing
to study and to work at speaking English. Gibbes took full advantage of the situation, and their sessions began to produce satisfying results. When Sir John Hanbury-Williams, Chief of the
British Military Mission, met Alexei at military headquarters a

year later, he was astonished by the boy's ability to speak foreign languages "well and clearly."[5]

In 1915 Gibbes could take only a brief summer leave in Russia before resuming work with his imperial pupils and also with his classes in St. Petersburg. But the pace got more and more hectic, the schedules more complicated for everyone, and especially for the Imperial Family, with the Grand Duchesses involved in their demanding hospital work and with regimental reviews, so important for their effect on wartime morale. In the summer of 1916, the Empress offered Gibbes a flat in the Catherine Palace, an offer he accepted gratefully even though it meant giving up some of his other commitments. However, for business and social reasons he retained his quarters in the city well into 1917. He found the atmosphere at Tsarskoe Selo invigorating and thoroughly enjoyed spending summer in the country . . .

> if you would call Tsarskoe Selo country; some people do; many, perhaps, do not. It would be truer to call it a ruralised town, or an urbanised wilderness, according to the way you look at it. It contains a number of houses and barracks, for it is also a great military centre. But besides this there are many charming palaces set round with vast artificial parks; also expanses of water that have come to seem natural to the place. While that is Tsarskoe Selo itself, the country round it is still in pristine savagery, barren swamp.

Gibbes was soon settled in and even adopted a cat, who came

---

[5] John Hanbury-Williams, *The Emperor Nicholas II as I Knew Him* (New York: E.P. Dutton, 1923), p. 283.

through his window each night to see what was left of the meal
sent over from the kitchen of the Alexander Palace. In his new
location he felt very much a part of the nation's struggle. At the
beginning of August he became even more deeply involved, for
the Empress asked him to proceed to the Imperial Military Headquarters at Mogilev and continue English lessons with Alexei.

Gibbes's comments on this development give us a hint of his
lingering mental and emotional uncertainties. He had not slept
well for several nights: "I felt that something was coming. I was
just beginning my supper when he [Gilliard] telephoned, and for
a while it was quite difficult to eat." This call was a summons to
the palace for his new assignment. He gave great significance to
a recent dream in which the Tsarevich had said to him that he
would soon be serving at headquarters. Gibbes also gave credence
to a prediction of the fortune-teller, Dyadya Misha, who had told
him he would be taking an important journey.

❧❧

The story of Russia in the Great War is from beginning to
end heart-piercing tragedy, though not without moments of true
glory. She was a gallant, chivalrous nation eager to serve her allies
with everything she had to offer, but she was out of step with the
modern world in which she suddenly found herself fighting for
her life. Many of her most admirable qualities—her incredible
fighting courage, her unfailing hospitality and kindness, her
deep Orthodox faith—worked against her even with her allies,
and certainly with the efficiently brutal war machine of the
Germans.

This war was not only a clash between the old world and a
strange new one, but between attitudes toward war itself. The

Russian concept of war had a traditional etiquette, a code of honor. The ranks of officers were filled primarily by men from the nobility, since this was one of the few careers open to them. They took great pride in their magnificent cavalry, especially the famous Cossacks, and continued to use it in the new warfare. With the bayonet the Russians were unsurpassed, and each infantryman was confident that if he could get to his enemy he had a beaten man.

The foe they faced had resorted to mechanized barbarism. In their *Conduct of War Manual*, the Germans approved the use of disguise in enemy colors, and Admiral Souchon had actually run up the Russian flag on the *Goeben* on August 4, 1914, when he fired on French troop transports in the Mediterranean. The Germans also resorted to the use of poison gas as an instrument of war, even though in armaments—heavy artillery, transport vehicles, airplanes, and the like—they were unsurpassed.

To counter that ruthless force Russia had only the matchless valor of her men, who poured out their blood with reckless abandon. "These people play at war," remarked Sir Alfred Knox in sad amazement, as he watched officers marching upright into battle—believing it cowardly to do otherwise—while commanding their men to crawl forward. Knox described the Russians as "great bighearted children who had thought out nothing and had stumbled half-asleep into a wasp's nest." [6]

Still Knox is wholehearted in his admiration for the Russian regular army. Despite miserable supply and planning—

---

[6] Alfred Knox, *With the Russian Army 1914-1917: Being Chiefly Extracts from the Diary of a Military Attaché* (London: Hutchinson & Co., 1921; rpt. New York: Arno Press & The New York Times, 1971), pp. 249, 86.

no patrols, late orders, contradictory orders, no telephone, no cipher, no notes of their units taken from prisoners, no roads assigned for transport, petrol short—the troops maintained "triumphant good temper as a substitute for order."[7] Almost completely lacking in artillery and machine guns, the Russians met the enemy onslaught with rifle and bayonet and with their bodies. It was Bernard Pares who noted that the Russians did with men what the Germans did with metal.[8]

Consideration for prisoners and refugees they gave to a fault, often sharing tea and bread they needed themselves. Hanbury-Williams remarked, "Hospitality, kindness, sympathy one found everywhere, and it sometimes strikes me that it is this intense desire to please, to make you happy and at home, which makes for weakness and want of stability."[9] In the first year of the war, enemy officers were not searched or questioned, or even disarmed. One wounded German officer being borne from the field by Russians drew his pistol and shot one of the bearers dead.[10]

The simple, daily evidence of the deep Orthodox faith of the men never ceased to amaze foreign observers. Each day began and ended with services—in the chapel at military headquarters, and in the open air or a tent in the field. On a tour of the battlefields with Bezobrazov in the spring of 1915, Knox records how touched the men were as the general gave them words of praise from the Emperor, and goes on to share his glimpse into the soul of the Russian soldier.

---

[7] Knox, *Russian Army*, p. 150.
[8] Pares, *Russian Monarchy*, p. 363.
[9] Hanbury-Williams, *Emperor Nicholas*, p. 7.
[10] Knox, *Russian Army*, p. 127.

Each place we stopped at the General gave a little lecture to the officers explanatory of the general situation, of which people in the trenches are very ignorant. . . . Here, again, I was struck by the wonderful simplicity of the Russian officers as well as the men. When we were in the underground hut of the Moskovski Regiment, the conversation ran on the tactics of the Germans and how best to circumvent them. The General discussed the possibility of break in our line of defence [and went on to describe how to deal with it]. . . . Then in the simplest possible way, without any change of voice or hypocritical flourish, he added: "You must always remember, too, the value of prayer—with prayer you do anything." So sudden a transition from professional technicalities to simple primary truths seemed incongruous, and gave me almost a shock, but was taken quite naturally by the officers crowding round with serious bearded faces, in the little dug-out. This religious belief is a power in the Russian army; the pity of it is that it is not turned to more practical account.[11]

For all his sincere admiration, Knox had put his finger on a prejudice shared by all Western allies of Russia. Her religion, centered as it was on divine mystery, had none of the utilitarian focus that had brought political, social, and economic progress to the West. The lengthy and elaborate Orthodox services did not seem to produce an advancing, modern society. Hanbury-Williams also records pleasant memories: the Great Blessing of the Waters in

---

[11] Knox, *Russian Army*, p. 263.

the Dnieper River at the Stavka in Mogilev with the thermom-
eter at twenty degrees below zero, and the midnight Easter service followed by a procession to the imperial house, where the
Emperor presented each of those present with a Fabergé egg.[12]

Even the French Ambassador, Maurice Paléologue, though
he thought the Orthodox services much too murky and mournful, could not suppress his awe at the Vespers service at Krasnoe
Selo, where sixty thousand troops were drawn up for review by
the Tsar.

> The sun was dropping towards the horizon in a sky of
> purple and gold. On a sign from the Tsar an artillery
> salvo signalled evening prayer. The bands played a hymn.
> Everyone uncovered. A non-commissioned officer recited
> the *Pater* in a loud voice. All those men, thousands upon
> thousands, prayed for the Tsar and Holy Russia. The si-
> lence and composure of that multitude in that plain, the
> magic poetry of the hour . . . gave the ceremony a touch-
> ing majesty.[13]

By the time Gibbes arrived at the Stavka headquarters,
the war had lasted for two hard and costly years, much longer
than most military and political observers had anticipated. One
German officer was quoted as saying he expected to be home
before the leaves fell—in 1914—and General Erdeli had told
Alfred Knox that they would be home for the New Year—1915.

---

[12] Hanbury-Williams, *Emperor Nicholas*, pp. 74, 89–90.
[13] Maurice Paléologue, *An Ambassador's Memoirs*, tr. F. A. Holt (New
York: George H. Doran Company, 1924), pp. 21–22.

Germany had long had a plan in place for taking down its main rivals with a two-pronged attack once the war for which they were waiting broke out. There would be a massive assault upon France sweeping through the Low Countries; already garrisons were stationed along the border with Belgium. Once France had been subdued, they would turn their attention to Russia, which would have been slow to mobilize because of primitive transportation and communication systems.

Russia was not unaware of Germany's ambitions and had its own strategy in place. Their action against Germany would be purely defensive, while they would hurl their most powerful forces in an offensive to knock out the Austrians. But once hostilities had exploded into reality, the situation for France was desperate. Menaced by the onslaught of the German war machine, she cried out to the Russians for immediate, aggressive assistance. Russia was more chivalrous than prudent in changing her basic strategy at the last moment and even before her mobilization had been completed for the campaign against the Germans.

Grand Duke Nikolai Nikolaevich, Commander-in-Chief, agreed to take the offensive. General Pavel Rennenkampf was ordered to invade East Prussia, which he did on August 12; by August 17 he had the German forces retreating before him to within 150 miles of Berlin. This initial success, together with the news that General Alexander Samsonov was advancing on the left with the second arm of the pincer, threw German Military Headquarters into near panic. Their first move was to recall the hesitant and frightened General Prittwitz and replace him with the seasoned veteran General Paul von Hindenburg and his chief-of-staff Erich von Ludendorff. Next, two army corps and a cavalry division were withdrawn from the western front and dispatched eastward. This, of course, violated the carefully laid German plans, but what good would it do to defeat France if Berlin were taken?

Meanwhile, on the eastern front, Samsonov was struggling to link his half-mobilized Second Army with Rennenkamph's left and then close in to surround and overwhelm the enemy. Success here depended on precise timing and good communications, a goal that was unrealizable for two reasons. First, the plan was activated too soon; second, Samsonov's under-strength army had to cross impossible terrain—the impenetrable marshland of the Masaurian Lakes, which as part of Russia's defensive strategy had been left without roads, without communication lines.

Thus the pincers did not close, and Samsonov's force, brought almost to a standstill in the mire, was totally annihilated by German artillery. Elation at Rennenkamph's early success was engulfed by the utter defeat at Tannenberg. General Samsonov had lost 170,000 men, and in despair took his own life. But this gallant sacrifice so costly to the Russians provided just the assistance needed for the French to hold off the invader on the Marne, and historians are unanimous in seeing this as the turning point in the war. The initial phase of the German strategy had been defeated, affecting all their subsequent plans. "God has dealt us a heavy blow," said Grand Duke Nicholas, even as he went on to say that he was happy to have helped the Allies. It has been remarked that the Russian soldiers who died at Tannenberg deserve as much credit for saving the Marne as the Frenchmen who died there.[14]

---

[14] See Pares, *Russian Monarchy*, p. 201.

Meanwhile, the Austrians had launched a massive invasion of Russian Poland. But here the Russians were ready, and in less than three weeks had driven the enemy forces out and followed them relentlessly into Galicia. Heavy artillery, of which the Russians had almost none, played very little part in this action. It was the skillful tactics and maneuvering of such generals as Plehve, Ruzky, Evert, Ivanov, Brusilov, and Lechitsky that took full advantage of the terrain and made effective use of the unbeatable Russian bayonet. The Austrian rout was so complete that she considered suing for a separate peace.

Before the fighting died down for the winter, the Germans to the north in a hard-fought battle drove Rennenkamph and his army out of East Prussia and a little way into Russia. Even here, with gallant fighting the retreating Russians managed to escape. The badly battered remnant of the army still stood facing the enemy, and Russian gains in Galicia more than made up for German gains in the north.

After the miserable showing by Austria, the Germans set out to provide sinew for their flabby ally by inserting their own troops in among them. It was this reinforced and steeled force that set out in Galicia in May of 1915 to accomplish what Austria alone had failed to do—capture Poland. This campaign revealed Russia's woeful shortage of munitions. The artillery had no shells and the infantry was short of rifles. Many raw new recruits were sent into the line without a weapon and ordered to wait for one until someone close at hand was wounded. The summer months for the Russian forces were one long, slow retreat, while the enemy conquered Galicia, Poland, and even part of Ukraine.

As stories of the huge losses (the regular army no longer

existed), the lack of guns and shells, and the horrible suffering of the men drifted back to the rear, spirits fell and indignation rose. There was a growing dissatisfaction with the Allies. Britain was not yet fully mobilized, while the French were constantly pressuring the Russians to do more than they were able, though they usually tried. The feeling was widespread in Russia that she was bearing the whole burden of the war. Panic reigned at headquarters and in the Duma, which began to press for a government of "public confidence" immediately and even talked of taking charge of military operations. Conservatives argued that concentrating on political reforms in time of war could only divert attention and resources and lead to catastrophe. The important thing was to win the war and then turn to political matters.

It was at this critical moment, when Russian military fortunes were at their lowest and civilian morale had plummeted, that the Tsar made his decision to take command of the armed forces. His ministers were horrified and begged him not to take on this extra burden, which would place on him the responsibility for every reverse and defeat. But these were arguments that bore no weight with the sovereign, who had three important reasons for his action. First and foremost, he felt his duty was to be with his troops at just such a time. Second, he believed his presence would lift morale, particularly among the peasant soldiers, who had little sense of nationalism but deep reverence for their Tsar. Third, it offered an opportunity for better coordination between the military and civilian authorities.

Critics of the Tsar expected the worst, giving him little credit as a strategist (which he never claimed to be), and predicting catastrophe if Grand Duke Nicholas were removed. Actually, his removal was beneficial. There is much truth in a remark that Brianchaninov had made earlier to Paléologue: "I'll grant you that he [the Grand Duke] is a patriot and a man of iron will, but he's in no way equal to his task. He's not a leader, but an ikon."[15] After the disastrous summer had revealed the frightening shortage of munitions and the incompetence of his aides, Generals Yanushkevich and Danilov, the Grand Duke was very near to nervous breakdown. He accepted his transfer to the Caucasus gracefully, perhaps even gratefully.

On September 6, 1915, Tsar Nicholas arrived at the Stavka and took charge. His presence did indeed make a difference. Hanbury-Williams gives his first impression: "I had always pictured him to myself as a somewhat sad and anxious-looking monarch, with cares of state and other things hanging heavily over him. Instead I found a bright, keen, happy face, plenty of humour and a 'fresh-air man.'" Months later, when the Emperor had returned to Stavka after an absence of some time, the Englishman again noted, "He is always so bright and cheerful that one cannot but be cheerful with him. It is a wonderful temperament for a man who must have such cares and anxieties on his mind, and I am sure is an inspiration for others."[16] In retrospect Gibbes noted the same qualities. "His genial personality, coupled with his authority and prestige were the centripetal forces that just made all the difference, as the Governments after his abdication soon discovered when it was too late."

Nicholas named General M. V. Alexeiev as his Chief of Staff, a man much more competent than his predecessors. Almost

---

[15] Paléologue, *Memoirs*, p. 45.
[16] Hanbury-Williams, *Emperor Nicholas*, pp. 15, 83.

immediately the military situation improved. Kiev, which had been threatened, was saved and the entire eastern front stabilized for the rest of the war. Just as important was the improvement in military supplies brought about by the collaboration between the Minister of War, Polivanov, and the leaders of Russian industry. "When the 1916 campaigning season began, the Russian army was larger and better equipped than at any previous time in the war."[17]

∾ ∾

In October of 1915 the Tsar brought the Heir to Stavka. Alexei's health seemed good at the time, and Nicholas felt that the disciplined military atmosphere would be beneficial for a boy who had had so much nursing and attention. The Tsarevich took to the altered atmosphere at once; he became a great favorite with the staff and provided many occasions for merry relief. But the Tsar intended this experience to be a serious part of his son's education, and when as new Commander-in-Chief he made a formal visit along the entire front, he took Alexei with him.

It was an arduous trip that did the troops and the father and son much good. The daily standing to reviews, walking the battle lines, and the travel itself were demanding, but Alexei's stamina and interest were remarkable. At one point they paid a surprise night visit to a dressing station in a small building lit by torches. "The wounded men could hardly believe that the Tsar was among them, and one of them raised his hand and touched his coat as he passed, to assure himself that it was no dream. Alexey was 'profoundly moved'."[18]

---

[17] Lieven, *Nicholas II*, p. 217.
[18] Gilliard, *Thirteen Years*, p. 126.

It was only as they were returning to Stavka that the Tsarevich's nose began to bleed profusely. It is not certain whether this was caused by a violent sneeze or by a jolt of the train when he had his nose pressed against the window. In any case, the bleeding intensified and the Tsar ordered the train to proceed on to Tsarskoe Selo. By the time they reached the station there, the Heir was very near death.

The doctors finally located the small blood vessel that had burst and managed to stop the bleeding by cauterizing that spot. Rasputin also played a role, for he had visited the sickbed, made the sign of the cross, and told the Empress not to be alarmed, the boy would recover. And recover he did, though it was early summer before he could return to Stavka. Meanwhile, his lessons resumed when he was strong enough, but they had to be worked in around the demands and ceremonies of Christmas, Epiphany, Lent, and Great Pascha (Easter).

When Alexei went back to Stavka in May, he was promoted to corporal and was as full of mischief and pranks as ever. Hanbury-Williams seems to have had a special rapport with the boy. Every day Alexei made a point of inspecting the attaché's coat to be sure each button was properly fastened and invariably found at least one intentionally overlooked. "Untidy again," announced the Tsarevich.

There were also more boisterous games: football with anything they could find for a ball, bread pellet fights at table, even water fights around a fountain in the garden, which involved plugging up all the holes with one's fingers, turning up the water to full power, and then letting go. This often gave everyone, including the Tsar, such a soaking they all had to go and change.

"Childish amusement no doubt, but which did one good all the same," commented Hanbury-Williams. The attaché also remembered more solemn moments. On the death of his eldest son, who had been mortally wounded fighting in France, Alexei came quietly into the room where he was sitting and said, "Papa told me to come and sit with you as he thought you would feel lonely tonight."[19]

When Gibbes arrived at Stavka on August 8, 1916, Pierre Gilliard had been granted a much-needed leave and Gibbes had to take over tutorial duties, which included monitoring Alexei's pranks and intervening when they became unruly. Gibbes was housed, like most other members of the staff, in the Hotel France, and each day after breakfast he made his way up the hill to the Governor's House, where the Tsar and Tsarevich lived and where the military headquarters were located.

Peter Vassilievich Petrov was also present, and the tutors worked their lessons into whatever schedule the Tsar had planned for his son. They accompanied him on drives into the town or the woods and took part in any games the boy found time to play. They usually dined with him in the evening alone, but lunch was a huge affair with the Tsar, the staff, and guests, sometimes as many as sixty or seventy people. In the presence of foreign dignitaries, Alexei could be very circumspect, speaking other languages well and asking intelligent questions.

As Gibbes took up his task, he began to write a diary from the point of view of the Tsarevich.

Oct. 8, 1916: Lessons as usual. Motored to the train at

---

[19] Hanbury-Williams, *Emperor Nicholas,* pp. 110, 139.

11 o'clock & after lunch motored to the wood on the Orshansky road where we played at "Robbers."

Oct. 13, 1916: Wrote to the Empress. . . . Came from play not feeling very well, by doctor's orders to bed at 6.30 pm. Very poorly all evening. Stomach quite upset. CSG read, but with difficulty could pay any attention.

Nov. 6, 1916: Had a bad night. . . . Dined all together as usual & after dinner played with geometrical puzzle & cat. [The cat, named Zoubrovka, was a kitten from Mogilev.]

Nov. 8, 1916: Feeling much better. Slept well & in good spirits but not allowed to get up until tomorrow. C.S.G. read and also P.V.P. . . . After dinner was carried into Emperor's study bed and all, while the room was aired. While there visited with the Grand Duke Nicholas & the Grand Duke Peter.

The entries reveal that despite the appearance of good health, there were constant small disturbances. A vein in his foot would swell until Alexei could not put on his shoes, one in his groin would interfere with walking, often his stomach was upset, perhaps from internal bleeding, and any slight cold brought the danger of coughing and sneezing.

Still, Alexei presented only boyish high spirits when he appeared among military observers, staff, and visitors. In addition to Hanbury-Williams, Baron de Ricquel, the Belgian military attaché, was a favorite and despite his huge girth joined in the impromptu games of football. The lessons also continued in as orderly a fashion as the tutors could manage under the circumstances. Among the interferences were the visiting dignitaries such as Prince Kolohito Kan-in of Japan, who came bringing presents, as did the ambassador from the Crown Prince of Serbia. The Empress and her daughters also came occasionally for a brief visit. At these times Alexei often went to visit their train and ride out with them for his daily outing.

There were many things to interest and entertain such a boy as the Tsarevich. There were flying exhibitions by the exciting new airplanes. He had playfellows from Mogilev to share boating and bathing in the Dnieper River. The Tsar and entourage often accompanied him on hikes through the woods, and the whole company would feast on roasted potatoes and chestnuts at the end of the trail. In the evening there was often a moving picture—another novelty—courtesy of the Pathé Company, which had sent the boy a reel and supply of film. *The Mysterious Hand* seems to have been the favorite, and the theater at headquarters was always filled when it was shown. In mid-December Alexei was not feeling well, and he returned with his tutors to Tsarskoe Selo to recuperate and prepare for the holidays.

The atmosphere on the military front was as optimistic and wholesome during this period as that at Stavka. According to Bernard Pares, the fine spirit at the front was "a wonderful unity in mind, thought and speech between those who lived in the constant reach of death, in the actual front line. . . . There was a zone which, in a very true sense, remained clean and even holy throughout."[20] Even in those dangerous conditions the bright Russian spirit often shone through.

---

[20] Pares, *Russian Monarchy*, p. 349.

It is astonishing what our soldier can do: what he can
simply arrange by himself with the greatest art. On a broad
field in front of the forest, in which were scattered the
dug-outs of this division, they set us down as spectators
of an extraordinary sight. Soldiers, dressed up as men of
all nations or as animals, paraded and danced and engaged in the sports of a county fair, and gave us a whole
programme of amusing items, dances, competitions, tricks,
choral singing, or rude country games. . . . All this music,
noise and hubbub were interrupted by the discharges of
the enemy's artillery, which were here considerably more
audible than at the staff; and among men and officers
there reigned such carefree merriment, as was a sheer joy
to watch.[21]

The opening of the 1916 campaign on the eastern front in
the battle of Lake Naroch was disastrous. Once again the movement in the north was begun in response to urgent French ap-
peals from the western front, where the Germans had launched
their tremendous assault on Verdun. The Russians advanced with
a vigor which completely surprised the enemy, who thought that
this part of the opposition had been permanently silenced. There
was now adequate ammunition, and under General Baluyev the
Russians made steady advances, until horrible weather and even
more horrible terrain brought them to a halt, causing enormous
losses in a morass of icy mud and blood. Still, the Russian spirit
seemed unconquerable.

The Germans had brought their heavy guns to within

[21] Brusilov, quoted by Pares in *Russian Monarchy*, p. 352.

400 yards of the Russian lines and unleashed a murderous attack, supported by poison gas, on the defenders, who had neither
steel helmets nor gas masks. Each time the Germans stopped the
bombardment to assess results, a burst of rifle fire came from the
other side. After five hours of this pounding, every battalion in
the front line had been reduced to less than a hundred men. But
for all this the Russians were only driven back a mile and a half,
and each night from their makeshift bivouack they could be heard
singing their Easter hymn, "Christ is risen from the dead, trampling down death by death." "One wondered whether that was
not the only weapon they had to fight with."[22]

The story in the southwest was quite different. General
Mikhail Brusilov was in charge there, and this outstanding commander was full of energy and ingenuity. He had remarked many
times that the regular army had been wiped out and what remained was little more than a militia. But he set about to make
up for their lack of training with drills, target practice, and en-
trenching methods there at the front. His tactics were also brilliant and daring, always relying on the attack. Realizing that any
massing of Russian forces in a particular spot would be detected
by the enemy, he devised a plan of multiple sites for simultaneous
assault. From early June to mid-September he advanced steadily
southwestward, recovering some of the losses of the previous summer and taking over 375,000 prisoners and a great deal of valuable equipment. However, he had paid the heavy price of 550,000
men, and with his reduced forces the advance began to lose steam.
Still, his successes had been some of the finest in the entire war.

At this point came another of those blows which fate seemed

---

[22] Pares, *Russian Monarchy*, p. 358.

to aim unremittingly at Russia. Rumania joined the Entente, and their presence proved to be much more of a hindrance than a help. They had thus far served as a neutral buffer, but their entry into the war greatly extended the Russian front line, and they needed much more assistance from their allies than they were able to give in return.

Still, as the winter of 1916–17 set in and the fighting died down, the Russian position was good and spirits were high. At the Inter-Allied Conference at Chantilly in November, the allied staffs laid plans for simultaneous offensives on both eastern and western fronts in early spring. The visible signs of demoralization in enemy prisoners, the failure of the Germans at Verdun, and the successes on the eastern front were grounds for the confident expectation that final victory in the war could be achieved.

6

⁂

Deeper Night

On the home front the outlook was not so bright. Despite the greatly improved military situation after Brusilov's brilliant offensive and the well-founded hope of winning the war in the next year, people in the large cities—especially St. Petersburg, now renamed the more Russian Petrograd—had another winter to get through. It would be their third winter at war, and it turned out to be one of the most severe. The major problems were basic: food, fuel, and transport. The very location of the city, at the most extreme distance from the food-growing regions, was a great disadvantage that combined with the crisis in railway transport to make food scarce and expensive. Prices soared while wages did not. There was little actual starvation, but there were acute shortages not only in food but in other necessaries. Living was hard. These problems were compounded by a flood of refugees from the war zone and workers coming from the countryside to find work in the munitions factories. Harsh living conditions began to take a toll, and war weariness set in.

Russia's transport systems were plagued from the outset by fateful and fatal misfortunes. Food, coal, and other supplies for the capital had formerly come through the Baltic Sea to ports such as Riga and Kronstadt, but the Germans had cut off that route from the beginning. Only Arkhangelsk in the north remained open and it was a hazardous route indeed, so little more than a trickle of supplies made it through from England and France.

Even before the declaration of war, Germany had the battle cruiser *Goeben* lurking in the Mediterranean, ready to move the moment Turkey aligned with the Central Powers. While awaiting a final confirmation, the commander, Admiral Wilhelm Souchon, proceeded with deliberation toward Constantinople, using stealth and cunning to elude all pursuers, and was in position when the go-ahead came. Joined by the *Breslau*, he slipped through the straits and into the Black Sea, where the two ships succeeded in closing off the only other warm-water ports available to central Russia. All other supplies and munitions had to be routed to Vladivostok and sent three thousand miles on the Trans-Siberian Railroad, already stretched beyond capacity hauling food and troops and fodder for their animals, which was of course top priority.

But there were other, even more intractable problems: the aggressive forces of discontent had been aroused, and it is always easier to incite resentment and anger than patience and restraint. Immediately after the declaration of war, there had been several months of apparent harmony within the government. However, once the Tsar made known his determination to postpone all parliamentary reform until after the war was won, the Duma members and liberal politicians found themselves with little to do except to plot and plan for that future.

In the spring of 1915, when the military losses were disastrous and the crippling shortage of ammunition and guns was exposed, the Duma's mood turned hostile. Blame for the shortages and defeats was laid at the feet of General Vladimir Sukomlinov, who was consequently impeached and removed as Minister of War. One of his aides, Colonel S. N. Myasoedov, was arrested for spying, court-marshaled at a secret and highly suspicious trial where he was convicted without defense counsel, and hanged that very night. These events provided a convenient alibi for the military disasters, laying the blame on espionage rather than the poor generalship that was actually responsible. In the eyes of the public, treason in high places had been proved. An hysterical spy-scare swept the capital, and there were whispers that treason had invaded the palace itself.[1]

In the wake of the scandal, Nicholas made an attempt to appease the nervous and restive Duma by agreeing to a shift in his cabinet. Four loyal and trusted ministers were replaced with men more inclined to work with the Duma and with the voluntary organizations, the Town Union and the Zemstvo Union, that had been formed to help with the war effort. The new Minister of War was Alexei Polivanov, an intelligent and energetic fellow despite some dangerous associations with men like A. I. Guchkov, who was an outspoken enemy of the Tsar. Polivanov began to

---

[1] George Katkov, who was a close personal friend of Gibbes in Oxford after WWII and one of the few people with whom Gibbes was willing to discuss his Russian experience, gives a detailed account of the intrigues at GHQ and the Myasoedov affair in *Russia 1917: The February Revolution* (New York: Harper & Row, 1967), ch. 6.

uncover the true situation at the Supreme Commander's Head-quarters, and the picture was so alarming that the Council of Ministers came up with a proposal to take charge of affairs by forming a Supreme Military Council, made up of ministers and Duma members, over which the Tsar would preside.

Nicholas's response to the situation was the decision to assume supreme command himself. His plan sent his ministers into near-panic, but he held firm despite all their efforts to dissuade him. His resolution contradicts the familiar picture of Tsar Nicholas as weak, witless, and without a will of his own—a view that has prevailed since the revolution of 1917. That view had been embraced earlier by his allies as well as his enemies and was promoted with great elaboration by the Soviet government.

As mentioned earlier, many pertinent archival documents have come to light since the defeat of Germany in World War II and the subsequent collapse of Communist Russia that make it worthwhile to give some attention to sorting out the details of the events leading to the abdication and the revolution in order to get a balanced account. These documents indicate not only the intrigues of the Tsar's political opponents but the significant amount of planning and resources spent by Germany on subversion, for the very purpose of bringing about such an upheaval.

The Council of Ministers was slow to recover from their pique at the Emperor's taking this momentous decision on his own—though it was certainly a traditional prerogative of tsars, and one this Tsar had mentioned to Grand Duke Nicholas when he was appointed Commander-in-Chief. They also blamed him for rejecting their proposal of a military council and ignoring their warning about the dangers of his taking over at a time when the military situation was so grave and he would bear the blame for every calamity. Prime Minister Ivan Goremykin, just after the Tsar's announcement, said that he too thought the decision very dangerous, but the Tsar was fully persuaded that it was his duty. "There remains for us only to bow before the will of our Tsar and help him."[2] But they did not try to help the Tsar. They set about trying to find some way to compensate for the lost political opportunities some of them had envisioned in a military council.

Their next move was to press Nicholas to cooperate with the Progressive Bloc, a recently established coalition of industrialists, members of the voluntary organizations, about two-thirds of the Duma members, and several from the Council of Ministers. They drew up a sweeping program of legislation, most of which would have to wait until after the war, but their primary purpose was to begin taking an active part in administration of the war effort and the economy. The Bloc called for a government of public confidence in which the Tsar would appoint a prime minister they approved, who in turn would name and direct the other ministers. Again the Emperor rejected the proposal, stating once more his firm conviction that any change in the form of government must wait until the Germans were defeated.

When the Emperor's arrival at headquarters brought about real improvement in morale, in military performance, and in the supply and delivery problems, public criticism softened considerably. These developments put the critics of the regime in an embarrassing position. Their dire predictions of impending disaster had proved false, and it began to dawn on them that their

---

[2] Lieven, *Nicholas II*, p. 214.

own bargaining position with the Tsar would be weakened once the war had been successfully concluded.

When military operations were curtailed as winter set in, the opposition intensified the campaign to vilify and discredit the monarch and his government. Every problem, every misfortune, every dissatisfaction was blamed on the autocracy. Nothing could be remedied, they alleged, until the entire system was changed. The press gave full support, publishing fact and rumor alike until the capital was gripped by doubt and uncertainty.

The Town Union, the Zemstvo Union, the War Industrial Council, and the voluntary organizations were a constant source of vexation. On the one hand, their excellent work in the supply and distribution of food, in care of the refugees and the wounded, in transportation of war materials was indispensable. On the other hand, their leaders missed no opportunity to insist that they were the ones who carried on these vital enterprises in spite of constant government attempts to thwart their efforts. They were the ones winning the war. Finally, the authorities were compelled to rebut this attack by pointing to the generous cash subsidies issued to these organizations, but the damage had already been done.

These organizations also provided political training grounds for many dissidents, and those who dealt directly with the military often found occasion to promote their own interests at the expense of the establishment. Despite the sometimes subversive suggestions, military commanders were unwilling to report these activities for fear of losing the organizations' assistance. A. I. Guchkov, friend of Polivanov, chairman of the Central War Industrial Council, and member of the State Council, was a particularly dedicated and wily leader in this movement. From his station in Moscow he was busily planning a palace coup he hoped to perpetrate in March, 1917. He flatly denied the existence of any such plot to the Tsar: "This is not the result of some conspiracy or coup planned in advance, but a movement that sprang from the very ground and instantly took on an anarchical cast and left the authorities fading into the background."[3] But Guchkov did have a plan, and the details were strikingly similar to the way actual events were played out. The Tsar was to be stopped at an obscure station between Mogilev and Tsarskoe Selo and forced to abdicate, and there would be antigovernment actions by the Petrograd garrison.

When the Duma convened in November, 1916, a spirit of confrontation prevailed. Pavel Miliukov made his famous speech, openly suggesting that the Emperor and Empress were guilty of treason. It has been called the first revolutionary act in Russia, and it had a stunning effect. He delivered an eloquent list of general accusations, each one followed by, "Is this treason or folly?" By this time the entire city of Petrograd had been infected with new doubts: the Tsar had previously been disparaged as unable to win the war; now he was accused of not wanting to win and of trying to make a separate peace. As tensions increased the possibility of revolution was openly discussed in the press, in drawing rooms, in factories, and on street corners.

❧ ❧

Sydney Gibbes had come to know Petrograd well in the

---

[3] From document in Mark D. Steinberg and Vladimir M. Khrustalev, *The Fall of the Romanovs* (New Haven and London: Yale University Press, 1995), p. 96.

fifteen years since his arrival. He had managed a variety of business interests and had never committed himself exclusively to his imperial duties, but kept active contacts in the capital. He had witnessed the rise of public dismay during the crisis months of 1915, when the military performance of the Russian Army was so dismal. Though he had spent several months at Stavka after the Tsar took command, drinking in the fine spirit that prevailed there, he was also aware of the harsh criticism directed at the Russian government, not only by opponents inside the country but also by her European allies—a unanimous call for immediate change to a Western-style constitutional government. But none of this kept him from taking another decisive step, actually two decisive steps, indicating a firm intention to establish himself permanently in his adopted country.

In mid-1916 Gibbes began negotiations to purchase Pritchard's English School for Modern Languages, an institution that offered courses in English, French, Spanish, German, Swedish, and Japanese. One of the specialties was business correspondence in any of these languages. The transaction was completed in November, though this was a time when political tensions were high and had gripped public attention. He had as his partner in the purchase Laura Anna Cade, an Englishwoman with whom he had worked at the school, where she was also a teacher. They contracted to purchase the school for five thousand rubles, to be paid over a period of three years.

Miss Cade had appeared as a special guest in at least one of Gibbes's programs of public reading in January of 1912. Unfortunately, there remains no correspondence between them, which was not too surprising so long as they worked together and saw each other regularly. But even in the papers generated after Gibbes had left Petrograd, there is only one tantalizing reference to Miss Cade by a third party. According to George Gibbes, Sydney's adopted son, they had intended to marry, but the revolution separated them and they were never able to make contact again.

In December Gibbes, Gilliard, and Petrov returned from headquarters to Tsarskoe Selo, bringing the Heir, who was ailing again. At the very time they were on their journey, on December 17, Gregory Rasputin was gruesomely murdered by three men, including two members of the Tsar's own family: Felix Yusupov, son-in-law of the Tsar's sister, Grand Duchess Xenia, and Grand Duke Dimitri Pavlovich, the Tsar's first cousin. The third assassin was a prominent right-wing member of the Duma, V. M. Purishkevich.

Luring their victim to Yusupov's palace, they plied him with enough cyanide to poison half-a-dozen men. When this had no effect, they resorted to shooting him. The first shot, fired by Felix, felled Rasputin, but shortly thereafter he revived, and rising up, made a lunge for his tormentor. Purishkevich later fired at him several times, and at least of two of the bullets brought him down. The assassins then weighted the body and dropped it into the icy river. The autopsy revealed that his death was caused neither by gunshots nor by poison—though both the bullets and the poison were present—but by drowning. One of the most potent elements in the legend that has gathered around this strange figure is his near-indestructibility.

When Alexandra learned of Rasputin's death, she died a death of her own. Gone was the one person who, she believed, could keep her son alive. She believed with all her being that this rough peasant, this man of the people, had been sent by God to help their beleaguered family. Moreover, he had left a strange letter predicting his own death before the year's end—and ruin for the Imperial Family if his killers were of the aristocracy. After this, Alexandra felt their doom had been pronounced; all they could do now was wait. And indeed a series of catastrophes, each one worse than the last, now began to unfold.

That Rasputin was able to help the Tsarevich is a fact established by many credible witnesses, though there has never been a satisfactory medical explanation for his cures. That he did the family great harm is also an established fact, but his influence and escapades have been sensationalized out of all proportion. His debaucheries, though real and shocking, never involved the Imperial Family, despite all the rumors and gossip to the contrary. But those tales did their poisonous work.

A deliberate campaign of slander suggesting that the Empress had intimate and improper relations with Rasputin had been launched by Guchkov in late 1916 and carried on with relish by several Duma members. This did enormous damage to the prestige of the monarchy, as the papers gave the stories sensational coverage, highlighted with mocking cartoons. Even more hurtful were the rumors, equally false, about "dark forces" surrounding the "German woman" who was their Empress, rumors insinuating that she and Rasputin were the center around which a "black bloc" had formed to work for a separate peace.

Given Gibbes's serious interest in mysticism, clairvoyance, and the like, it is surprising that he did not pay more attention to this notorious character, Rasputin, or at least try to get a glimpse of him. Gibbes is certain to have been aware of the stories circulating in the capital and appearing in the press. On the other hand, he still did not know the nature of his pupil's illness, and there may have been other family matters, such as visits by their "friend," that were just as guarded. His only comment in later years was that Rasputin was an uncouth *muzhik* who did not visit the palace nearly as often as people thought. Gibbes never saw him, and Gilliard, who was constantly on the premises, saw him only once.

As one would expect, the atmosphere in the palace when the Tsarevich arrived was one of gloom and foreboding, though the Empress was well-practiced in hiding her feelings. A few days' rest with treatments and compresses applied by his doctors had the boy feeling well enough to join in preparations for Christmas. There were Christmas trees to visit at various sites throughout the Tsar's Village and presents to distribute, and of course there were church services attended by the entire family and members of the court. The Tsar had hurried home at the news of Rasputin's murder and remained through the holidays, during which the family kept up a brave appearance.

But even during that festive time the boy continued to have intermittent episodes of swelling and nausea, and when bed rest was prescribed Gibbes began reading *Robinson Crusoe,* a story Alexei thoroughly enjoyed and often asked to have repeated. *King Solomon's Mines* was another favorite. There were times, however, when the pain was severe enough to require morphine, and then the Tsarevich could not pay attention to anything. After Christmas he was unable to return to Headquarters with his father.

Illness and ill luck seemed to stalk the palace. In mid-February, Pierre Gilliard came down with influenza, a killer during World War I. No sooner had the Tsar departed than Alexei came down with measles, another very serious disease in those days. Then one by one, or rather two by two, the Grand Duchesses were infected: first Tatiana and Olga, then Anastasia and Marie. The first pair had troublesome ear infections, Marie developed double pneumonia, and with Alexei every cough was dangerous. For weeks all of them lay in darkened rooms while the Empress, already exhausted by her hospital nursing and anxiety over the political situation, made her way back and forth among seven very sick patients. (Anna Vyrubova, her closest friend who was now living in the palace, had also come down with the same plague.) Alexandra insisted on doing the nursing herself, and Gibbes, who found himself on call at all hours, was given quarters in Alexander Palace. Alexandra wrote her husband that "Sig"—the nickname the family used among themselves—when summoned late to read to Alexei, came in his dressing gown. (Privately the family called Gilliard "Zhilik," though they used formal address to the tutors themselves. Gibbes was Sydney Ivanovich and Gilliard, Pyotr Andreevich.)

❧ ❧

Before the Tsar returned to Stavka on February 22, 1917, he had been bombarded with warnings of the growing threat of civil upheaval. The warnings came not only from the liberal politicians, but also from the aristocracy, from the officers' corps, and from the Grand Dukes within his own family. He was not blind to the situation in Petrograd and had in fact extended his holiday stay to deal with it. Plans were in place for handling violence should it erupt.

There are conflicting accounts as to the reasons for the Tsar's decision to return to Stavka. Rodzyanko in his memoirs reports that he had it from Prince Golitsyn, the Prime Minister, that the Tsar planned to meet with the Duma on February 22, but changed his mind. Other recollections suggest that he was just tired of the tensions in Petrograd and elected to return to the bracing atmosphere of Headquarters. Sophie Buxhoeveden, lady-in-waiting to the Tsaritsa, provides an eyewitness account, as she was present when the Tsar came into Alexandra's mauve boudoir with a telegram in his hand. "General Alexeiev insists on my coming. I cannot really imagine what can have happened to make my presence at Headquarters so urgently necessary now. I shall have to go and see myself. I am determined to stay only a week at the utmost, for I must be here."[4]

The journey to Stavka did lift his spirits, for there were enthusiastic welcomes at each stop along his route. Only a day or two before the great storm broke he told the Governor of Mogilev that he knew conditions were alarming, but "Soon, in the spring, will come the offensive and I believe that God will give us the victory and then moods will change."[5]

No sooner had Nicholas departed than there was a massive strike in Petrograd as women workers poured into the streets to mark International Women's Day. It was supposed to be peaceful, but their numbers were swelled by others, men and women, many of whom had poured out of the munitions factories, incited by special agents paid by the Germans to foment unrest. Others said they were striking because they were hungry and

---

[4] Buxhoeveden, *Tragedy*, p. 246. Gibbes considered Baroness Buxhoeveden to be an unimpeachable witness.

[5] Steinberg and Khrustalev, *Fall*, p. 231.

needed to search for food. And, of course, socialist revolutionaries joined the fray to fan these sparks. Though the mood of the crowds was volatile, the police and soldiers patrolling the streets had orders to withhold their fire. Instead of the calming effect this was designed to have, the demonstrators were emboldened and began to attack the police and officers, loot bread and wine shops, stop streetcars and drag off the passengers, whom they forced to join them.

News of the disorders reached Nicholas at headquarters, but the reports were conflicting. Letters from Alexandra dismissed the demonstrations as a hooligan movement that would die out if the weather turned really cold. Her letters also broke the news that their children were seriously ill. The official dispatches gave a much more complete picture of the disturbances, including attacks on the policemen and widespread looting, but they also reported that the situation was under control, which was not true.

With the surging crowds growing in number and becoming more unruly, on February 25 the Tsar wired General Khabalov: "I command you tomorrow to stop the disorders in the capital, which are unacceptable in the difficult time of war with Germany and Austria."[6] The general met with his unit commanders immediately to give the necessary instructions. He also posted notices throughout the city banning all demonstrations, warning that force would be used and that those arrested would be conscripted into the army at once. Despite this, hordes of people poured into the streets, and the troops followed their orders to fire, causing many casualties and at least forty deaths.

Order was restored, the crowds dispersed, and the soldiers

---

[6] Steinberg and Khrustalev, *Fall*, p. 50.

returned to their barracks, and Khabalov notified the Tsar that calm had been restored. But it was a calm that tingled ominously. The soldiers who had been mingling with the people during the past few days were sickened at the prospect of now having to fire on them. The first mutiny occurred that evening in the Pavlovsky Guard and the contagion spread rapidly from unit to unit, infecting the entire Petrograd garrison.

When Mikhail Rodzyanko wired the Tsar late that night to say, "State authority is totally paralyzed and utterly unable to reimpose order," Nicholas could not believe it and did not respond.[7] The Duma president had cried wolf too often. What Rodzyanko did receive that evening was an order postponing the Duma until a time in April 1917. According to George Katkov, the Tsar had left two incomplete manifestos when he went to Headquarters, one for proroguing the Duma and the other calling for a brief recess. The Council of Ministers and Prime Minister Golitsyn must have chosen between the two on their own responsibility, for there is nothing in the recorded official communications to indicate the Tsar's being consulted.[8]

The people who poured into the streets on February 27 were armed and ready to do battle, but instead of war it was fraternity when they found the soldiers joining their ranks. On this day the autocracy effectively ceased to function. Military authority had collapsed, and civil authority soon followed. The Council of Ministers, on hearing Khabalov's stark report on the increasingly volatile situation, first called for a military dictatorship and then formed a committee to try for cooperation with the Duma. But

---

[7] Steinberg and Khrustalev, *Fall*, p. 50.
[8] Katkov, *Russia 1917*, p. 287.

within a few hours, they decided the wisest course would be to abandon their responsibilities and tender their joint resignations. The Tsar rejected the resignations, wiring the ministers to remain in their posts. He informed them that General Ivanov was on the way with loyal troops and full authority as military dictator to restore order, and that Nicholas himself was returning at once. Despite orders to the contrary, this message was delayed by General Alexeiev, but it would probably have done little good had it arrived on time. The ministers had already retreated to their homes or gone into hiding.

Early next morning Nicholas boarded the second of the two imperial trains, which were to proceed by way of Smolensk and Bologoe to leave the more direct line to Tsarskoe Selo open for Ivanov. The Tsar expected to be home within two days and was confident that his presence along with that of the loyal troops could turn the tide. He had no inkling of the forces plotting to converge over the next three days to challenge him, there in his own railway carriage, and wring from him decisions that would change Russia forever.

As Nicholas proceeded, governors and honor guards were out to meet him at stations along the way. But arriving in Bologoe, he learned that rebel forces were blocking the way ahead, and it was decided to divert the train westward to Pskov, headquarters of the northern front. As they approached, word came that there would be no honor guard, though the governor of the province was on hand and assured the Emperor that the city was calm in spite of the news from Petrograd. General Ruzsky, commander of that front, was not present to greet his Commander-in-Chief, but came late and barged into the Tsar's salon car wearing muddy galoshes and a heavy scowl, signals of trouble to come.

The Tsar welcomed him with his usual cordiality. Ruzsky expected to find Rodzyanko there, but the chairman of the Duma had failed to appear at Dno as planned, though Nicholas had waited thirty minutes for him to keep the appointment Rodzyanko himself had requested. Nor had he come to Pskov. This meant that Ruzsky faced alone his assigned task of pressuring the Tsar to grant the concessions the Duma and liberal ministers had been calling for. Ruzsky was a very brusque and tenacious man with the tact of a bulldog, and he laid before Nicholas in the plainest terms the state of affairs in Petrograd, arguing that only a government in which the people had confidence could bring order out of the chaos. The Tsar was just as adamant, insisting that these matters would be handled effectively when he arrived at the capital the next day.

The struggle was confused by misinformation, manipulated information, and outright deception. The aim of the military leaders now was to persuade the Tsar to grant political concessions that would appease the people and remove the necessity of using troops to stop the riots. The Emperor was not told that a Provisional Committee had already been formed, with Rodzyanko as chairman, and had taken matters into its own hands. Nor did the Tsar know that the chairman had imprisoned his ministers, with the exception of those of War and the Navy, in the Peter and Paul Fortress. The military commanders on all fronts received continuous reports about the situation from Rodzyanko and from Alexeiev at Headquarters, and their greatest fear was that use of troops to quell the disturbances in Petrograd would result in total demoralization of the army. They were under the impression that

Rodzyanko was the man of the hour in Petrograd, the one who was in control of the situation, so that once the Tsar conceded a representative government the need for military intervention would be erased.

Meanwhile General Ivanov had arrived in Tsarskoe Selo with his troops, and the intriguers now bent their efforts to prevent his taking action. General Alexeiev took it upon himself to wire Ivanov from Mogilev that the Tsar seemed likely to agree to a representative government, in which case Ivanov's assignment would be changed. Alexeiev then sent an impassioned wire to Nicholas at Pskov, emphasizing the growing danger of anarchy, the disintegration of the army, and the diminishing hopes of winning the war, and urging him to agree to a representative ministry led by Rodzyanko. This is the argument that broke the Tsar's resistance. He agreed to sign the manifesto and wired Ivanov to take no action until further orders. Drained by the grueling events of the day, Nicholas retired in the wee small hours of the morning.

But Ruzsky did not retire; he contacted Rodzyanko by direct telegraph and held a four-hour conversation in which he learned that the revolution was roiling out of control, that soldiers were disobeying and even murdering their officers, that the chairman had imprisoned the ministers, and that hatred of the dynasty was rising and could not be contained. The Tsar's concessions had come too late, Rodzyanko said, and only abdication in favor of the Tsarevich could save the situation. Ruzsky was surprised to learn that matters were so completely out of hand, and that the man who had maneuvered them into a position where abdication seemed the only solution was himself losing control.

When Alexeiev received a copy of this telegram, he dispatched a message to all his commanders reviewing the situation and stating his opinion that in view of the rising hostility, abdication was now the only way to save not only the dynasty, but the army and any prospect of winning the war. He requested that the commanders send their response to this proposal directly to the Tsar at Pskov with copies to him, Alexeiev, at Headquarters.

On the morning of March 2, Ruzsky awoke Nicholas to read him the transcript of his conversation with Rodzyanko. Immediately afterward responses from the commanders began to arrive, along with Alexeiev's copies and his own statement of support for abdication. All recommended that course, and only General Sakharov, commander of the Rumanian front, delayed his vote until the others were in. The Council of Ministers had simply dissolved, and now the Tsar's generals, without whom the war could not be won, had abandoned him.

Nicholas walked to the window of the car and looked out over the winter landscape for a long time. Then, turning, he said, "I have decided to abdicate."

He then entered his own car and wrote out two telegrams. One went to Alexeiev at Stavka:

> For the sake of the well-being, peace, and salvation of Russia, which I passionately love, I am prepared to abdicate from the throne in favor of my son. I ask you all to serve him truly and sincerely.

He included instructions for drafting an abdication manifesto. The second message he addressed to Rodzyanko:

There is no sacrifice that I would not make for the sake of the true well-being and salvation of our own mother Russia. For that reason I am prepared to renounce the throne in favor of my son, assuming that he will remain with me until his coming of age, under the regency of my brother Grand Duke Michael Aleksandrovich.[9]

While waiting for a response to these messages, the Tsar had a long conversation with Dr. Fyodorov about the health of the Tsarevich. The doctor told him that the boy's hemophilia was incurable, and though long life was a possibility, there would always be the threat of an accident and his condition would severely limit his activities. This information moved Nicholas to change his mind and abdicate in favor of his brother.

These painful discussions and arrangements were prolonged by further failures in communication. The Provisional Committee had sent two delegates, the hostile A. I. Guchkov and a more moderate Vasily Shulgin, to persuade the Tsar to abdicate. They were dumbfounded to discover that the Emperor had already made his decision and had indeed drawn up his own manifesto. Guchkov, who had long been anticipating just such a confrontation, must have been sorely disappointed that the matter had been settled without him. Recalling that solemn day, Shulgin remarked, "How pitiful the sketch we had brought, and how noble his parting words."[10]

The two delegates expressed their anxiety at the withdrawal of Alexei as successor, for they had counted on the child's having

---

[9] Steinberg and Khrustalev, *Fall*, p. 61.

[10] Quoted in Edvard Radzinsky, *The Last Tsar;* tr. Marian Schwartz (New York: Doubleday, 1992), p. 188.

a softening effect on public opinion. The naming of Michael in his stead was worrisome for two reasons. First, it violated the laws of succession, and second, he was married to a twice-divorced commoner, another disqualification.

In the end both matters were academic, for at the Tauride Palace, where crowds had gathered along with the Duma members, the announcement that Grand Duke Michael would succeed was greeted with loud protests: "Long live the republic!" "Down with the dynasty!" "Down with the autocracy!" "Down with the Romanovs!"

Even those officials who had tried to preserve the monarchy in a constitutional form realized it had become impossible and any attempt would only lead to bloodshed. When Prince Lvov, who was now Chairman of the Provisional Government, told Grand Duke Michael that they could not guarantee his safety, he also decided to abdicate, though he added to his manifesto that he would be willing to ascend the throne if requested by a constituent assembly. And so the three-hundred-year rule of the Romanovs ended on March 3, 1917, though very few actors in the drama appreciated the true significance of the event or the consequences it would precipitate.

❧❧

The ex-Tsar was permitted to return to Stavka to bid farewell to his troops. As the train was pulling into Mogilev, General Voeikov, palace commandant, went into the car where Nicholas was sitting alone, with only an icon lamp burning. The former Emperor, who had maintained such self-control throughout the tragic day, rose to embrace his old friend and finally wept. When the train arrived, Nicholas went with General Alexeiev to the

Governor's House, where he wrote out a moving farewell to the troops he loved so. He encouraged them to obey the new government and their commanders and make their best effort to win the war. "May the Lord God bless you and may the Holy Martyr and Conqueror St. George lead you to victory." On orders from the Provisional Government, this message was never published, and the troops knew nothing of this final act of devotion.

Next day Nicholas said farewell to his staff and officers. Once again his main concern was encouragement to pursue the war to a successful conclusion; with his incredible calm and emotional control he thanked them for their loyalty and service. As the men gave a cheer for the leader they truly loved there were tears in every eye, and many officers fainted.[11] To his diary Nicholas confided that his heart nearly broke.[12]

The following day his mother, Dowager Empress Marie, came by train from Kiev to say good-bye. The abdication had been a terrible blow to this regal woman, and she was unable to maintain the poise that was her trademark. The three-day visit must have been agonizing for them both; she was unable to restrain her sobs, but the son she had trained so carefully maintained his calm. He listened attentively to her laments at the humiliation and tried to reassure her that they would all meet again soon and in safety in the Crimea or in England. He smiled and waved as her train pulled away and both made the sign of the cross, neither realizing that they would never see each other again.

Back in Petrograd, the Soviet of Soldiers' and Workers' Deputies were making such insistent demands for revenge on the

---

[11] Katkov, *Russia 1917*, p. 351.

[12] Steinberg and Khrustalev, *Fall*, p. 115.

Imperial Family that the Provisional Government decided to "deprive them of their freedom," and for their safety to confine them to the Alexander Palace at Tsarskoe Selo. On March 8, four officials of the Duma arrived at Mogilev to arrest the former Emperor and conduct him back to his prison home.

As their train moved out, General Alexeiev, with tears in his eyes, removed his cap and made a low bow. Only a few hours after the abdication he had told an aide that he would never forgive himself for "having believed in the sincerity of certain people, for having followed them, and for having sent the telegram suggesting the Emperor's abdication to the commanders-in-chief."[13]

---

[13] Katkov, *Russia 1917*, p. 347.

7

Prisoners

Alexander Palace, that haven of domestic tranquillity for this close and affectionate family, was also something of a fortress. Since the assassination of Alexander II, the traditional guards of the Imperial Family had become much more than ceremonial. The élite *Garde Equipage,* the Composite Regiment, the Cossacks of the Emperor's Escort, and the Railroad Regiment were constantly on duty, for the threat of terrorist attacks was very real, as the frequent assassinations attest. On February 28, 1917, the fortress came under siege. Inside were the Empress, her friend Lili Dehn, wife of the *Standart's* first officer, the children—three of whom were stricken with measles along with Anna Vyrubova—and members of the palace suite and servants.

The Empress had invited Lili that Monday to join her for a pleasant drive and then tea. Over the weekend there had been no urgent bulletins about disturbances in the city, and Alexandra thought this meant order had been restored. It was only after their excursion that she learned the Petrograd garrison had mutinied, murdering their officers and pouring into the streets to join the unruly demonstrators. Not only that, the mob was rampaging through the city, looting shops, burning buildings, seizing cars after throwing the drivers out. Under such conditions Lili decided to stay the night, and a bed was made up for her in the family quarters.

In the early hours of March 1, Rodzyanko made an urgent telephone call to the palace. The family there was in danger from the hostile mob and should be moved immediately. Grand Marshal Benckendorff did not disturb Alexandra, for they had stayed up very late discussing the threatening situation, and he knew that she was sorely in need of rest. However, he did send word to the Tsar and received instructions to make the necessary arrangements for their evacuation. When the Empress learned of this development, she adamantly refused to budge. She would never leave without her children, and they were too sick to be moved. Benckendorff called to report her decision, and Rodzyanko informed him that the crisis had deepened to the point where no train would be available, and even if there were the railroad workers would not let it pass.

Anxiety filled that day, putting even more strain on already taut nerves. The Empress was unable to make contact with the Tsar; all her telegrams were returned with the ominous notation, "Whereabouts of this person unknown." She tried to convince herself that this meant he was on the way home. Toward evening came word that a gang of mutinous soldiers in Petrograd had murdered their officers and set out in commandeered trucks for Tsarskoe Selo, shouting that they were going to get the "German woman." Benckendorff ordered additional men to beef up the guards stationed around the palace.

When night fell the women watched from the upstairs windows as bonfires were lit and mess wagons drawn into place. They were comforted by the sight of their own soldiers silhouetted in battle order against the snow, those in front kneeling and the line behind standing with rifles at the ready. But raucous sounds could be heard from the town, where the rebels had stopped to loot the wine shops and were now drinking, shouting obscenities and threats, singing revolutionary songs, firing random shots. They were getting closer.

Gibbes in later years would often recall how the Empress surpassed herself when courage was called for. Around 9 P.M. she threw a fur coat over the nurse's uniform that had become her regular attire, and taking Marie with her went out into the dark, accompanied by Count Benckendorff and Count Apraksin, to speak with their soldiers. She passed along the line thanking each man, assuring them all of her trust, and reminding them the life of the Tsarevich was in their hands. Then she made arrangements for groups of men to be brought into the palace to warm themselves and have hot tea. When she came in out of the frigid night she was confident, "These are our friends."[1]

There was little sleep that night. The Empress, Lili Dehn, and Lady-in-Waiting Baroness Sophie Buxhoeveden lay down but did not undress, and from time to time Alexandra would get up to look out into the night. The unruly soldiers did get within five hundred yards of the palace, but a howling blizzard, plus the

---

[1] Paul Benckendorff, *Last Days at Tsarskoe Selo: Being the Personal Notes and Memoirs of Count Paul Benckendorff.* (London: William Heinemann, 1927), p. 8.

rumor that a huge force was guarding the palace and had machine guns pointing at them from the roof, threw the drunken, leaderless men into confusion, and they decided to give up their adventure.

Next day, Alexandra rose well before daybreak to greet Nicholas when he arrived. He did not come, and though she tried to believe that he had been delayed by the blizzard, everyone knew that if this were the case, they would have had word. On one of her trips to the windows, she noticed that the soldiers were now wearing white bands at the wrist. These turned out to be tokens of a truce worked out during the night with the revolutionary troops. The rebels had agreed not to attack the palace on condition that the palace guards not interfere with their wild activity in the town.

On March 2, events took a sharp turn for the worse. The men of the élite regiments, men whose loyalty was never doubted and who were regarded as personal friends, had defied their officers and gone to join the mob. Even more incredibly, Grand Duke Cyril Vladimirovich, the Tsar's first cousin, had pinned a red cockade to his cap and led the sailors of his *Garde Equipage* into Petrograd to pledge allegiance to the Duma.

Still no word from the Tsar. Terrible suspense and uncertainty hung over the palace, which had now become rather like a huge dungeon. Lights and water had been cut, so the long corridors and cavernous rooms were dark and cold. Water could only be obtained from ice on the pond, and there was no steam in the pipes for warmth. But with the indomitable will that amazed them all, the Empress insisted on maintaining a semblance of normal order. Her elevator to the children's quarters was not working, but despite her seriously ailing heart and painful sciatica, she labored up the stairs to make regular rounds of the sickbeds.

Gibbes had been sleeping in Alexander Palace during the epidemic to be on call through the night. On this evening he and Alexei played a quiet game of dominoes in the classroom, where there was a fire, as the playroom could not be heated. They also made a few model houses of paper to add to the village they were developing and molded some bullets, but their hearts were not in it. "The boy knows nothing of passing events," Gibbes wrote, "but feels them all the same." Later in the evening Syd read Russian fairy tales by candlelight until the boy fell asleep.

The Empress insisted that Gibbes take the next day off, so Thursday night he went over to the Catherine Palace and slept once again in his own rooms. No trains had run that day, but he went to the station very early next morning and found that a train was being made up. He boarded, wondering all the while how and when he would get back. Once in the city he went through streets littered with debris and scarred by burned-out buildings to check on his flat, make sure things were in order there, and pick up a few books. Then he set out for his newest enterprise, Pritchard School, where he spent several hours getting a thorough briefing on the progress and prospects there.

Gibbes emerged into an altered city. The streets were filled with agitated people—some crying, some standing silent and bewildered, some shouting and cheering. Word was spreading that Tsar Nicholas II had abdicated the throne. Russia no longer had a tsar. Gibbes was staggered, and the full import of the news took a while to sink in. When he was able at last to focus his mind, he set about gathering the most authoritative newspapers he could find and hurried back to his flat.

Once convinced that he had to believe the unbelievable, Gibbes set out for Tsarskoe Selo—he would be needed on such a night. There were no trains now, so he hired a cab. A number of servants from the palace had also gone into Petrograd for the day. Perplexed and frightened, they set out to walk the fourteen miles home through the ice and snow with the news, but the Tsaritsa could not believe them.

The stunned members of the imperial suite and officers of the guard read the papers through tears. In the evening Grand Duke Paul Alexandrovich came to break the news to Alexandra. She emerged from the interview pale and shaken and made her way into the red drawing room, where Lili Dehn was waiting. *"Abdiqué,"* she gasped and fell into a chair, her head in her hands. It was long before she could speak. Then all her concern turned to her husband, "all alone down there. What he has gone through, oh my God, what he has gone through. . . . And I was not there to console him."[2]

It was late indeed before anyone thought of retiring. Faithful members of the suite came one by one to assure Alexandra of their loyalty. She was deeply touched and spoke her heartfelt gratitude, and also her faith that somehow all was God's will. When at last everyone had retired, most lay staring into the dark pondering, fearful of what lay ahead.

But the sun did come up next morning and even shone brightly, a sign Alexandra took for good. She decided to delay

---

[2] Lili Dehn, *The Real Tsaritsa.* (Boston: Little, Brown, and Company, 1922), p. 165.

telling the sick children, at least for a time. In her mauve boudoir, she and Lili spent much of the day burning her letters and diaries. There were tears as she read again the letters of Queen Victoria, who had loved and guided her motherless granddaughter since Alexandra was six years old. She kissed each letter before committing it to the flames. There were letters from her sisters and brother and from the friends she bombarded with her lavishly affectionate correspondence. The hundreds of letters from Nicholas she did not burn, intimate and tender as they were, intended for no eyes but hers. There were now loud demands to put the deposed couple on trial, and she realized these letters would be valuable as proof that there was no treasonable conspiracy on their part to make peace with the Germans.

The day brought one enormous relief: Nicholas telephoned from Pskov. The faithful servant Volkov, who came with the word, was so excited that he forgot all formality, and just burst in and blurted out his message. The telephone connection was abominable, and both knew others were listening as they spoke, but to hear his voice and know he was safe was the best news Alexandra could possibly have. He asked whether she knew of the abdication. "Yes," she said, only that. He could not say exactly when he would be returning, but expected it to be soon. They ended their conversation speaking briefly of the illness of the children. Later she poured out her heart in a letter:

What relief & joy it was to hear your precious voice, only one heard so badly & one [i.e., someone] listens now to all conversations. And your dear wire this morning. I wired you yesterday evening about 9 1/2 [9:30] & this morning before 1. . . . The invalids upstairs & downstairs know nothing of yr decision—fear to tell them, & and also as yet unnecessary. Lili has been an angel & helps one being like iron.[3]

She adds that Gibbes, now their reporter and courier in Petrograd, had seen two daughters and the seriously ailing wife of Count Fredericks, Minister of the Imperial Court and Domain, crammed into a single room in an officers' hospital since their home had been burned down. None of the Imperial Family dared go out while the streets and rails were in control of the revolutionaries, but Sig was able to get about; he brought news and ran various errands on request. One errand was a special trip to the home of Lili Dehn to find out about her seven-year-old son, Titi, who was ill, and to bring some fresh clothing for the lady.

Very late on Sunday evening, 11 P.M., two unexpected visitors arrived at the palace: A. I. Guchkov and General Lavr Kornilov, new commandant of the Petrograd garrison. Arrival at such an hour seemed ominous; had they come to arrest Alexandra? Count Benckendorff summoned Grand Duke Paul from his bed to come and be with her. About twenty members of the revolutionary council of Tsarskoe Selo had accompanied them. These ruffians roamed through the palace, peering into rooms without knocking, insulting officers and members of the suite, taunting the servants.

Guchkov and Kornilov conducted themselves with restraint, though a cold formality prevailed. They assured Alexandra that they had come only to make sure she and her children were safe

---

[3] Steinberg and Khrustalev, *Fall*, pp. 11–12.

and had the things they needed, particularly medicine. She replied that they had adequate provisions, but she requested that the palace utilities be restored for the sake of the sick children and that order be maintained around the palace. She also asked that the delegation check with the military hospitals in Tsarskoe Selo to be sure their supplies were ample. Guchkov promised to carry out her wishes.

Once news of the abdication spread among the troops remaining in the palace garrison, the men "became more and more down-hearted. They began to say that as the Emperor had abdicated, they were absolved from their oath, and that they would make their submission to the Provisional Government." The worried officers consulted together and decided that the wisest course was to form a deputation of officers and men and present a formal declaration of intent to the new authorities. This was done in the night, and their document pledging loyalty to the new authority also stated that they intended to do their duty to protect the Imperial Family and their palace. Rodzyanko received the deputation and gave his enthusiastic approval. "When this was over, the morale of the troops was completely restored and routine went on as before." Heartened by this development, Count Benckendorff prepared similar papers for the palace police and the servants.[4]

After this, Gibbes noted, there was a pronounced change in atmosphere. All the comings and goings of ministers, foreign dignitaries, petitioners, and friends ceased. Even the servants, though still respectful, seemed somehow different. On March 8 Gibbes made another trip to Petrograd.

---

[4] Benckendorff, *Last Days,* p. 16.

That very day General Kornilov returned to the palace to place the family officially under arrest. The palace guards were replaced by troops loyal to the Provisional Government. All doors in the family wing of the palace were sealed except for the main entrance and the kitchen. Members of the suite, including officers, were free to go, but those who left could not return, and those who remained would be under house arrest. Not surprisingly, the majority left, and many of them may have heard the general's disgusted, "Lackeys," as they made their retreat. All correspondence going out or coming in was to be examined by the palace commandant, Colonel Yevgeny Kobilinsky. Telephone lines were cut, except one in the guardroom. Later the prisoners were permitted to use that phone, but only in the presence of a guard and speaking Russian.

Gibbes returned from the city that day to find himself barred from Alexander Palace. When Tsar Nicholas returned on March 9, the tutor had to watch the sad spectacle from the Semicircle of the Grand Palace. The new contingent of soldiers on guard were a sorry sight, slouching and unkempt, their hair uncombed, their uniforms untidy. The ruinous Order No. 1, posted on March 1 as a manifesto granting soldiers civil rights, had totally demolished military discipline and morale. Soldiers no longer saluted or used "Sir" in addressing their officers. They refused to obey any order that displeased them. They often beat their officers, and in some cases killed them. Just such a disreputable crew greeted the former Tsar with humiliating surliness. Ignoring his salute, they first pretended not to recognize him and went through a crude, theatrical verification of his identity before allowing "Citizen Romanov" to pass.

His true welcome came from the family waiting so anxiously within. Alexei and the girls had now been informed of the abdication and something of its implications, but not a word was said about it as they showered their father with kisses and told him how glad they were to have him home at last. When he emerged from their darkened quarters, the light exposed the ravages of his ordeal. He had grown pale and much thinner, the hair at his temples had turned gray, his face was deeply lined, and there were dark circles around his eyes.

Nicholas smiled feebly and sat down with Alexandra and Lili. He made an attempt at casual conversation, but it was more than he could manage. He decided to go for a walk to unwind. As Alexandra and her friend looked on from their window, the sight was heartbreaking. No matter which direction he took along the path leading to the canal, a soldier would step up to block his way, prodding him this way and that with the butt of a rifle as if herding an animal. Nicholas retained his usual calm and nodded to each one of his tormentors before finally turning back toward the palace. The imperial prisoners were face to face with the hard facts.

Valia Dolgorukov, stepson of Benckendorff, had come back with Nicholas from Pskov, and he described the abdication to the suite and officers.

His narrative was dramatic, and made a deep impression on us. It seemed to us inexplicable that the Emperor, who had never been able to make up his mind to grant a constitution and to appoint a responsible minister, had so quickly consented to abdicate. The part played by the Generals and Staff seemed to us like treason.[5]

Gibbes now found himself outside the palace and a free man. Many in that position would have considered themselves lucky, but he had no intention of abandoning his duty. Still, what should he, what could he, do? His first move was to seek the aid of the British Ambassador, Sir George Buchanan, who listened sympathetically and immediately dispatched a letter to the head of the Provisional Government requesting that Gibbes be permitted to return to his duties. Weeks dragged by before a response signed "Five Commissars of the State" denied the request. A second letter was sent, and Buchanan advised patience, promising to use his office to do everything he could. On his own, Gibbes took his plea to every revolutionary authority he could reach, but with no success.

He had also written at once to the ex-Empress telling her of his efforts to return to duty. Correspondence was permitted, though all letters, whether going out or coming in, were read by the palace commandant, who very early began to complain at the huge volume of mail. Gibbes kept in touch by writing to his pupils and to members of the staff who had stayed on. His colleague, Pierre Gilliard, who was forbidden to leave the palace, wrote often asking Syd to run various errands for him in the city— shopping, banking, acting as business representative. Censorship did not allow the tutors to exchange much meaningful information, though it is possible that they worked out some sort of code. In his letters Gibbes gave careful, factual reports of the news in Petrograd that had been made public, and Gilliard reported that

[5] Benckendorff, *Last Days*, pp. 43–44.

the imperial students were back in a routine of lessons. The Tsar
was teaching Alexei history and arithmetic, Alexandra taught
religion, Gilliard continued French lessons to all but Olga, who
no longer had lessons. He also helped coordinate all the instructions. Baroness Buxhoeveden had taken over the English instruction (she and Gibbes exchanged notes on this), Countess
Hendrikova taught art, and Mlle Schneider Russian.

Gibbes made his rooms in Catherine Palace his regular lodging so as to pick up what snippets of information leaked out about
the family and their faring. He was still able to purchase his meals
from the imperial kitchen, and when his servant went over to
pick them up he was able to get bits of inside gossip. These reports gave some indication of the state of things, at least among
the servants. Some had been infected by the revolutionary propaganda and were sullen; others were loyal but unhappy at the
confinement; still others were ready to serve to the end. A long-
standing custom allowed families of the kitchen servants to come
each evening to receive leftovers. After their visits, these folks
were usually bursting with information, though truth was hard
to extract from the gossip. Unfortunately, as the more radical elements began to dominate the palace guards, this practice was
stopped. Another source of inside news opened up whenever the
guard made one of its periodic decisions to reduce the number of
servants. The dismissees immediately found themselves the center of attention, for everyone was anxious to know what was going on inside the palace.

Despite a firm resolve to return to his tutorial duties, Gibbes
was a practical man. He took steps to follow up on a proposal
made by his Uncle Will to market an efficient kitchen stove in

Russia, the Barnsley Smokeless Cooker. The presentation to the Burgomaster of Petrograd was promising. In early April he wrote his uncle,

> There is no trace of any previous proposition of the kind in the annals of the Town. . . . They realize the advantages that may result from such a scheme and would be glad to consider a more definite proposition. Can you send me as early as possible particulars of the Barnsley Smokeless Fuel Company, Ld? What they now wish to obtain is some idea of the financial side of the question and a comprehensive view of the Barnsley Co.

But political tensions continued to worsen to the extent that the Provisional Government on April 26 had to acknowledge it was no longer able to maintain order—and little wonder, since their first actions upon coming to power had been to abolish the death penalty, then the police department and all regional governors and their deputies. Without authority to enforce the law and with discipline in the army destroyed, chaos was inevitable. The breakdown in communications ended any possibility of commercial negotiation. Did Uncle Will even receive Syd's letter?

Newspapers were full of conflicting reports about the Imperial Family. The radicals pictured them enjoying extravagant luxury in a palace when they deserved to be in the Fortress of SS. Peter and Paul. The moderates tried to make it plain that, though severely restricted, the family was being treated humanely. The actual details are in the Tsar's diary, letters from the family to friends, memoirs of some of those who were with them, and even reports of their adversaries. One feature that stands out in all accounts is the absence of bitterness. The faith of the entire family enabled them to hope that good could come out of even this cruel and threatening situation and to conduct themselves with dignity and grace in the face of deliberate insult and deprivation.

❧❧

Inside the palace, tedium sat heavily on each day. No guests came in, no inmates went out, and activities were always the same. Alexandra's routine for studies seldom varied. Lessons filled the morning hours and occupied the entire family, now that Nicholas and Alexandra had joined the faculty. Only Olga was excepted, and in consequence she sometimes grew sluggish during their confinement. Morning tea provided a recess, and afterward Nicholas walked out, accompanied by members of his staff and one or more of the children, before resuming their studies. Other walks were permitted, but only in specified areas during daylight hours and always attended by touchy guards. An outing might be ended abruptly because Count Benckendorff walked too slowly, because Gilliard said something to one of the Grand Duchesses in French, or because a servant was pushing Alexandra in her chair—a practice particularly resented by the revolutionary soldiers, who shouted and swore that she should be made to walk.

The school day ended around midday for lunch, then the long afternoon stretched ahead to be filled somehow. Here Nicholas's active, enterprising nature redeemed the time. He and his children and willing members of the suite spent hours and hours in humble, hard manual labor. Wood would be needed for next winter's fires, and the former Tsar and some of his men set to work felling trees around the park and sawing them up, while

Alexei and the girls stacked the brush. In mid-July they were "nearly up to sixty sawed-up trees."[6]

At the end of March, they began work on a vegetable garden. Dirt was hauled by the barrow-load to create raised beds in which they set out five hundred cabbage slips. They also planted onions, cucumbers, and other vegetables. "All the servants who wished to, took part, and they were happy to have the opportunity of working for a few hours in the fresh air."[7] The Grand Duchesses worked side by side with them, wearing heavy work boots, plain woolen skirts, blouses, and sweaters. Their heads, which had been shaved during their illness, were tied up in kerchiefs. The garden work went on every day from two to five until they left Tsarskoe Selo. In May, the fruits of their labors began to appear on the table. One fine Tuesday in June, Nicholas noted that "all the daughters came out to gather the mown grass."[8] They actually took pleasure in doing the hard, outdoor work of peasants.

Neither Alexei nor his sisters ever complained about this labor. Their steady good humor and courtesy touched many of the guards, and some even pitched in to help. But this depended on the contingent of the day. Some resentful types taunted the prisoners in their abasement and looked for occasions to make trouble. One soldier reported to the Soviet of Soldiers' and Workers' Deputies that he had seen two officers kiss the hand of one of the Grand Duchesses. This made such a stir that the officers were subjected to an inquiry and then transferred to other

---

[6] Steinberg and Khrustalev, *Fall*, p. 165.
[7] Benckendorff, *Last Days*, p. 79.
[8] Steinberg and Khrustalev, *Fall*, p. 162.

posts. It could be dangerous to be civil to the Imperial Family.

After dinner in the evenings, the women often did needle-work while Nicholas read aloud. The adventures of Sherlock Holmes were favorites; he also read *The Count of Monte Cristo*, and lighter fare like *The Millionaire Girl*. On at least two occasions, Alexei invited everyone, including the suite, to his room to see a cinema. These were the Pathé films he had taken with him to Stavka.

> He enjoyed acting as host, and received us with a childish animation which was charming to see. He is very intelligent, has a great deal of character and an excellent heart. If his disease could be mastered, and should God grant him life, he should one day play a part in the restoration of our poor country. He is the representative of the legitimate principle; his character has been formed by the misfortunes of his parents and of his childhood. May God protect him and save him and all his family from the claws of the fanatics in which they are at present.[9]

The first prison of the family in Alexandra Palace was the easiest because it was home, and they were surrounded by their own things. Even so, the March days must have been hard, unaccustomed as they were to confinement, insult, and being ordered about. The soldiers were particularly obnoxious; intoxicated by their new authority, they delighted in harassing their prisoners. On one occasion a guardsman thrust his bayonet into the spokes of the bicycle Nicholas was riding, then guffawed as he struggled

---

[9] Benckendorff, *Last Days*, pp. 95–96.

to his feet and walked the machine back to the palace. Another
day as the ex-Emperor and his company returned from their walk,
they found the sentry lounging in a fine gilt chair he had dragged
from the palace; he had his boots on the ottoman.

In March, Kerensky burst onto the scene. He had replaced
Rodzyanko as leader of the Provisional Government. This curious man could not hold himself still. He was so charged with
nervous energy that he shouted when he might have talked, ran
when he might have walked, gesticulating wildly. On March 21
he darted in at the kitchen entrance of the palace and ordered
the servants assembled. He then delivered an inflammatory
speech, telling them "they no longer served their old masters,
that they were paid by the people, and that their duty was to
watch all that took place in the Palace and to consider themselves under the orders of the Commandant and the officers of
the Guard."[10]

But he had another purpose in this visit: to order the Empress separated from the Emperor and the children, a step that
was needed, he said, because the extreme parties believed her to
be the head of a counter-revolutionary movement. Benckendorff
and Sophie Buxhoeveden finally persuaded him that the Empress should remain with the invalids, but Kerensky insisted that
if this were the case the Tsar must be kept apart and permitted to
see the rest of the family only at meals and at worship services in
the presence of guards.

Kerensky had also come to arrest Anna Vyrubova. When he
entered the room where Anna lay still recovering from measles,
he was dumbfounded to discover that this woman, whom rumors

---

[10] Benckendorff, *Last Days*, pp. 54–55.

had painted as the seductive mistress of Rasputin and even of the Tsar, was a rather pudgy, middle-aged woman who could not walk without crutches. Nevertheless, he ordered her taken to the Fortress of SS. Peter and Paul, where she was held in cruel conditions for several months. Lili Dehn was also arrested, and though released after a few days, she was not permitted to return to the palace.

The separation of Nicholas and Alexandra lasted only two weeks, but Kerensky took advantage of the time to question them separately about government policies and appointments just before the revolution. Alexandra responded to his questions with a clarity and frankness that astonished him, explaining that she and the Emperor had been in total agreement on all matters and that she made no decisions without his approval. Most of her meetings with ministers had related to hospitals, the Red Cross, prisoners of war, and other charitable projects. The ex-Emperor, on the other hand, felt no obligation to explain or defend his decisions and made no attempt to keep the conversation going. Kerensky was impressed with his calm reserve and later acknowledged that he had found no trace of treason or counter-revolutionary activity in either of them.

The long, hard month of March ended with Holy Week and the promise of Easter. Father Afanasy Beliaev had been summoned to the palace early in the month to bring the revered Icon of the Sign, depicting the Virgin Mary with the Holy Child encircled on her body, and conduct a service for the birthday of Alexei and for the sick. He arrived in procession, accompanied by deacons and subdeacons, and all were passed in by the soldiers. He was deeply moved when "on her knees, with tears in her eyes, the earthly tsaritsa asked the Heavenly Tsaritsa for help and intervention."[11] Count Benckendorff recalled how the procession left the palace, and everyone went out on the balcony and watched as it disappeared. "It was as if the past were taking leave, never to come back. The memory of this ceremony will always remain in my mind, and I cannot think of it without profound emotion."[12]

For the celebrations of Holy Week and Pascha, the priest was allowed to move into the palace. His diary records some of the items featured in their Lenten meals: shredded cabbage with pickles and potatoes, cabbage soup with mushrooms, rice cutlets, fried smelts, dry biscuits in sweet syrup, fruit compote. That intimate contact with the royal family exhilarated and inspired him, but broke his heart.

> One has to see for oneself, be near enough to understand and be convinced of how fervently the former tsar's family pray to God, in an Orthodox manner and often upon their knees. They stand at worship with such obedience, meekness, and humility, giving themselves up completely to the will of God. And I, a sinner and unworthy servant of the altar of the Lord, feel my heart stop beating, the tears flow; and despite the oppressive difficulty of seclusion, the Lord's abundance fills my soul.[13]

At the first Divine Liturgy in the presence of the former Emperor, when it was time to pray for "the Provisional Govern-

---

[11] Steinberg and Khrustalev, *Fall*, p. 139.
[12] Benckendorff, *Last Days*, p. 103.
[13] Steinberg and Khrustalev, *Fall*, p. 142.

ment instead of the Devout Autocrat Sovereign Emperor and so
on, I could not at first find the strength and almost started weeping. With a cracking voice, stumbling over the words, I finished
the commemorations."[14]

Everyone in the palace, including the servants, made confession during Holy Week: on Wednesday fifty-four, on Friday
forty-two servants and members of the suite, including the two
doctors; then followed the confessions of the ladies of the suite
and the members of the Imperial Family. The confessions of the
Grand Duchesses and Alexei made a deep impression on Father
Beliaev.

> I will not say how the confession went. My general im-
> pression was as follows: Lord, let all children be morally
> as upright as the children of the former tsar. Such mild-
> ness, restraint, obedience to their parents' wishes, such
> absolute devotion to God's will, cleanliness in their lodg-
> ings, and complete ignorance of worldly filth—either
> passionate or sinful—amazed me and I was totally at a
> loss; as a confessor, do I need to remind them of sins that
> perhaps they do not know?[15]

He was even more affected by the confessions of the parents.

> Her Majesty came in an agitated state . . . to confess the
> illnesses of her heart before the holy cross and the Gos-
> pels. His Majesty came for confession after her. . . . Oh,
> how unspeakably happy I am that I was favored by God's

---

[14] Steinberg and Khrustalev, *Fall*, p. 140.
[15] *Ibid.*, p. 144.

grace to become the mediator between the Heavenly Ruler and the earthly one.... Until this time, this was our God-given Anointed Sovereign . . . And now Nicholas, a humble slave of God, like a meek lamb, benevolent toward all his enemies, harboring no offense, fervently praying for Russia's prosperity, believing deeply in her glorious future, on bended knee, gazing at the cross and Gospels, in the presence of my unworthiness, tells the Heavenly Father the innermost secrets of his unfortunate life and, prostrating himself before the greatness of the Heavenly Tsar, tearfully asks forgiveness for his voluntary and involuntary sins.[16]

Then came the great Bright Feast of the Resurrection, when masters and servants gathered together at midnight to hymn the great, glad happening. After Liturgy the family and the suite broke fast, and next morning Nicholas exchanged the traditional triple kiss with all the servants, while Alexandra gave them porcelain eggs left over from former reserves. "There were only about 135 people."[17]

After this, their days fell back into the same old pattern of study, walks, and work. The isolation weighed on them all. There was a momentary lift in spirits when a promising offensive was launched on the southwestern front, but within a fortnight hopes were dashed. The troops refused to advance when ordered, and even retreated when there was no enemy pressure. Nicholas was devastated.

---

[16] Steinberg and Khrustalev, *Fall*, p. 145.
[17] *Ibid.*, p. 154.

Gibbes was not having a pleasant time of it either, though he was free and had affairs enough to occupy him in Petrograd. He was having trouble just getting his belongings together. Quite a few of his possessions were inside Alexander Palace, and even more had been left in his quarters at the Hotel de France in Mogilev. When he had accompanied the Tsarevich home to Alexander Palace in December 1916, he had fully expected to return to Stavka, though of course that never happened.

Not knowing who was now in charge of the hotel or under what ministry such matters would fall, he wrote Sir Hanbury-Williams for help. The British Attaché made inquiries at the hotel and wired Gibbes that his property had been turned over to the servant he had sent for it. This information was not reassuring, for Gibbes had sent no servant; the soldier assigned to serve him at the hotel had been part of the regular rotation and reported to his own commander. Apologizing profusely for further trouble, Gibbes wrote Hanbury-Williams again, enclosing a list of the things left in his room. It is an interesting assortment: a quantity of books, a large Persian rug, a pair of high boots, some clothes, toilet necessaries, electric light wire, a walking stick, an umbrella, and some picture posters. These things were never recovered.

Word that his father had died in the spring of 1917 reached Syd two months after the event, and the news stirred his family affection. He wrote poignant letters home, especially to Aunt Hattie, who had attended John Gibbs in the years since the death of his wife. His first thought was to thank her "for all the love and care that you have bestowed on him during the last years of his life."

Without you it is difficult to imagine what he would have done, he certainly could not have lived so long nor been so happy. . . . I should have much liked to come once more before all is broken up, but putting aside the question of authorisation to travel which is not given at the present moment, you will doubtless by now know the position in which we are placed here from the turn of political events. It therefore seems out of the question at the present time, for nobody knows what is going to happen, and my duty as well as my interests call for my presence here. Our fortunes are completely broken, and it is more than possible that I shall leave Russia and return to England with my pupil.

The news that his aunt would be selling the things from the family place at Normanton prompted him to ask apologetically for a few pieces of furniture and pictures, "just some of the things that are always associated in my mind with home." He insisted that she have the things valued and let him know the price, mentioning again that "it is possible that we may come over to spend our exile there."

Nor was he alone in expecting to go to England. Upon abdication, Nicholas had made four requests of the Provisional Government: (1) that he be given safe conduct to Tsarskoe Selo; (2) that the family be permitted to stay there until the children were completely recovered; (3) that they be given safe conduct to Murmansk, which implied embarking for England; and (4) that they be permitted to return after the war to take up permanent residence in the Crimea, at Livadia. General Alexeiev presented the first three petitions, which were approved by the Provisional Government. The fourth he did not mention.

The safe conduct turned into arrest and the stay at Tsarskoe Selo into confinement, but the third item still had official approval. Miliukov sent a formal request to the King's Government through Sir George Buchanan, who added his own opinion that such a move would help calm the situation in Russia. At first the government agreed; after all Russia was an ally and King George was cousin to both Nicholas and Alexandra. But there was one reservation: that Russia provide financial support for the family.

During the months that followed, radical sentiment in Russia began to fester, and any plan for supporting the family at public expense would have caused a violent eruption. The shaky new government realized it could not fulfill its pledge. Public opinion in Britain was not much friendlier, for the liberal and labor factions, with strong encouragement from Prime Minister David Lloyd George, were vehemently opposed to accepting the fallen monarch. Buchanan was notified of the King's decision to withdraw the offer, but instructed not to mention it unless another official request was made. Of course, the prisoners knew nothing of these developments, but when they were finally informed that they would not be going to England their reaction was almost one of relief, for they had always been reluctant to leave Russia.

During July serious disturbances broke out in Petrograd, and Kerensky realized that the family would have to be moved. He held out a vague hope of their going to Livadia, though he probably knew this would never happen. In the end he decided on Tobolsk, a sizable town in Siberia, but one that had dozed off after the Trans-Siberian Railway bypassed it. The political atmosphere there was conservative and, so far, free from radical activity. This choice was quite astute, because it achieved the purpose of the Provisional Government by removing the family from harm's way, and at least for a time pacified some of the growing radical demands for punitive measures by sending them away to the desolate land notorious as a place of exile. Kerensky's move undoubtedly added a year to the lives of the Romanovs.

Informed that they would leave on July 31, 1917, they started packing warm clothing, a few household items such as lamps, vases, linens, rugs, pictures, books, and papers. Alexandra also took many of their jewels, worth approximately a million rubles. On the morning of their departure, Alexei and the girls rushed about the palace, saying good-bye to friends and servants and leaving little gifts.

Nicholas made a more solemn round to bid farewell to all, and instructed Benckendorff to distribute the garden produce among the servants who had helped with the work. Count Benckendorff was not accompanying them because of age and the state of his wife's health. In a thoughtful gesture, Kerensky had arranged for Grand Duke Michael to pay a final visit, but it turned out to be only awkward, since neither Nicholas nor his brother could think of much to say under such circumstances and in the presence of an observer. After a few strained remarks they bade one another good-bye, then Michael kissed Alexei and left hurriedly in tears.

That afternoon the family and those accompanying them gathered in the round hall where their crates and trunks were

stacked. Wearing heavy coats and hats, holding two of the beloved family dogs, they were ready to proceed. Their evacuation
was being conducted in utmost secrecy, and for one reason or
another delay followed delay. They were kept waiting all evening
and on through the night. Every attempt to lie down or doze off
was frustrated by yet another report that the moment for departure had come. In the wee hours of the morning Madame
Benckendorff decided to order tea for the party, but a painful
incident marred this final courtesy. When Nicholas took his cup
and sat down, the officers rose from the table, saying they would
not sit with a Romanov. They later confessed to Count
Benckendorff that they had done this for fear of being reported
to the soviet by the soldiers—one more depressing commentary
on the state of the army.[18]

The trains—there were two, marked with signs reading "Red
Cross Mission" and flying a Japanese flag—scheduled for one
A.M. did not arrive until six. The family and their companions
entered one car, most of the military escort the other, and their
long journey eastward began just as the sun was coming up.

---

[18] Benckendorff, *Last Days,* p. 110.

Left:
Grand Duchesses
Tatiana and Olga.

Below:
Grand Duchesses
Anastasia and Marie.

Left:
The Empress reading on
the balcony at Tsarskoe Selo.

Photos, page 1

Above:
Alexei with his three tutors,
Pierre Gilliard, P.V. Petrov,
and Charles Sydney Gibbes.

Left:
A portrait of Tsarevich Alexei,
by an unknown artist.
(courtesy Wernher Colection, Luton Hoo)

Below:
Alexei out for a drive with his tutor,
Charles Sydney Gibbes.

Left:
The Empress, Olga, and
Tatiana as Sisters of Mercy.

Below:
Charles Sydney Gibbes
giving a lesson to Anastasia.

Bottom:
The imperial classroom
at Tsarskoe Selo.

Left:
Marie and Anastasia in
amateur dramatics (1912).

Left:
Guards at the gate of the palace.
For a time, Charles Sydney Gibbes
was not allowed to enter.

Below, left:
Tsar Nicholas and Pierre Gilliard sawing
wood at the compound of the Governor's
House, Tobolsk (1917).

Below, right:
Tsar Nicholas riding a biccycle during his
time of captivity in Tobolsk (1917).

Left:
A revolutionary procession outside the Governor's House, where the Imperial Family was being held in Tobolsk.

Below:
Alexei and Olga on board the *Rus* at the beginning of their last journey.

Below:
The Ipatiev house in Ekaterinburg, where the Imperial Family was confined and murdered.

Two photos above: Investigation underway at the Four Brothers mine, where some human remains of the Imperial Family were found.

Left:
Box containing the human remains of the Imperial Family found at the Four Brothers mine area. (This box was in Charles Gibbe's charge for a time.)

Photos, page 6

Above:
St. Nicholas House, 4 Marston Street, Oxford; George Gibbes in doorway.

Below:
Chapel at St. Nicholas House, containing some of the treasures of the Imperial Family Charles Sydney Gibbes had collected.

Above left:
Charles Sydney Gibbes
in 1925.

Above right:
Charles Sydney Gibbes,
soon after his ordination
to the priesthood
(as Fr. Nicholas)
in 1935.

Right:
Archimandrite
Nicholas Gibbes
(at right)
with Archbishop
Nestor in 1938.

Photos, page 8

8

Sent to Siberia

No sooner had the Romanov family departed on August 1 than Gibbes received the long-awaited permit to enter Alexander Palace, dated August 2. He went over at once to retrieve the items he had left there. The walk through the heavily guarded halls was painful as he passed the familiar rooms, their doors now closed and sealed—the classroom, the playroom, the sickroom where he had so recently kept vigil, the dining room where the staff took their midday meal. All those lively, lovable friends and colleagues had departed into an unknown, menacing future, and he was left behind. He stopped now and then to listen, hoping perhaps for some echo of the happier days. In his own room he picked up books, clothes, toiletries, and that dressing gown the Tsaritsa had commented on.

Next day he sought out a commissar, seeking permission to travel to Tobolsk, and was surprised to learn that he was free to go whenever he wished. Sydney Gibbes had never considered any other course than following the family when permitted, even though he expected to be imprisoned; now he could leave at once, and might even overtake them. He hurried into the city and set about disposing of his considerable interests there. He turned in his resignation at the Imperial School of Law, arranged instructors for his private pupils, and then turned to dissolving his ten-month-old partnership at the Pritchard School.

One cannot help wondering about the effect of this decision on the relationship between himself and Miss Cade. They were affianced, and she would be understandably distressed at his going, but dissolving the partnership implied a deeper breach; it may have so offended her that she made a renunciation of her own. She may well have felt that his pledge to her ranked higher than his loyalty to the former monarch and the family he had not seen for five months, who had now gone off into the unknown. Besides, as an Englishman, Gibbes was not a subject of the Tsar nor of the present government, nor was he dependent on them for his livelihood.

An intriguing item among Gibbes's papers may provide a hint. There is a single postcard from Katya, a former servant in Petrograd, where he had maintained his flat on Nevsky Prospekt up until his departure. "Dear Master," she writes in December, 1917, she is sending the book he requested to Tobolsk, and in response to his query adds, "Miss Cade is in good health." Apparently, the lady herself was not communicating and expressed no concern about his faring. Their parting seems to have been a more definite rupture than the vague loss of contact during the revolution that has been suggested. Whatever happened there, it did not delay his buying a ticket to Tiumen. However, yet another railroad strike erupted, and he was delayed a month longer.

≈≈

Meanwhile, the "Red Cross" trains made their way across the Russian heartland. The cars in which the family and their entourage rode, though not luxurious, were comfortable, modern sleeping cars, and Nicholas reported that their meals were "very tasty." Several loyal members of the suite accompanied the royal exiles: General Ilya Tatishchev; Marshal of the Court, Prince Vasily Dolgorukov; Pierre Gilliard; Dr. Evgeny Botkin; Alexei's faithful sailor companion, Nagorny; Countess Anastasia Hendrikova; and Mlle. Ekaterina Schneider. There were also about thirty servants and retainers, including cooks, a barber, a wine steward, chambermaids, wardrobe attendants, valets, a nurse, and the like.

The second train carried the armed guard, numbering over three hundred. They were under the command of Colonel Evgeny Kobylinsky, the same considerate commandant who had done as much as he could at Tsarskoe Selo to ease the situation of the prisoners. Before the trains departed, the soldiers had been lectured by Kerensky: they were to behave with respect and decorum. Rude or vindictive behavior was unworthy of the revolution. Kobylinsky was just the man to enforce such orders.

The soldiers had been issued new weapons, including machine guns, and their mission as defined by the Provisional Government was more one of protecting the prisoners from outside interference, and even attack, than of trying to prevent their escape. Each day a contingent of the guard rode shotgun on the outside, while at least four soldiers plus an officer were stationed inside each car with the prisoners. All window shades were drawn, all doors locked when going through a station in towns or cities of any size. Stops for water or mechanical problems were only permitted in smaller stations, and then on the most remote siding with guards posted. Each evening the trains stopped in open country, and those who wished could walk in the fields and run the dogs. Their guards seem to have been lenient in remote country, judging from the account Anastasia sent to a friend, of which Gibbes saved a copy.

> Once in the evening I was loking out of the window we stoped near a little house, but there was no staition so we could look out. A little boy came to my window and asked: "Uncle, please give me, if you have got, a newspaper." I said: "I'm not an uncle but an anty and have no newspaper." At the first moment I could not understand why did he call me "Uncle" but then I rememberd that my hair is cut and I and the soldiers (which were standing next to me) laught very much.

All went smoothly until the caravan reached Perm. There the train was halted, a rough, gray-bearded man barged into Kobylinsky's cabin, and, "calling himself chairman of the railway workers, declared that the 'comrade' railway workers wished to know the purpose of this train, and until they were told, they would not let it pass."[1] When the general brought out the authorization signed by Kerensky, the man seemed satisfied, and the trains were permitted to proceed on their way. On August 4 Nicholas noted in his diary, "Crossed the Urals and felt a substantial cooling. Passed Ekaterinburg early morning," with no

---

[1] Steinberg and Khrustalev, *Fall*, p. 170.

inkling that this city was destined to be the scene of the terrible end of their long journey.[2]

Through the wearisome steppe country, the trains seemed to be dragging; nevertheless, they reached Tiumen the same day. Their train pulled in close to the platform, where motorcars were drawn up beside the station to transfer the passengers to boats waiting on the Tura River. As Nicholas emerged from the car, he saw the military authorities of the town standing at attention some distance behind the lines of guardsmen and saluting as he passed. The Romanovs and their company boarded the *Rus,* while the soldiers, servants, and baggage followed on the *Kormilets* and the *Tiumen.* At the point where the Tura and Tobol rivers meet, they passed a village that had significance for them all. It was Pokrovskoe, Rasputin's home, and the whole company crowded against the railing to gaze at the hamlet in which his two-story house stood out clearly. He had once told Alexandra that she would see his home before she died, and this was yet another of his prophecies fulfilled. An omen?

On August 6, as the *Rus* rounded a bend in the Tobol, the passengers saw a low, symmetrical hill crowned by massive, crenellated stone buildings and walls that had once been the city's fortress. The golden domes of the cathedral also shone out over the town from high on the hill, and the adjacent archbishop's residence stood like a palace. The rest of the town had arranged itself around that hill and along the river. In its prime Tobolsk had been a provincial capital and an important river port, trading fish and furs from the Arctic north, though only a trickle of that trade remained since the railroad had bypassed

---

[2] Quoted by Radzinsky in *Last Tsar,* p. 210.

the town. Many of the twenty thousand or so remaining inhabitants lived in modest wooden houses close to the river bank, while others occupied more imposing homes that climbed up the hillside above the town. There were at least twenty small whitewashed churches with green roofs and golden crosses in the lower town, brightening the clusters of shops and houses along the planked streets.

As the boats pulled up to the dock of the West Siberian Steamship and Trading Company, all the church bells were ringing and the streets were filled with people. The commissars of the Provisional Government were taken by surprise and alarmed: was this a monarchist demonstration? Their reconnaissance party returned to report that it was the Orthodox Feast of the Transfiguration and the people were keeping traditional festival.

The former governor's mansion was to house the prisoners. A large, white house with two stories across the front and three facing the back garden, it was located in the center of town and surrounded by other old, but still sturdy, civic buildings. Just across the street stood an equally commodious house owned by a rich merchant named Kornilov. His house was commandeered for members of the suite.

When Kobylinsky, Tatishchev, and Dolgorukov went to inspect the premises, they found them far from ready. Nicholas wrote:

> The lodgings were empty, unfurnished, dirty, and unfit to move into. So we remained on the steamer and began to wait for them to bring back the necessary baggage for us to retire. We had supper, joked about people's

astonishing inability to arrange even for lodgings, and went to bed early.[3]

The family and some of the servants remained on the *Rus* for another week, and an enjoyable week it turned out to be. The captain cruised up and down the river by day, stopping wherever the bank seemed to offer a likely spot for hiking or even a picnic. These were to be their freest, happiest days. Even Alexandra went ashore to walk a bit or sit and watch the others.

Meanwhile, most members of the suite, the commandant, a commissar from the government, and numerous servants went to work on the house. Rooms were scrubbed and painted, windows washed, furniture, including a piano, bought and arranged, pictures and draperies hung. Even so, when the family moved in and had "examined everything in the house from the bottom to the attic," Nicholas confided to his diary that "everything has an old, neglected look," and the garden he found "nasty."[4]

The family occupied the entire second floor. On either side of the salon at the head of the staircase were the drawing room and a study. Along the corridor behind these were the bedrooms. Nicholas and Alexandra occupied the main one and all four girls shared a large corner room just behind it, where each put her personal stamp on her own narrow space with its camp bed, single straight chair, and side table. They filled the tables with icons, books, combs, brushes, scent bottles; their beds with favorite cushions, afghans, and clothing for which there was no wardrobe space. The wall behind each headboard was plastered with photos of

---

[3] Quoted in Radzinsky, *Last Tsar,* p. 212.
[4] *Ibid.,* p. 213.

friends and relatives, the *Standart,* their military regiments, their pets, special outings, and the like.

Alexei had his own room on the other side of the hallway, with Nagorny occupying a small room adjacent to it. Pierre Gilliard took a room downstairs just off the drawing room, while the rest of the suite found space in the Kornilov house across the street. The top floor at the back of the Governor's House was occupied by the servants and unpacked luggage.

At first the atmosphere was easier and more pleasant than at Tsarskoe Selo. The soldiers were for the most part more professional, less surly, though the Second Rifle Regiment remained hostile as ever. Members of the suite were free to come and go as they pleased, several of the servants were permitted to live in town with their families who had followed them, and Dr. Botkin even set up a private practice.

The Imperial Family itself was not allowed the same freedom, though in the beginning Kobylinsky set no guards inside the house. However, when the family ventured across the street to visit the Kornilov house, the men of the Second Rifles were incensed and demanded that they be more closely guarded. Traffic from the Kornilov house was to be strictly one way. Colonel Kobylinsky was forced to have a high stockade erected around the house, the grounds and service buildings, and a portion of the dingy street alongside. This dusty, treeless space was their only exercise area. Nicholas's frequent requests for permission to walk under guard into the town or beyond it were always refused on the grounds that their safety could not be guaranteed, an excuse he considered "stupid." Up to the very end, neither he nor Alexandra could comprehend the animosity that had been engendered toward them in the very people they had trusted as the "true Russians."

The second story of the Governor's House was graced by small balconies running along outside the windows and a large commodious one on the west front, which the family put to full use. In fine weather they took morning tea there and came out frequently during the day to enjoy fresh air. From here they had a fine view of the comings and goings, the flow of normal life, going on around them in the center of town. The citizens also had a fine view of them.

The revolutionary spirit had yet to make much headway in this region. People there, many of whom were descendants of exiles or political prisoners, still revered the Tsar as the God-anointed ruler, who could not be touched by earthly authorities.[5] Yet here he was in their midst under circumstances that were bewildering. Members of the imperial suite walked about the town in uniform, the faithful servants in livery, while the Tsar himself and his family were closely confined behind the stockade. Guards stood at the gates and constantly patrolled the perimeter. Occasionally a belligerent soldier would disperse the citizens who

---

[5] Jacob Walkin has interesting comments in *The Rise of Democracy in Pre-Revolutionary Russia* (New York: Frederick A. Praeger, 1962) on the nature of prison and exile that put these institutions in a surprising new light. Brutality and harsh conditions there certainly were, but "Czarist prisons seem 'mild, almost humanitarian,' compared to the concentration camps of modern totalitarian states. Political prisoners were segregated from common criminals and given more privileges and better living conditions." They were not required to work, and if they had no means of support, the government gave them an allowance. Books, paper, pencils were allowed. "Lenin wrote the whole of his *Development of Capitalism in Russia* while in jail or in Siberian exile. The book was then published legally in 1899, during his last year of exile. . . . Neither Lenin nor Stalin worked while in exile. Both were men of leisure and engaged largely in hunting, fishing, and reading (pp. 67–68)."

flocked daily for a glimpse of the august presences. At times the always-regal Tsaritsa could be seen in her chair doing needlework, the beautiful young princesses more often, and they always acknowledged friendly greetings with a bow. The Tsar and Tsarevich were less disposed to sit out, but the appearance of either became the event of the day. The people crossed themselves and bowed, some fell on their knees. The people also brought offerings of food. There were sweets and pastries from the nuns, butter and eggs from peasant farmers, fruits and other delicacies from the merchants. "Little gifts from heaven," Alexandra called them.

By September a routine very like that established at Tsarskoe Selo was in place, a way of giving order to their days and substance to their hope in a future for which they were preparing their children: lessons in the morning, a break for tea and exercise at eleven, more lessons, lunch, and exercise again. Afternoons were freer, but assignments had to be prepared for the next day. The girls practiced on the piano, a pleasant interlude, for all but Anastasia were accomplished enough to provide pleasant listening.

After dinner everyone assembled in the large downstairs drawing room to fill the long evenings as best they could. Often Nicholas read aloud while Alexandra and the daughters did needlework. Sometimes there were games of cards or dominoes, or music from Mlle Schneider and on rare occasions from Alexandra herself, who played and sang beautifully and lost some of her shyness in this close-knit company. This was also a time for writing letters.

September brought a change in the prison environment. Vasily

Pankratov had been appointed by Kerensky to be commissar in charge of the captives, and he and his deputy, Alexander Nikolsky, arrived on the second day of the month. Pankratov, though a dedicated revolutionary, was a decent, self-educated man who brought high principles to his task. Nikolsky was of another disposition; Kobylinsky described him as "rude," "uncultivated," "obstinate as a bull," "rough and distant."[6] Though Pankratov was in charge, Nikolsky's bold, defiant attitude had more influence with the guards, and after his arrival the family began to experience more sharply the hostile and vindictive attitude they had tasted at Tsarskoe Selo.

∾ ∾

At the beginning of October, Gibbes finally made it to Tobolsk after a suspense-filled journey. After his delayed departure, he had barely managed to catch the last boat leaving Tiumen before the winter brought river traffic to a halt for seven months. Now that he was here, it was not certain that he could join the family, because Pankratov insisted that the soldiers' committee must decide whether to permit his entry. After two days of debate they did agree, and again it was close as he was the last person to be admitted. Baroness Buxhoeveden, whose illness had prevented her traveling with the original party, arrived by sleigh in November, but was not allowed to join the household and took up residence in the town. Gibbes was assigned a room in the Kornilov house.

Later that day he was conducted across the street and upstairs to Alexandra's drawing room, where she was lunching with Alexei. Gibbes was shocked to see how the Tsaritsa had aged in

---

[6] Steinberg and Khrustalev, *Fall*, p. 175.

five short months, her hair gray and her face quite drawn, while Alexei appeared to be healthier than usual. Both welcomed him with joy. The Tsar came to join them the moment he heard, and after a warm handshake, "he positively pounced on me," Gibbes recalled. Gibbes was an Englishman, and the venomous barbs continually slung by the English press had wounded Nicholas deeply. His abandonment by their government hurt even more. These were the very people to whom he had been so steadfast, for whom he had sacrificed so much, diverting the Germans at enormous cost while England was still trying to mobilize. Gibbes himself was just as vexed, but had no response other than his own loyalty.

His arrival turned out to be a tonic for the chronic boredom that had become even heavier since the arrival of winter, when it was still dark at eight in the morning and dark again by midafternoon. Gibbes brought fresh, though not very encouraging, news from the world the Imperial Family had left, messages and tokens from friends and relatives, a new supply of books, and an idea for sparking up the evenings. They could stage plays, and Syd with his dramatic flair would produce, direct, and sometimes act. Performances were scheduled for Sunday evenings, but the preparations provided entertaining work for many folks during the week. Alexandra and her maids worked at putting costumes together from stuffs they had on hand, others wrote out programs and copied parts for the actors, still others helped assemble the stage properties, and of course there were rehearsals, usually held between tea and supper.

Their most ambitious undertaking was Chekhov's one-act play, *The Bear*. Nicholas was the star of the show as Smirnov, a

landowner trying to collect the debt owed him by the late husband of the young, dimpled widow Popova. In deep mourning,
she is refusing to see anyone—though we learn from her solilo-
quy that she is actually trying to avenge herself on the unfaithful
and neglectful husband, hoping to cause him pain in the afterworld
by her sorrowful fidelity. Smirnov is so desperate for the money
that he refuses to leave. Finally Popova appears and orders him to
go, explaining that she cannot pay until the day after tomorrow
when her steward returns. Smirnov needs the money today, and
with furious tirades and threats vows to stay a month, a year, if
need be. He finally challenges Popova to a duel. She accepts, but
while teaching her to handle a pistol, Smirnov discovers that he
is in love with her.

Olga played the part of the widow, and Marie was the servant who could not get Smirnov, the Bear, to leave. In the final
scene Nicholas, on his knees in front of Olga, makes an extravagant declaration: "I love you as I have never loved before: I have
left twelve women, and nine have left me, but I never loved one
of them as I love you."[7] The play ends in a kiss. Even before the
cast could take their bows, the audience filling the drawing room
was on its feet, clapping wildly and roaring with laughter.

The most popular presentation by far was *Packing Up*, a light
little farce by Harry Grattan, one that Gibbes thought a bit
coarse but very funny. Anastasia played the part of the husband,
Marie the wife, and Alexei had a bit part as their porter. The
husband and wife bumble their way through a slapstick packing-
up routine getting ready for a trip, then the porter takes away

---

[7] *Plays of Anton Chekov*, tr. Paul Schmidt (New York: HarperCollins,
1997), pp. 22–31.

their luggage. Gibbes describes the show-stopping scene.

> . . . the husband has to turn his back, open his dressing-gown as if to take it off—Anastasia wore an old one of mine [that dressing gown again]—and then exclaim: "But I've packed my trousers; I can't go." The night's applause had excited the little Grand Duchess. The piece had gone with a swing and they were getting through the "business" so fast that a draught got under the gown and whisked its tail up to the middle of her back, showing her sturdy legs and bottom encased in the Emperor's Jaegar underwear. We all gasped; Emperor and Empress, suite and servants, collapsed in uncontrolled laughter. Poor Anastasia could not make it out. All were calling for a second performance, but this time she was more careful. Certainly I shall always remember that night; it was the last hearty unrestrained laughter the Empress ever enjoyed.

There were enough comical sketches of this sort to run through the holiday season and up until Lent. Gibbes himself, wearing a long, white beard, played the lead in *The Crystal-Gazer,* a light comedy in which he allowed himself to poke fun at a fortune-teller who gets his clients confused; he offers serious advice to one about the lover he has lost when what he has actually lost is his dog. Unabashed, the charlatan declares, "I mistook you for another person. If you insist on calling without a proper appointment, it is no fault of mine if you have to put up with a vision intended for somebody else."

Of course, Gibbes worked at more than entertainment. He had assumed his place in the instruction routine, teaching the three younger Grand Duchesses and Alexei. Two composition books in which Marie and Anastasia had written Gibbes's dictation and their translations he kept through the years. Anastasia was the cut-up of the family, and during one session when she was full of nonsense and would not stop talking, he snapped in exasperation, "Shut up!" "How do you spell that?" she asked and wrote it carefully after her name on the cover of her book. She had a new nickname.

Nicholas more than anyone else felt the pinch of their restricted walks, and as at Tsarskoe Selo he turned to sawing wood for the needed exercise. Pankratov had logs brought and a cross-cut saw and "was astounded by his physical stamina and even strength. His usual coworkers in this work were the princesses, Alexei, Count Tatishchev, and Prince Dolgorukov, but they all quickly tired and kept relieving one another while Nicholas II continued working."[8] He also built a platform on top of the greenhouse with steps leading up so that he and members of the family could get the best of the wan winter sunshine.

❧❧

Meanwhile, in Petrograd the Provisional Government was in its death throes. As we have seen, by the end of April it had to acknowledge its impotence. In Moscow as well as Petrograd civic and social order had completely broken down, while the army garrisons had become little more than bands of brigands. Only officers and some of the older veterans retained any sense of duty, but they had no control over the men. Workers and soldiers were

---

[8] Steinberg and Khrustalev, *Fall*, p. 265.

violently demanding control of the government. In factories the workers asserted their new power by wrecking machinery and attacking the supervisors and owners, often throwing them physically out of the building.

In an attempt to combat the spreading chaos, a number of conservative organizations were calling for someone to take control and restore some measure of discipline and order. General Lavr Kornilov, who had been appointed Commander-in-Chief of the Army by Kerensky, responded with a plan to amass a sizable body of loyal troops and march on the city to impose military rule. He had outlined the plan in detail to Kerensky, including the important role he would play in the reformed government. Believing he had Kerensky's approval, Kornilov swung into action, and on August 26 was ready to move.

But when the moment came, Kerensky's socialist convictions prevailed, and he balked at relinquishing power into the general's hands. He publicly denounced Kornilov as a traitor who was trying to overthrow the revolution, and in his panic turned to the Bolsheviks for help—even providing the weapons for them to use. Met by mobs of armed workers and unruly garrison soldiers, impeded as well by the railroad workers who would not let his forces advance, Kornilov's movement collapsed. By September 5 it was all over.

Immediately Kerensky was faced with the consequences of his action. The Bolsheviks laughed when ordered to return the weapons they had been issued, and when a Constituent Assembly was finally convened in October, Lenin's party, though in the minority, took over by force using those very rifles and grenades. The slogan, "All Power to the Soviets," became their justification for the vicious class war, the Red Terror, that became official state policy in the new government. This policy turned hatred and vengeance into virtues and urged destruction of every institution, every monument, every symbol, every person of authority connected with the old order, so that a totally new life could begin. The unfortunate Kerensky was last seen speeding out of Petrograd in a borrowed automobile. He hid for a time in the south of the country before slipping secretly out of Russia, never to return.

When news of the October Revolution reached Tobolsk in November, Nicholas was stunned, and for the first time openly expressed regret over his abdication. The generals and Duma members who had assured him that they and only they could restore order and win the war had been unable to do anything. The intelligentsia who had been so scathing in their criticism of the Tsar and the bureaucracy found the task of governing much more difficult than they had thought once they came to power in February 1917. According to Richard Pipes, the new leaders "allowed the state and society to disintegrate in a matter of two or at most four months—the same state that the bureaucrats [and the autocrat] had somehow managed to keep intact for centuries."[9]

The triumph of the Red Bolsheviks in the capital was ominous for the family and those with them, and the sense of growing danger drew them all closer together. They began to speak in whispers about the possibility of being rescued and to scan the streets for some glimpse of new arrivals who might be on such a mission. Several plots were indeed developing in Tobolsk, Petrograd, and Moscow, and notes were smuggled into the

---

[9] Richard Pipes, *The Russian Revolution* (New York: Alfred A. Knopf, 1990), p. 69.

Governor's House from supporters indicating that help was on the way.

The most notorious of the conspirators was Boris Soloviev, who secured the trust of Anna Vyrubova by marrying Rasputin's daughter Maria in September of 1917. Once convinced of his intention to rescue the family, Anna used him as her courier, taking letters, money, and little gifts to those in Tobolsk. Alexandra's confidence in the man was complete, as is evident in a letter she wrote in January, 1918, when it seemed he was about to act.

> I see by your tradesman's clothing that contact with Us is not safe. . . . Let me know what you think of our situation. Our common wish is to achieve the possibility of living tranquilly, like an ordinary family, outside politics, struggle, and intrigues. Write frankly for I will accept your letter with faith in your sincerity. I am especially glad that it is you have come for us.[10]

Soloviev boasted that he had a force of three hundred officers in Tiumen who were ready to march on Tobolsk dressed as ordinary soldiers and rescue the family. Despite the hopes he raised, his plots came to nothing, and most of the money entrusted to him disappeared. Many monarchists and even the chief White Army investigator after the murder of the Tsar and his family believed that Soloviev was a Bolshevik *agent provocateur;* others thought he was a double agent, and there is some evidence to support each charge.

---

[10] Steinberg and Khrustalev, *Fall,* p. 222.

In the end all plans for a rescue fizzled. Not one took more definite shape than a vague dream, and the true reasons for the failures are impossible to determine, because accounts by the participants are invariably self-serving and unreliable. "If only" is the recurrent theme, always seeking to lay blame for failure on someone else. The rumors of rescue attempts were as much of a danger to the prisoners in Tobolsk as the actual plots, because as the Bolsheviks struggled to establish their power, they realized what a compelling symbol the Tsar would be in rallying opposition. They too started making plans for the family; however, their attention was diverted temporarily when the Germans and the Austrians renewed hostilities and invaded parts of western Russia.

When the weather turned really cold, Alexandra abandoned her embroidery and began knitting woolen socks for Alexei, patching the Tsar's trousers, and mending the girls' nightgowns. She was also at work on Christmas presents for everyone, including servants and soldiers.

Perhaps it was her remembrance of past Christmases that moved Alexandra to ask Sydney Gibbes to perform a special task. She wanted him to write a letter as if from himself, but addressed to Miss Margaret Jackson, a former governess for whom she had deep affection and respect. Alexandra had corresponded with "dear Madgie" over the years, confiding both joys and sorrows, and they kept in touch even after Miss Jackson retired to a Home for Governesses in Regent's Park, London. Now, as hope for rescue by their countrymen was fading, Alexandra made one last attempt to enlist support from the

English court, where her ties had always been strong.

Gibbes's assignment was to send enough detailed information about the situation in Tobolsk to be helpful without betraying the true identity of the sender. In his papers there is a draft revised and re-revised to achieve the right tone, that of an Englishman writing a friend at home.

> You will have read in the newspapers of the many different changes that have taken place. In August the Provisional Government decided to change the residence from Tsarskoe to Tobolsk.

He goes on to describe the town and its precise location, the arrangement of quarters in the Governor's House, who sleeps where, and details of the daily routine. Then:

> It is ages since you wrote, or maybe your letters have not arrived. Try and write again, perhaps the next will reach its destination. Send news of everybody, how they are and what they are doing. I hear that David is back from France, how are his mother and father? And the cousins, are they also at the front?

David! he was the Prince of Wales, and Alexandra was sure his name would signal Madgie to take the cry of distress to the queen.

Once again nothing happened. Gibbes was able to determine later that the letter, sent from Tobolsk in a diplomatic pouch on December 15, did reach Petrograd, but there the trail stops, and there is no such letter in the English Royal Archives, though there are other mentions of Gibbes.

❧❧

Despite her brave efforts to make the Christmas season a happy one, Alexandra confessed in a letter to a friend, "How sad these holidays are now!" Since their imprisonment she had taken the precaution of keeping her diary in abbreviated form, listing events usually without comment. On Christmas Eve she arranged the presents she had made. At noon there was a religious service in the house, after which she went downstairs to join everyone for lunch—not her usual practice. She dressed trees for the family, the suite, and the servants, and after tea took a tree out to the soldiers along with some tasty holiday treats. For each of the men on duty she had a Gospel—these were from the stock she had had on hand for distribution in her hospitals—with a bookmark she herself had painted. At dinner Kolya Derevenko, son of the doctor, was allowed to come as Alexei's guest. In the evening gifts were presented to the suite. For Gibbes she had copied in her own hand a prayer that seems so appropriate to his state that she may have composed it herself and just for him.

I pray
That Christ the Xmas King may stoop to bless,
And guide you day by day to holiness,
Your Friend in joy, your Comfort in distress;
I pray
That every cloud may lead you to the light,
And He may raise you up from height to height,
Himself the Day-Star of your darkest night;

I pray
That Christ, before whose Crib you bend the knee,
May fill your longing soul abundantly,
With grace to follow Him more perfectly.

1917

Tobolsk

Alexandra

On Christmas Day Alexandra was up a little after six A.M. and the family walked through the city park to attend Nativity Liturgy in the church. Once again she lunched downstairs and afterwards "saw Isa at the window. Went to sit on balcony." Interpreted this means that Sophia Buxhoeveden was standing in the street, and a significant nod passed between the two friends, for Isa, as she was known in the family, had been invited to spend Christmas Day with them, but it was not allowed. She had come now to deliver greetings as best she could and perhaps conceal a note in some crevice or knothole.

At Liturgy on one of the Christmas holy days, the deacon intoned the traditional prayers for Tsar, Tsaritsa, and the children by name, asking "many years" for them all. This caused a near riot among the soldiers present. The soldiers wanted to drag deacon and priest out immediately and put them in prison, but while their crime was being classified in preparation for a trial, Bishop Hermogen, an erstwhile but now disillusioned supporter of Rasputin, ordered the deacon to safety in another parish and Fr. Vasiliev to the Abalaksky Monastery, a measure that further infuriated the soldiers. The event brought an end to attendance at the church.

The men were becoming more and more infected with the Bolshevik propaganda and, led by the committee formed in the radical Second Rifles Regiment, began a campaign of deliberate harassment. Back in September, they had staged an angry protest when a case of wine was sent to Nicholas by Kerensky. Nikolsky saw to it that the bottles were smashed and thrown into the river.

Immediately after the Christmas Liturgy uproar, the soldiers wired Petrograd asking that Pankratov be replaced. This request was not immediately granted, but orders were sent to Kobylinsky to reduce the expenditures of the household and to put the Tsar and his family on soldiers' rations. Half in jest, Nicholas organized a "committee" to work out the new budget that would enable them to live on the 600 rubles a month allowed each person. The solution was to eliminate sugar, coffee, cream, and butter from the menu. However, within a week they were receiving "meat, coffee, biscuits for tea, and jam from various good people who found out about the curtailment of our expenditures for provisions. How touching!"[11]

Next the soldiers' committee declared that beginning with the new year no officer would be allowed to wear epaulettes. Kobylinsky, who had to remove his own, pleaded with an outraged Nicholas to follow the directive. It was bitter to remove the colonel's epaulettes given him by his father, the rank he had kept even as commander-in-chief. In the end, he and Alexei wore their emblems in private but covered them with overcoats when they went out.

During the holidays everyone had pitched in to build an ice hill, that favorite winter amusement of Russians young and old.

[11] Steinberg and Khrustalev, *Fall*, p. 228.

Tatiana described some of the capers for their old tutor Petrov.

> [W]e often take very funny falls. Once Zhilik [Gilliard]
> ended up sitting on my head. I begged him to get up, but
> he couldn't because he had sprained his ankle and it hurt.
> Somehow I crawled out. . . . Another time I was going
> down the hill backwards and banged the back of my head
> really hard against the ice. I thought nothing would be
> left of the hill, but it turned out that neither it nor my
> head burst.[12]

The fun was brought to an abrupt and senseless end in early
February. The beloved Fourth Regiment, the men who had been
so kind and friendly, was leaving and the family climbed the hill
to wave as they marched away. They were ordered down and the
hill destroyed forthwith on the pretext that they might be shot
while in view—even though they appeared on the balcony daily.
Gilliard described the replacements for the men of the Fourth as
"black-guardly looking," and appearances were not deceiving.
They turned out to be crude and disgusting, carving obscene words
on the seats of the swings in the yard and vulgar graffiti on the
walls of the girls' lavatory.

March 3 brought the cruelest blow so far for Nicholas. The
Bolsheviks surrendered to the Germans and signed the Treaty of
Brest-Litovsk, giving back four thousand square miles of the territory won with so much blood and sacrifice, and in the process
obliterating any sense of patriotism in the army. With the war
disposed of, Lenin and his men were able to turn their attention

---

[12] Steinberg and Khrustalev, *Fall*, pp. 222–23.

once more to the Tsar. The original plan seems to have been to bring him to trial in Moscow, which had just become the capital. However, there were challenges from several sides. A military challenge was developing among the opposition on the right. Spurred by the humiliating surrender, loyalists were organizing an army of their own, the Whites, who intended to defeat the Reds and rescue the Tsar. Radical Siberian soviets in Omsk and Ekaterinburg, fearful that the Tsar would be sent out of the country, were competing with each other for custody of "Nicholas the Butcher" in order to wreak vengeance.

The special commissar dispatched to remove the imperial prisoners from Tobolsk, convey them around these obstacles, and bring them safely to Moscow was Vasily Yakovlev. He arrived at the Governor's House on April 22, 1918, with authorization from the Central Executive Committee to take control of all local institutions, to establish a revolutionary tribunal, and to shoot anyone who disobeyed his instructions. Restrictions on the prisoners had been rigidly tightened in anticipation of Yakovlev's arrival. Servants could no longer go into town, and occupants of the Kornilov house were to be brought into the Governor's House. When every inch of that space had been taken up, the two doctors, who were useful to the citizenry, and Gibbes, who had been last to arrive, were permitted to remain across the street. The commissar and his entourage took over the rest of that house.

Yakovlev's first order of business was to meet the Tsar and his family and inspect their house. Alexandra was not ready when he came, but Nicholas and his daughters were assembled in the drawing room to receive him. He was quite polite, addressing the Tsar as Your Majesty and inquiring about the comfort of the family.

Alexei was very ill at this time with hemorrhaging as severe as that at Spala, and his right foot was paralyzed. He had injured himself careening down the stairs on a makeshift sled after their ice hill had been destroyed. He lay in bed and Gibbes was reading to him when Nicholas entered with Yakovlev: "This is my son, and this is his tutor." Yakovlev was shocked at the sight. "The yellow-complexioned, haggard boy seemed to be passing away."[13]

This would mean a change in plans. Yakovlev was anxious to leave with his charges as soon as possible, for the spring thaw was almost upon them, as he knew from the slush and mud he had encountered, and once the river thawed all sorts of attempts to get at the family might be made from every direction. He wired Yakov Sverdlov, chairman of the Central Executive Committee of the Workers', Soldiers', and Peasants' Deputies in Moscow, telling him of the situation. Sverdlov authorized him to take away the main "baggage," Nicholas, and return for the rest when Alexei could travel. However, for reasons that are not clear from any of the documents, there had been a change in the original plan: the destination was now Ekaterinburg in the Urals.

Yakovlev went over right after breakfast to inform Nicholas that he would be taken away at four o'clock the next morning. Though he did not say where they were going, everyone thought the destination would be Moscow. Alexandra had to make an agonizing decision: she could not bear to let Nicholas go and face a trial alone, and yet Alexei was so very ill. All day the family struggled with the decision, and in the end it was decided that Alexandra, Marie, Dr. Botkin, Count Dolgorukov, and four

---

[13] Steinberg and Khrustalev, *Fall*, p. 238.

servants would accompany the Tsar. Olga would look after Alexei, Tatiana the household, and Anastasia would "cheer all up" until the family could be reunited.

On this day too Gibbes had been reading to Alexei. The Empress had promised to look in on him after lunch, and when she did not come Gibbes went out into the hall to see where she might be. He saw the distraught family standing in the hall and soon had details of this ominous new development. Alexandra went to sit with Alexei for a while and emerged calm but red-eyed. The boy had also been weeping.

That evening the Emperor and Empress dined alone, and later took tea with the whole company in the upstairs drawing room. "It was the most mournful and depressing party I ever attended," Gibbes recalled. "There was not much talking and no pretence at gaiety. It was solemn, tragic, a fit prelude to inescapable catastrophe. After the party the suite went below and just sat about and waited." Alexandra's maid, Anna (Niuta) Demidova, confided to him, "I am so frightened of the Bolsheviks, Mr. Gibbes. I don't know what they might do to us." In the cold darkness of predawn, Gibbes gathered with the rest of the household on the glass porch to say good-bye. Nicholas "had a handshake and a word for everyone, and we all kissed the Empress's hand."

❧❧

Nicholas records details of their departure in his diary dated Friday, April 13, though under the new calendar it was April 26. In mid-February the Bolsheviks had moved the calendar ahead thirteen days to conform to the Gregorian calendar used throughout the Western world. For a short time Nicholas used both dates, but within a month had gone back to the old method, and Friday the thirteenth seems sadly appropriate. More significantly, at this very time Christians throughout the land were commemorating the Passion of Christ, looking forward to the great Paschal celebration.

"At 4 in the morning we said farewell to the dear children and sat down in the tarantasses: I with Yakovlev, Alix with Maria, and Valia with Botkin. From among our people, Niuta Demidova, Chemodurov, and Sednyov went with us." The tarantasses to which he referred were actually wretched peasant carts without springs or seats, more like big baskets slung between two poles. There was a frantic search for straw and a mattress to put down for Alexandra. Dr. Botkin gave her his fur coat, and another was brought for him. The pitiful procession of carts set off into the darkness surrounded by a mounted escort. "The road was very difficult, and we shook terribly from the frozen ruts."[14]

There was worse to come. On the first day they crossed the Irtysh, which was still half frozen, but the horses were in water up to their chests. There were four changes of horses by the time they had gone ninety miles, and they stopped to spend the night in the village of Ievlov, where the food was good and the beds clean. Next day the Tobol River had to be crossed on foot over a precarious bridge of planks laid on the breaking ice, and a change of horses was made in Pokrovskoe. "For a long time we stood right before Grigory's [Rasputin's] house and saw his whole family looking through the window."[15]

All the while, Yakovlev and the mounted escort were on the alert, watching for an ambush. The disputes among the rival

---

[14] Steinberg and Khrustalev, *Fall*, p. 243.
[15] *Ibid.*

soviets in Omsk and Ekaterinburg and the guard at Tobolsk had grown so intense that machine guns had been positioned around Governor's House. Yakovlev had information that Ekaterinburg men were planning to waylay him on his way to Tiumen and capture or kill the Tsar, so he stationed his own troops at intervals along the route to give advance warning.

Once in Tiumen the prisoners were hurried onto a train. Yakovlev again wired Sverdlov, informing him that he had made it this far with the "baggage," but was reluctant to follow the old route because of the dangers posed by the Ekaterinburg soldiers, who had another ambush set up along that route. He further expressed his opinion that once in the hands of the Ekaterinburg detachment, "the baggage would be destroyed." At this time the Bolsheviks appeared anxious to preserve the Tsar alive, and Sverdlov authorized his commissar to take the train immediately to Omsk and await further instructions. But angry, suspicious eyes were watching his every move. The train left the station in the direction of Ekaterinburg, but at the first station changed direction and headed east for Omsk.

At this the telegraph apparatus started humming with messages summarized below.

Ural Regional Soviet to Sverdlov—from Ekaterinburg, 28 April 1918: Yakovlev headed for Ekaterinburg, then switched directions and headed east toward Omsk. This is a traitorous action.

Sverdlov to Ural Regional Soviet—from Moscow, 28 April 1918: Trust Yakovlev, he is acting on orders. Wire Omsk to give every assistance.

Beloborodov, Chairman of Ural Regional Soviet to Sverdlov—from Omsk, 29 April 1918: Yakovlev treacherously disobeying orders to deliver former Tsar to Ekaterinburg. He is headed for Omsk.

Sverdlov to Ekaterinburg regional committee—29 April 1918: Trust Yakovlev. Everything is direct fulfillment of orders.

Sverdlov to Yakovlev in Omsk—29 April 1918: Understanding reached with Ekaterinburg Soviet. They will control the men. Return to Tiumen hand the baggage over to Uralites and accompany them yourself to Ekaterinburg. Inform Beloborodov and Sverdlov of your departure from Omsk.

Yakovlev to Sverdlov—from Omsk, 29 April 1918: Submits to all orders but warns that once baggage is in Ekaterinburg "you will not be able to drag it out. . . baggage will be in utter danger at all times. Thus we warn you one last time and free ourselves from any moral responsibility for future consequences." [16]

With great misgiving Yakovlev followed the orders given by Sverdlov, and his fears were confirmed when the train pulled into the station at Ekaterinburg. A huge, angry crowd was waiting at the platform, shouting threats: "Show us the bloodsucker!" "Let us at him!" Even the stationmaster wanted to spit in his face. The situation became desperate as the crowd began to push forward,

---

[16] Complete texts of these messages shed light on the reasons for Yakovlev's actions, reasons that have long been shrouded in controversy as to just what he was up to. See Steinberg and Khrustalev, *Fall*, pp. 245–254.

threatening the patrols that were in position. So when Yakovlev spotted a freight train idling on a siding between his train and the platform he gave orders to move it at once in between them. Protected by the freight train he hurried to platform no. 2, where no one was waiting. From there he notified the chairman of the soviet and handed his passengers over to them after getting a signed receipt.

He stayed long enough to see the Tsar and his company situated in a large private house surrounded by a fourteen-foot paling fence. The guard was increased and the regimen revised to resemble that of a true prison. Only a few days before, this house had belonged to a wealthy merchant named Ipatiev, which means "special purpose"—an ill omen indeed, particularly as the guard was called the Special Purpose Detachment. Yakovlev set out on his way back to Tobolsk to collect the rest of the family, fully realizing that it meant a death sentence for them all.

9

The Triumph of Darkness

When Yakovlev arrived at Tiumen, he paused to act on the compunction that had plagued him throughout his journey. The moral responsibility for these lives he had expressed to Sverdlov was genuine, and he refused to complete the mission to Tobolsk and deliver the rest of the family as victims to the unbridled brutality of the Ekaterinburg soviet. In the wire informing Sverdlov of his decision, however, his stated grounds were the counter-revolutionary charges made against him by the Ural Regional Soviet. They did not trust him, and he did not trust them. Having relieved his conscience of this burden, he headed to Moscow for reassignment, and was sent to command a military unit in Siberia, where the fighting between the White and Red forces was becoming a full-scale civil war.

Back in Tobolsk, gloom settled heavily on the isolated remnant of the Romanov household and their faithful attendants. The heart and soul of the family had been taken away. Where were they being taken, what was going to happen to them? And what would happen to those left behind? When and where, if ever, would they all meet again? Formal lessons had been all but abandoned as the sisters and tutors concentrated their attention on Alexei, whose illness was aggravated by the loss of his mother and father. The girls took turns sitting with him at breakfast to be sure he ate, they took tea with him, they wheeled him about in the yard or pulled him on a sled if there was a sudden spring snow.

The tutors took turns reading to the boy and trying to comfort him. Gibbes was reading James Fenimore Cooper's adventure *The Pathfinder* at the time and tried to make rough illustrations on scraps of cardboard salvaged from two old boxes, one that had held sweets and another a card game. He also pulled out some wire from his store of oddments to make chains for a model ship they were building. During the long evenings the prisoners read, wrote letters, or just sat talking and speculating about the bewildering events swirling around them.

After what seemed an eternity, a telegram did arrive from Tiumen. It had been days getting to them, but they learned only that the travelers had gotten safely that far. More long days passed before a letter came from Marie in Ekaterinburg with a message from Alexandra, instructing her daughters to begin packing and to take care of "the medicines" as planned. The "medicines" became their primary work, particularly in the evenings, when there was less chance of the guards looking in on them. They were actually stitching jewels—the only resources the family had left—into their clothing, sewing them into hems, hat bands, and coat linings, and often covering them with fabric to make buttons.

Their corsets made especially good hiding places because of the stiffness. The girls encrusted the undersides of these garments with diamonds, pearls, and other precious stones and then covered them over with a lining.

The situation in the Governor's House had deteriorated markedly. Colonel Kobylinsky and his men had been expelled by the Bolsheviks, and a crude, foul-mouthed, and brutish company led by Nikolai Rodionov took over. Insults became ever more a part of the daily ordeal for the defenseless young captives. The grand duchesses were forbidden to lock their bedroom door at night, and those gentlemen of the staff who were still in Tobolsk organized their own secret vigilance, taking turns staying awake at night to be sure the innocent young women were not molested. Gibbes came over to the main house regularly to take his turn.

These woeful events were unfolding during Passiontide, Holy Week, and Easter. In fact, when Yakovlev first came to inform Nicholas that he was to be taken away, Alexandra thought he had come to arrange for services in Passion Week. It turned out to be the beginning of their sad journey toward their own Gethsemane, following the pattern of our Lord. Easter services were held in the Governor's House, and Anastasia reported to those in Ekaterinburg that the girls themselves had decorated the icon screen with spruce and flowers. No services could be held in Ekaterinburg, but the Tsar read the prayers and hymns to the little company there. Every letter during this period begins with the traditional Easter greeting: "Christ is risen!" or the response, "Truly He is risen!" Marie, writing from their new and harsher keep, greets those in Tobolsk on "this joyous holiday," even though she goes on to suggest how different their present situation is from the "cozy" one they had left behind. Anastasia in her reply sent not just the traditional triple kiss, but "hundreds of kisses."

By mid-May the Tsarevich was judged ready to travel, though he was still unable to walk. Rodionov had burst in upon the morning tea and found the boy sitting up. That was enough; the rest of the prisoners would leave immediately. The commissar now in charge of their transfer, Pavel Kokriakov, was alerted and the steamer *Rus*, the very one that had brought them to Tobolsk, was readied.

On the night before their departure, Gibbes and his colleagues decided to call for the last two bottles of wine to spark up the all-too-familiar dinner of "veal garnished and macaroni." Spirits certainly needed brightening, they could not take the wine with them, and drinking it seemed the best thing.

> While we were doing so the new Commandant was heard sneaking down the corridor. We had only just time to hide the bottles and our glasses under the table, concealed by a long trailing cloth, when in he walked. He stood by the door, giving a quizzical look all round, and immediately we felt like little schoolboys caught doing something naughty at school. The situation was so ludicrous that as our eyes met we could contain ourselves no longer, and burst into a wild yell of uncontrollable laughter.

The baffled commandant withdrew, probably concluding that such merriment did not indicate a conspiracy.

On May 20 according to the new calendar, the party boarded

the familiar ship. Here too Rodionov asserted authority in his usual spiteful way. The cabin where Nagorny and Alexei slept had to be padlocked, despite the sailor's insistence that the boy might need immediate medical attention, but not the rooms of the young women, whose safety was very precarious as the unruly men of the detachment, many of them drunk, roamed the decks. Well into the night, when the danger became obvious, the commandant finally had to relent and lock their door.

This voyage, like each previous one, brought contact with the legacy of Rasputin, this time with his daughter Maria. She had come to Tiumen to buy tickets for a train trip she and her husband, the notorious Boris Soloviev, were planning when she happened to see a heavily guarded ship at the dock. No one was allowed to approach, but when she made her way through to the cashier "suddenly Nastia [Hendrikova] and the little one [Alexei] saw me through the ship's window; they were terribly happy. . . . They were like angels."[1]

At Tiumen the party was to be transferred from the ship to a train. Rodionov appeared and directed the boarding according to a list he had prepared. First, members of the suite and some of the servants were called by name. They rose and departed. The imperial children were called next, and they also rose and left; with Nagorny carrying Alexei they entered their railway car. Rodionov returned and barked, "The rest of you," and Gibbes, Gilliard, Baroness Buxhoeveden, Mlle Schneider, and Countess Hendrikova were put into a fourth-class wagon, which turned out to be little more than a heated freight car.

It was near midnight on May 23 when their train reached

---

[1] Steinberg and Khrustalev, *Fall*, p. 305.

Ekaterinburg, but, "we kept moving backwards and forwards, halting for a short time in some inaccessible place in order to change our direction." This went on until seven in the morning, and then the train stopped. Gibbes looked out to see that, though they were not at a station, there were several drozhkies drawn up on the bank, obviously waiting for passengers. He and Gilliard watched through the windows as the girls struggled up the slippery embankment in ankle-deep mud, Tatiana trying to manage heavy suitcases with one hand while holding her little dog in the other arm. The sailor Nagorny came to assist, but was roughly brushed aside by the guards, who insisted that she be made to carry her own bags. When those passengers had been seated the drozhkies took them away, and the train proceeded on to the Ekaterinburg station. There General Tatishchev, Countess Hendrikova, and Mlle Schneider were arrested and taken away under guard. None of them was seen alive again.

These dramas continued all day outside the windows of the railway carriage. A few more servants were removed and taken to Ipatiev House. The watchers saw animated consultations among various local commissars and Rodionov. Nagorny came back to fetch the girls' beds and more luggage. Finally, at five in the evening, Rodionov burst into the wagon and told those remaining they were free to go wherever they wished, but they would not be allowed to join the Imperial Family.

As counter-revolutionary challenges were developing rapidly, Gibbes and his colleagues ended up having to use that poor fourth-class car as their headquarters for about ten days, because Rodionov soon had to revise his first pronouncement. They would be sent back to Tobolsk, but even before they could get under way, the White Russian Army had cut off that route, and they were stuck in the Red Urals. Those were difficult days—no facilities for bathing or preparing food, only the most rudimentary provisions for sleeping—but they managed somehow. Each day they walked out, usually one or two at a time and at staggered intervals so as not to draw attention, and passed Ipatiev House hoping to get a glimpse of the family. Only once did Gibbes see the arm of a woman raising a window and concluded that it was probably Anna Demidova. Another day, as Gibbes and Gilliard were passing the house together trying not to look too curious, they saw the sailor Nagorny being led out by soldiers with fixed bayonets. He saw them as well, but gave no hint of recognition. Four days later he was shot.

Alexander Avdeiev, a rough and vengeful member of the Executive Committee of the Ekaterinburg Soviet, quickly turned the House of Special Purpose into an even harsher prison. It was now surrounded by a double fence that reached to the eaves of the house. The lower floor was occupied by the commandant and soldiers of his guard. The thirteen members remaining in the Tsar's company were confined to five rooms on the upper floor. Alexandra, Nicholas, and Alexei occupied one bedroom, the four grand duchesses another, Anna Demidova slept in the dining room, Dr. Botkin, Kharitonov, two Sednovs—uncle and nephew—and Trupp the valet in the hall. On the night of their arrival the daughters had to sleep on the floor, as their beds had arrived too late to be set up.

Prison conditions prevailed everywhere. Food was scanty and repulsive: tea and black bread made breakfast; at dinner rewarmed soup and other items brought from a public soviet kitchen were dumped into a single bowl and set before them without linen or silver. If there happened to be meat in the dish, Avdeiev would often appear and reach in to snatch out the largest piece for himself. After good, faithful Kharitonov arrived, he managed to arrange a kitchen of sorts on the second floor, and their food improved even though he had to prepare most meals from leftovers. The girls also volunteered to learn cookery and in the evenings would knead bread for baking in the morning. After Avdeiev was removed as commandant, the supply of milk, eggs, butter, and cream that nuns in the nearby convent had been sending all along began to get through to those for whom they were intended, and the menu improved markedly. The company enjoyed fairly decent meals for the final two weeks of their lives.

There were other privations. The piano had been taken from their hall by the men, and in the evenings the soldiers could be heard singing loudly in the guardroom. Sometimes the songs celebrated the revolution and at others they were bawdy and coarse. Alexandra and her daughters often drowned out the noise by singing, as Anatoly Yakimov recalled in his deposition during Sokolov's 1919 investigation:

> The only thing I personally remember about the Imperial Family was their singing. I heard them sometimes singing sacred songs; I especially remember the Cherubim's Song. But they also sang a secular song. I could not hear the words, but the tune was very sad. This was the tune of the song, "A Man Died in a Soldiers' Hospital."[2]

---

[2] Robert Wilton, *The Last Days of the Romanovs: From 15th March 1917* (London: Thornton Butterworth Ltd., 1920), p. 271.

They were permitted to go out for only one hour a day, and everyone was required to go out at the same time and walk in a severely constricted space, guarded closely by soldiers who had orders not to speak to them unless someone asked a question about the rules or made a request, which was automatically refused. Guards were stationed by the upstairs bathroom, which they had decorated with obscene drawings of Rasputin and the Tsaritsa, but the prisoners were not allowed to close the door when they went in.

In mid-May, just as the weather was warming, Avdeiev conceived a particularly cruel torment. He had the windows locked and whitewashed on the outside. They no longer had any view of the greening outdoors or the bustle in the city streets, and the air in the crowded upstairs rooms was stifling.

Despite the discomfort, the inconvenience, the insults, the terrible monotony, the apprehension about the future, there was so little complaint. Not a word of bitterness appears in the diary entries of Nicholas or Alexandra or in any of the letters written during this period. They report the facts about what was happening to them, but without condemning their persecutors—Nicholas even expressed some sympathy for Avdeiev when he was dismissed for permitting thievery of the prisoners' belongings—and there was always space to mention pleasant things: bright sunshine or beautiful weather when they walked out, the fragrance from the gardens in the town. It was a season of family birthdays, and each was mentioned with affectionate gratitude, using old-style dates. Nicholas was fifty on St. Job's Day, May 6, Alexandra was forty-six on May 25, Tatiana turned twenty-one on May 29, Anastasia seventeen on June 5, and Marie nineteen June 14. There was thanksgiving for every religious service permitted.

From June 19 through July 4, dated in the new style, an intriguing series of letters was smuggled into the house, arousing hope that serious preparations were at last being made for their rescue—an episode the Tsar recorded in his diary. Some anonymous person, signing himself "An Officer of the Russian Army," indicated that a group loyal to them was ready to act. The advancing Czech Legion was now only fifty miles from Ekaterinburg, and the rescue would be coordinated with their arrival. "Be attentive to any movement from the outside; wait and hope." The captives did hope and sent as requested a sketch of their sleeping arrangements: who slept in which beds and how they were arranged, their time of going to bed, location of windows, and the like. Someone was to stay awake on specified nights for further information. On the night of June 14/27, following the latest instructions, they dressed and sat up all night anticipating deliverance.

Several items in those letters suggest that the supposed rescue conspiracy was actually a cruel hoax perpetrated by the Bolsheviks themselves and designed to lure the family into providing an excuse for shooting them "as they were trying to escape." One letter instructed the family to contrive some sort of rope to lower themselves from a certain window, some of which had finally been opened on June 9/22 after two weeks of daily inspection by various Bolsheviks. Of course, any such exit would be impossible for Alexei and Alexandra, and besides there was a machine-gun trained on the windows.

The response bears moving testimony to the family's greatness of heart.

We do not want to, nor can we, escape. We can only be *carried off* by force, just as it was force that was used to carry us from Tobolsk. Thus, do not count on *any active help* from us. The commandant has many aides; they change often and have become *worried.* They guard our imprisonment and our lives conscientiously and are kind to us. We do not want them to suffer because of us, nor you for us; in the name of God, avoid bloodshed above all.[3]

A subsequent note indicated that their friends "D. and T." were safe. There is little doubt that this was a reference to Count Dolgorukov and General Tatishchev, who were "safe" only because they had already been shot. By the end of June it became apparent that once again nothing was going to happen. The collapse of these final hopes took a heavy toll on morale. As all hope of escape evaporated, the imperial prisoners seemed to realize and resign themselves to the fact that death might be their fate. Fr. Storozhev and his deacon came to celebrate the Divine Liturgy on Sunday, July 14; this service would be their last rites. When the customary prayers commemorating the dead were read, the entire family dropped spontaneously to their knees. As the clergymen were leaving, the deacon remarked that the family, who had always somehow managed to remain cheerful, were altered, almost as if they were different people.

A momentary respite in their ordeal had come with the arrival of Jacob Yurovsky on July 4. At first it seemed as though a gentler policy might be introduced, because he made a great show

---

[3] Steinberg and Khrustalev, *Fall,* p. 320.

of recovering a number of valuable items that had been stolen from their stored luggage by the guards under Avdeiev's command. Yurovsky brought the items, many of them gold, and carefully catalogued them in the presence of the Tsar before returning them to "storage." Within a week, however, Nicholas commented to his diary that "things had not changed one bit."

That was because Yurovsky had come as the executioner. Immediately he replaced the guards inside the house with ten men from the Cheka, referred to as Latvians by Nicholas. Discipline of the existing outside guards was tightened rigorously. They were not to converse with one another or read newspapers and magazines on duty; they were to march in single file and keep extra close watch on the prisoners, who, they were told, might try to escape at any moment.

The question of just who issued the order to kill the family has always been an intriguing mystery, and a definite answer is still impossible, even with evidence from the documents that have come to light since the fall of the Soviet Union. Yurovsky's own accounts of the murders indicate that a trial of the Tsar had been planned, but the approach of the White Army made this impossible. His 1920 report states that on July 16 a coded telegram came from Perm, ordering the extermination of the Romanovs. In 1934 he explained to a meeting of Bolsheviks at Ekaterinburg, by then renamed Sverdlovsk, that the decision for "liquidation" had been made at "the center," that is, Moscow, as early as July 10 or 11, because of the military situation; Yurovsky was instructed that preparations should begin.[4]

Yurovsky began those preparations at once, and in the most

[4] Steinberg and Khrustalev, *Fall,* pp. 351, 356–357.

methodical way. First, he selected twelve men as the firing squad, and each one was given a Nagant revolver and assigned a particular person to shoot. At the last minute two of the Latvians had to be replaced because they refused to shoot girls. "They didn't have it in them," scoffed Yurovsky. There was one small act of mercy: the young kitchen boy, Sednov, was sent away early in the day, supposedly to meet his uncle, who had been arrested.

Next, guard commandant Pavel Medvedev was ordered to alert his men that there might be firing in the night, but they were not to be alarmed or take any action. A truck was scheduled to arrive at midnight to carry away the bodies. As details of the plan for their execution were falling into place, the family went through their daily routine: they walked in the yard, ate the dinner Kharitonov had prepared, passed yet another evening reading and playing cards, read evening prayers, and went to bed.

About midnight Yurovsky himself went to their rooms to awaken them. He ordered them to dress at once and come downstairs, as there were disturbances in the town that threatened their safety. In about half an hour they were ready, and according to Medvedev, "Her Majesty and the daughters were in dresses with no outerwear and uncovered heads. The sovereign walked ahead with the heir." No one asked any questions and "[t]here were no tears, no sobbing, either" as Yurovsky led them downstairs and into a semi-basement room. Alexandra did complain that there was not even a chair, and two chairs were ordered. She sat on one and Alexei on the other. Nicholas and the others, including the daughters, Dr. Botkin, Kharitonov, Demidova, and Trupp, were ordered to line up behind them.[5]

---

[5] Steinberg and Khrustalev, *Fall*, p. 348.

The firing squad marched in and Yurovsky announced that they were to be shot. "Nicholas turned his back to the detachment, his face toward his family, then, as though collecting himself, turned to the commandant: 'What? What?'" The men had been told whom to shoot and to aim for the heart in order to avoid an excess of blood. As the Tsar turned again toward the assassins, Yurovsky shot him dead. A frenzy of shooting began now: the Tsaritsa died next, then the footman Trupp and Kharitonov fell. The Tsarevich, three of the grand duchesses, Demidova, and Dr. Botkin were still alive and had to be shot again. This was an unexpected development, since the marksmen had aimed for the heart. "It was also surprising that the bullets from the pistols ricocheted off something and jumped about the room like hail. When they tried to finish off one of the girls with bayonets, the bayonet could not pierce the corset. Thanks to all this, the entire procedure, including 'verification' (feeling the pulse, etc.) took about twenty minutes."[6]

The soldiers filed out, and for a time silence filled the room where the anointed Tsar of Russia, the Heir, the Tsaritsa, the grand duchesses, lay in pools of blood along with the four devoted attendants who had remained steadfast to the last. All were struck down in what should have been the prime of their lives, and the Russia they had known and loved—a Russia that stood on the brink of victory in the Great War, its economy and industrialization developing rapidly, its culture rich and strong, its plans for governmental reform in place—was struck down with them.

❧ ❧

There was much more blood than had been anticipated, and

---

[6] Steinberg and Khrustalev, *Fall*, pp. 352–353.

heavy blankets were put down in the truck and wrapped around some of the corpses to prevent leaving a trail. While loading the bodies, the men began to steal from them, but Yurovsky put a stop to this at once and recovered the stolen things. The truck expected at midnight had not arrived until about one-thirty, and so many other unexpected difficulties developed that it was three o'clock in the morning before the vehicle set out with its dreadful load to the place of burial.

By this time Yurovsky had lost confidence in Commissar Yermakov, to whom the burial had been assigned, and decided to follow and oversee that operation himself. As matters unraveled, it took three days and nights to accomplish an effective burial for the eleven bodies they had on their hands. The matter-of-fact tone in which Yurovsky relates the callous lugging about of the corpses, the gross indecencies, the grizzly mutilations that followed says much about the Bolshevik doctrine of hate that had possessed the souls of these men. Having drowned their basic human sensibilities in torrents of resentment and malice, they had become brutes who could occupy themselves for three days disfiguring, trampling, tearing, dismembering, and burning eleven human bodies without revulsion or pity.

Preparations had not been made at the intended burial spot, a mine some few miles outside the town; not even shovels had been brought. The truck bearing the dead was halted briefly by twenty-five men on horseback, who were outraged to find that the Romanovs had not been brought to them alive; they had expected to be the executioners themselves. The carts brought to transport the bodies beyond the point where the truck could go no farther were inadequate; then it turned out that no one knew just where the mine was.

With dawn breaking, they had to make some short-term arrangements to hide the corpses. About eleven miles beyond Ekaterinburg, they came upon an abandoned mine shaft, known as Four Brothers, which was eight or so feet deep and partially filled with water. Here Yurovsky ordered the bodies to be stripped and a huge fire built to burn the clothing and other items. During this process the jewels sewn into the clothing of the women were discovered, and a halt had to be called while they were removed. The gems altogether weighed eighteen pounds. These were put into bags, the clothing was burned, and the bodies were thrown into the mine.

After posting reliable guards, Yurovsky returned to report to the Soviet Executive Committee and seek further instructions for a burial site. Three deep mines located along the Moscow highway were suggested, and Yurovsky went out to inspect them and found them satisfactory, though just getting to them was a journey so beset by misfortune that it consumed another entire day. At midnight on July 18, he set out once more with carts and ropes to drag the bodies out of the first mine, but when it began to grow light he decided to bury at least some of the corpses in this spot, and digging was begun. Even this plan had to be abandoned when a friend of Yermakov's arrived and observed what they were doing. The bodies would have to be moved to the deep mines, but the carts on hand were too flimsy, and Yurovsky went back to town for motorcars.

This grim comedy of broken-down carts and mired motorcars continued into the wee hours of July 19. They were hardly underway before once again one of the vehicles got hopelessly stuck, and it was decided to bury or burn the corpses right then and there. Yurovsky said later that they decided to burn Alexei and Alexandra, but got mixed up and burned the maid Demidova instead of the Tsaritsa. "We then immediately buried the remains under the fire and lit the fire again, which completely covered up traces of the digging." By seven in the morning the men had managed to dig a common grave for the rest. "We piled the corpses in the pit, poured sulfuric acid onto their faces and generally over their whole bodies to prevent them from being recognized and from stinking as a result of decomposition (the pit was not too deep)." Dirt and brush were piled on and railroad ties laid over it; then the truck drove over it again and again.[7]

The gruesome job had been done so thoroughly that when the White forces arrived a week later, they did not find the graves. They did, however, find enough evidence in a few gems carelessly dropped around the Four Brothers shaft and some fragments of singed cloth to confirm the suspicions raised by the empty Ipatiev House and its bullet-riddled basement room, where traces of blood remained even after obvious sand scrubbing.

Moscow issued a terse announcement stating that the approach of counter-revolutionary forces and a serious plot to free the former Tsar had forced a decision by the Regional Soviet to shoot him. His wife and son had been removed to a safe place. This false and enigmatic version of events, with no mention of the daughters, prevailed even after the investigation of 1919.[8]

---

[7] Steinberg and Khrustalev, *Fall*, p. 356.
[8] The Bolsheviks were forced to admit by the end of 1919 that the entire family had been killed. However, they tried to lay blame for the deed elsewhere and held a fraudulent trial, convicting and shooting eleven innocent Socialist Revolutionaries.

10

On the Rails

Gibbes and his colleagues, eighteen in all, remained more or less confined to their fourth-class rail car standing isolated on a siding in Ekaterinburg. They were under orders by the Bolsheviks to leave and were waiting to be sent away. In the meantime, they had limited freedom to walk about during the day in the city, and indeed had many friends and associates there. However, they were not permitted to take up residence or even stay out overnight, but had to return to this miserable shelter in the evening, where they spent long hours trying to come to grips with the shattering of their world. The Imperial Family they had committed to serve with a loyalty and courage that brought them to this place were in the hands of a cruel enemy. As for themselves, where could they go? What could they do? How would they live in the present hostile environment?

Gibbes and Pierre Gilliard made regular calls on Thomas Preston at the British Consulate, trying to find out what they could about the situation of the imprisoned family and the progress of White forces in the developing civil war. Preston knew nothing of any rescue attempt and was convinced that any such essay would be futile because of the numerous Red troops in Ekaterinburg, not to mention their spies everywhere. All hope seemed to hang upon the arrival of the White forces, who were indeed advancing rapidly and seemed to be carrying all before them. As we have seen, however, that very success was a determining factor in the Reds' decision to exterminate the Tsar and his family. It probably influenced as well the decision to free the Swiss and English tutors and Baroness Buxhoeveden, who was Danish. The Bolsheviks were not anxious to incur hostile scrutiny by any foreign power at a time when their own grip on power was so precarious. As for the rest of the surviving household staff, they had been too numerous to accommodate in Ipatiev House, but their devotion to the Imperial Family made them unwelcome in Ekaterinburg.

After ten days their carriage was attached to a train headed for Tiumen. However, at the first station along the way they were halted because Czech troops were closing in. There they stayed for another ten days, and miserable days they were, for the small village of Kamyslov was not only primitive but also in the grips of a typhus epidemic, conditions that kept them close to their base. After much haggling, negotiation, and perhaps some bribery, Gibbes and Gilliard persuaded the stationmaster to detach their car and hitch it to another train. Finally they pulled into Tiumen in mid-June, expecting to travel right on to Tobolsk by steamer, only to learn that the city was now in the hands of the White forces. "We only regretted that we were not too," Syd wrote Winnie. "But so it was and we were not allowed to cross the lines." This meant another two weeks in their tiresome railroad car.

At last, in Tiumen they were able to obtain a certificate from the commandant of military transport allowing "the former employees of the ex-Tsar to be billeted in private flats and hospitals." Gibbes found a room much to his liking. He was at the very top of a nice house overlooking the town, and its five windows gave him a view all around. "Not much furniture in the room, just necessaries; not even them, you might think, for there was no washstand," he wrote his Aunt Kate. No doubt Syd, with his fastidious ways, had been longing for one. "At first, I used to go down to the kitchen, get a basin, and take it down to the washhouse and wash there until the horrid landlady objected, and then I had to manage in my bedroom: not so nice for it was impossible not to spill much water."

During the first weeks of July, as the refugees were trying to find accommodations in Tiumen, their beloved family was being prepared for the terrible slaughter of July 16. On July 25 and 26 the White forces took Ekaterinburg, and as soon as they got the news Gibbes and Gilliard made the necessary arrangements to go there and find the family. They had no trouble getting permission to enter Ipatiev House, and they were deeply troubled by the ominous ruin visible everywhere.

All signs pointed to a desperately hasty attempt at obliterating all traces of the former occupants—much too hasty an attempt to succeed. Fireplaces and stoves had been so stuffed with family belongings that the fires lit by men of the Special Purpose Detail did not burn, and half-charred books, icons, picture frames, and photos filled the grates. Bits of clothing, needlework, knitting needles, combs, brushes, buckles, and buttons protruded from the rubbish bins.

Most disturbing of all was the eloquent basement room, its walls gashed and torn, a door wrenched from its hinges, bullet holes in the floor that, despite mopping and scrubbing, still showed outlines from pools of blood. The physical evidence indicated slaughter on a huge scale, but what to make of the official Soviet Central Committee announcement that the Empress and the Heir were in a safe place? What of the daughters, the servants, who were not mentioned? Gilliard was inclined to hold out some hope; Gibbes was more skeptical.

Back in Tiumen, Syd stayed in the nice room with its lovely view and horrid landlady for the rest of the summer, and he and his friends met often to linger over tea or a meal, trying to make some sense of the bits of information that filtered through about the family and discussing prospects for a very uncertain future. In September Gibbes was issued permission to proceed to Ekaterinburg and take up residence, billeted temporarily in a Lutheran church. He found a suitable accommodation at 10 Soldatskaya Street. Once settled, he had to return to Tiumen and retrieve the luggage he had left behind when traveling was so fraught with uncertainty that he hesitated to drag along too much baggage.

Back in familiar territory, Gibbes had no trouble finding pupils for his English classes; 40 rubles was the fee for class lessons and 75 for private ones. His account book shows his earnings: 920 rubles in October, 1780 in November, and 2180 for December and part of January. The atmosphere of the town suited him well, as there were quite a few English residents. His association with the British Consulate brought invitations to affairs involving the military personnel passing through now that the White forces were in ascendancy; many of them he had known previously in Petrograd or at Stavka. He was also introduced to Sir Charles Eliot, the British High Commissioner in Siberia, who halted his official train in town for a few days. Eliot became acquainted with Gibbes and learned of his command of Russian.

An official investigation was being conducted by General Dieterichs, chief-of-staff to Admiral Kolchak, into the murder of the Imperial Family. Gibbes followed the investigation closely and was always welcome as one who could identify many of the objects discovered. He gave a deposition and painstakingly copied those taken from eyewitnesses and from others, even those who supplied only hearsay or secondhand accounts. These were kept among his papers, and originals for many of these documents surfaced decades later in the official archives after the collapse of the Soviet Union.

On November 2, 1918, he recorded in his journal: "Have this morning been for the third time in the small cellar room under the Ipatiev House." He noted ten bullet holes in the wall opposite the door, all at a height of less than fourteen vershoks (24 1/2 inches), indicating that the victims were probably kneeling. Nine of the holes were bloodstained, but the tenth higher up was not. Numerous bullets had been fired into the floor, but these had been sawn out in square pieces for investigation. The space where the shooting occurred was so small that Gibbes wondered whether they had been shot one after the other.

❧ ❧

Gibbes's colleagues remained in Tiumen and from there sent

numerous requests to 10 Soldatskaya Street begging Syd to send along the boxes, bags, and crates of personal belongings they had left behind when expelled in June. The stream of requests was endless: a reel of fine white cotton, bottles of perfume, books, ointment for Gilliard's eczema, and the like. Syd always tried to accommodate the requests. Some arrangements were complicated; for example, Baroness Buxhoeveden was planning to leave Siberia for Japan. Her luggage, including some valuable jewelry, had to be sent to Omsk by courier, and there were several mix-ups. Before she left Gibbes also needed to collect the 1300 rubles he had lent her, which she had forgotten about. Gilliard had been a witness and could vouch for the transaction, and Gibbes in his meticulous manner enclosed a detailed statement. The records do not show whether he recovered his money, but he did continue to offer whatever assistance he could in arranging transportation for the baroness and her luggage.

Despite his improved situation, Syd dreaded the thought of another winter in Siberia and felt that with the Russian situation so uncertain, his best option was to return to England, though he was not sure how he could manage it. After the physical and emotional strain of the last months, he was feeling genuinely homesick. There had been no word from England since a letter from Aunt Kate posted in November, 1917. Now, more than a year later in December, 1918, a telegram from the Foreign Office arrived at the British Consulate asking whether Gibbes was dead or alive. Evidently none of his letters had gotten through, and that thought only increased his depression.

This was his state of mind when Thomas Preston told him that the High Commissioner was offering him a position as secretary on his staff. Gibbes leaped at the chance. The position was attractive for several reasons. First, he would be on an official British train, the next best thing to being on a piece of British soil. He would be with fellow countrymen of culture and reputation and have a box seat from which to observe as the White forces "laid the Bolsheviks low," which he hoped would happen by the end of the summer. After that he would proceed home by way of Petrograd.

On January 23, 1919, Gibbes received a formal letter from Preston confirming the verbal proposal of the Commissioner:

> I herewith beg to inform you that I have received a further telegram from Sir Charles Eliot, H.B.M.'s High Commissioner, in which he offers you a position as a secretary on his staff at Omsk, on the terms mentioned in his telegram of January 20, viz., £25 (twenty-five pounds sterling) monthly with board and lodging. Sir Charles, in his telegram of January 22nd, states that a compartment on his train will be placed at your disposal.
>
> If you are agreeable to accept these terms, His Excellency wishes you to leave with the utmost despatch.

This would mean living once again on a train, but this time a comfortably appointed one, which he described as a "very fine collection of railway carriages. The High Commissioner has a very comfortable car with bed-room, saloon, bath and a room for his Secretary. . . . Then there is a beautiful dining car, in one half there is a dining table and in the other there is a sort of drawing room." Here members of the company, several officials, and a small contingent of soldiers often gathered in the comfortable seats and chairs arranged around occasional tables. "We have a large first class coach for our accommodation and for the office." This Chancery, as it was called, had a safe, a stationery cabinet, a couple of tables, and a typewriter. "I have also a similar compartment and a writing table which can also serve as an office on occasion."

Gibbes had proceeded at once to Omsk, his way eased at every point by official orders for assistance—a far cry from other journeys he had recently made. In fact, he had grown so accustomed to obstacles and delays that he left much of his luggage in Ekaterinburg, not quite ready to believe this change of fortune. In Omsk he learned they would be going east three thousand miles to Vladivostok, where a headquarters for arriving Allied forces was being set up. They would be leaving right away, along with General Knox, head of the British military mission, so Gibbes wrote Preston asking to have at least one piece of luggage, a box of silver deposited in the State Bank of Ekaterinburg, sent to him there. He would be grateful if Colonel Lash could bring that box, "which needs to be well corded before delivery as the lock is not very secure and sometimes comes undone. . . . I hate to put you to so much trouble but the outlook is so gloomy that I am afraid to leave the box where it is."

This gloom had descended because of news from Paris: the Allies at the Versailles Peace Conference in January had declined to give official recognition to the White Russian government, pretending to be neutral in the country's civil war. Expectations had been high following the armistice of November 11, 1918; the White forces had absolutely no doubt that the Allies would come to their aid. Germany had been unconditionally defeated; surely the Bolsheviks could be knocked off in short order. Some Western leaders, such as Winston Churchill, wanted to wage war on the Bolsheviks, but others were afraid a White victory would revive Russian imperial aspirations and preferred to leave things as they were. This was a severe blow to effective organization of a military campaign against the Bolsheviks. However, the Allies did agree to supply aid, and Britain, spurred by Churchill, supplied the most. Troops and equipment were beginning to flow in through Vladivostok, and Gibbes found himself positioned at an important nerve center of communications, translating, coding, and decoding messages that indicated the fluctuating fortune of White forces.

There had been some fighting between Bolsheviks and counter-revolutionaries since November of 1917, but it was desultory and indecisive. Shortly after the Bolshevik seizure of power in October, Generals Alexeiev and Kornilov had organized loyal officers and troops into the Volunteer Army that became the nucleus of the White forces. In December 1917 they established themselves in Novocherkassk on the steppes in the Don Cossack region, enlisting the assistance of those famous warrior horsemen and their leader, General Alexei Kaledin.

From here an attack was launched on December 9, 1917, on the city of Rostov. It was the first battle of what would become a full-scale civil war, and Kornilov and Kaledin drove the Red Guards from the city and took possession. Their primary aim was to get the Bolsheviks out of the way in order to continue the war with Germany, and they were off to a promising start.

The Bolsheviks had yet to organize a disciplined fighting force, though there were Red Guard units stationed in strategic spots and revolutionary soldiers in Petrograd, Moscow, and other cities to enforce the Bolshevik edicts. For the first year the fighting had been for the most part on the rails, so to speak, without definite fronts or objectives. Troops were moved by train in what was called the railway war, and "it became a question of loading a handful of men and some machine-guns on to a train and moving off to the next station—which would then be 'captured' along with the town."[1]

However, more than troops were on the move. The Red Terror had been launched, particularly in the cities of the northern provinces, and was creating thousands of refugees, who streamed out of central Russia southward, toward the region of the Don River, or eastward into Siberia. Some managed to board a train, but most made their way by horse, in carts, or on foot. They were dispossessed landowners and their families whose estates had been seized, aristocrats, former factory owners, business and professional men, professors, shopkeepers, all reduced to penury as the state commandeered their establishments and requisitioned their property. They now had to beg for a place to sleep at night, and by day they lined the streets trying to sell what remained of their possessions—clothing, jewels, shoes, household items—to buy bread.

Mingling with the soldiers and refugees were students and intellectuals, many of whom had once been fierce opponents of the tsarist regime, but now felt betrayed by the unbridled malice

---

[1] Orlando Figes, *A People's Tragedy: A History of the Russian Revolution* (New York: Viking, 1996), p. 557.

of the revolution that was despoiling the country and turning its people into barbarians. Roman Gul' might have been speaking for them all: "I saw that underneath the red hat of what we had thought of as the beautiful woman of the Revolution there was in fact the ugly snout of a pig."[2]

Before the end of February, 1918, the Reds had marched south and recaptured Rostov and then Novocherkassk, gaining control of central Russia. But the war was not over, as Lenin thought. Even as the Soviet troops were entering Novocherkassk, General Kornilov led his men out over the ice-covered steppes on a trek that has been transformed into legend as the Ice March. Day and night they tramped southward in freezing temperatures, fighting the enemy every step of the way, and followed by the miserable file of civilians who dared not stay behind. This great feat of survival transformed Kornilov's men into a solid fighting force, one willing to take on anything.

When they reached the city of Ekaterinodar, Kornilov decided to lay siege. After a few days, it became evident that they could not succeed with their ammunition practically exhausted and the men half-starved. To add to their troubles, Kornilov himself, their most inspiring leader, was killed when his headquarters was shelled. The command fell upon General Anton Denikin, who had no option but to lead his forces in retreat northward, back to the Don. Here, luckily, they found the Cossacks more than eager to join them and wreak vengeance on the Bolsheviks, who had administered a strong dose of the Red Terror in their region. Together the two forces secured that rich territory and began preparations for a counter-offensive.

---

[2] Quoted in Figes, *People's Tragedy*, p. 556.

Another stronghold of anti-Bolshevik activity was Samara on the Volga, where some members of the first Constituent Assembly attempted to organize a provisional successor to the Provisional Government to maintain order and form a fighting force capable of defeating the Reds. It was called Komuch, acronym for Committee of Members of the Constituent Assembly. Though this administration was too tentative to succeed, it did receive enormous help in its war effort when the famous Czech Legion burst onto the scene in May.

This was a contingent of some 35,000 Czech prisoners of war who had been fighting alongside Russia against Austria in order to gain their independence. After the Treaty of Brest-Litovsk, these men decided to head back to the Western Front in Europe to continue their fight for a free Czechoslovakia. To avoid crossing enemy territory, they were taking the long Pacific route from Vladivostok right around the world. They set out on the Trans-Siberian Railway, breaking up into six companies. However, hostile soviets at several stations stopped and harassed their trains. In one Ural town several men from one Czech company were jailed after a brawl broke out; then the Red Guards tried to disarm the rest. This was provocation enough for the Czechs to occupy the town and free their comrades. From then on they were the force to be reckoned with along the railway, taking one town after another, advancing, as we know, on Ekaterinburg while the Imperial Family was held there.

In the Volga region they joined forces with the Komuch, calling their combined forces the People's Army, and on June 8 secured the city of Samara, driving out the Red Guards. In July of 1918 they captured Ufa and Simbirsk, Lenin's birthplace.

In August they took Kazan, where a large tsarist gold supply was stored.

However, during the summer months the Bolsheviks had begun preparing a genuine army to launch a campaign along the Volga, and by September had 70,000 troops at the ready. By this time the Czech soldiers were growing weary of fighting someone else's war and began to drop out to continue their way home. The gap left by their departure had to be filled by calling for volunteers from the peasants of the area. Much to the surprise of the Komuch, the response was feeble, and they had to resort to forced conscription, a measure that deeply alienated the people. The authorities had expected the peasants to join eagerly in the effort to defeat the Bolsheviks, whose cruel policies had certainly angered them. But the typical peasant felt that the war was not really his affair and cared little about another constituent assembly, since he now had enough land and freedom to suit him. On October 7 the Reds took back the city of Samara, and the weakened Komuch fled eastward to Ufa.

In Omsk, even before the Bolsheviks seized power, members of the Kadet party and the Socialist Revolutionaries had organized to form a government there in Siberia, with the idea of breaking away from central Russia and establishing an independent state. As more, and more varied, counter-revolutionary factions were attracted to Omsk, the friction between them became intense. Most officers in the Siberian Army distrusted the left-leaning government and felt that socialist experiments should be postponed until the civil war was won and a constituent assembly convened to make policy. In November 1918, the officers staged a coup and installed Admiral Alexander Kolchak as Supreme

Regent in Siberia, establishing a military dictatorship. Kolchak was at first reluctant to accept such a post, but at the urging of the officers and the insistence of General Knox that this was his duty, he consented. As High Commissioner for Britain in Siberia, Sir Charles Eliot was credited to Kolchak, and Gibbes was part of this company.

Before leaving Omsk, Gibbes sent a note to his servant, Dimitri, saying that he had waited as long as possible. The train was leaving, but he was giving Mitya's passport to Mr. Semyonov for safekeeping so that the young man could get a job in the city. Gibbes expected to be in Vladivostok about two months and asked his servant to send by way of the Consul the "glass negatives of corpses of people killed by the Bolsheviks, including the sailor Nagorny."

On the long journey to Vladivostok, Gibbes often found himself the center of attention at dinner and afterward, for everyone was anxious to know all he had to tell about the Imperial Family, details of their daily life, details of the final days. When they had first met in Ekaterinburg, Sir Charles had asked him to write an account of life with the family in Tobolsk, which he did.

Upon reaching their destination on the far eastern coast of Siberia, they found things buzzing. In fact, Gibbes felt a bit taxed by the hectic pace. Troops and supplies were coming in from Britain, France, Italy, Canada, the United States, and Japan, but their efforts resembled what Orlando Figes calls "a poor man's game of poker: none of the players wanted to be left out . . . but none of them would play with very high stakes."[3] President Woodrow Wilson, for example, sent some troops with one hand while

---

[3] Figes, *People's Tragedy*, p. 574.

putting out peace feelers to the Bolsheviks with the other.

On February 28, Gibbes was invited to visit his old friend General Michael Dieterichs, with whom he had worked during the first investigation in Ekaterinburg and who was now in Vladivostok. Dieterichs informed him that he had brought all the evidence along with him and was making preparations to send it to England. That same evening the captain of *H.M.S Kent*, the vessel that would be transporting these important items, joined them to get some details about his special cargo. The items, some as bulky as the wheeled chair of the Empress, were described and Dieterichs explained that boxes of appropriate size were being prepared for the shipment.

The Allies had great confidence in Admiral Kolchak, and their aid helped him strengthen his forces for a spring campaign, for which General Knox took on the task of training the troops. On Christmas Eve, 1918, Kolchak took Perm, an important industrial center, and from there pushed ahead in a three-pronged movement, despite the wintry weather. By mid-April his forces—about one hundred thousand strong—were within two hundred miles of the Volga River with their sights on the cities of Viatka, Ufa, and Orenburg. The master plan was to join forces with the White Volunteer Army from the Don area, commanded by General Anton Denikin, and then march triumphantly on to Moscow—Syd mentioned the possibility in a letter to Uncle Will.

As Kolchak was advancing, the British Commissioner and his staff set out on May 29 for the long trip back to Omsk to be near the action, traveling through a landscape studded with such varied and beautiful scenery that Syd laid aside his family letter-writing to look out the window. He did, however, dispatch an urgent message to his friend Colonel Leggett on May 30.

> I quite forgot to go to my room and take away some papers I had left there. In the second drawer of the dressing table there are two reports and some letters belonging to Pares. One report entitled "Special Service for Russia" or something like that and another of the same kind, I think with only the title "Memorandum." On the back of one of the reports is an address in Pares' handwriting to which they are to be sent. Be so very kind as to collect them if they still exist and send them off in a big envelope, it isn't necessary to put any word with them but just send them off as they are. Please let me know and if the worst is the case I will make my peace with Pares when I see him in Omsk. If it is all right, end your message with 36, and if it is all wrong with 18. . . . As the arrangement was a private one between me and P—s, I would rather you not mention the matter to R-b-rts-n (or any one else).

Bernard Pares happened to be the foremost British authority on Russia. He had been attached to the Russian Army during the war and in 1917 was Ambassador in Petrograd, so his papers would be important. He had shown great interest in the information Gibbes could supply during their conversations on the train and in Vladivostok, and in his book on the fall of the monarchy pays tribute to Gibbes's honor in joining the family in their imprisonment. This episode involving his papers must have turned out well, for there was talk of their traveling back to England together later in the year.

Meanwhile, the Reds, though decisively routed at Perm, had not been idle. They were preparing a counter-offensive, which they launched on April 18. In the ranks were several thousand members of the newly organized Communist Youth League, who added strength and enthusiasm to the other thousands of party members and peasant conscripts who had been forcibly mobilized for the campaign. Within two months' time they had pushed Kolchak's forces back east of Ufa, wiping out all his gains. Once in the Urals, the Reds captured Orenburg and Ekaterinburg, cutting short the second investigation into the massacre. By mid-August they had taken the important rail center Chiliabinsk, and Perm itself was threatened, at which point the Allies added insult to injury by reducing their aid to the Whites.

Much blame for the failure of Kolchak's campaign has been laid at the feet of General Denikin, who failed to follow the original strategy and bring his forces up to join those of Kolchak. He had decided instead to intercept the Red forces then driving into the rich coal fields of the Don basin, protecting at the same time his Cossack allies. These were threatened with mass terror by the Bolsheviks, who declared their intention to "decossack" the region and exterminate them to the last man. Denikin's decision, while understandable, was deeply costly and spoiled the Kolchak strategy.

Denikin was not the only one to blame, however. Kolchak's campaign exposed areas of serious dysfunction in the administration and coordination of the White forces, and yet those in authority were never able to understand the problems well enough to remedy them. Most of the leaders were military men who viewed counter-revolutionary activity in battle terms only, but in the present situation there were too many officers and not enough soldiers; rivalries of rank bred such resentment, insubordination, and independent adventuring that effective cooperation was seldom achieved.

Conflicting political ideas added to this discord and made it impossible to define a unifying purpose. Everyone agreed that the Bolsheviks had to be dispatched, but then what? Were they fighting to restore the old regime? To bring back the Constituent Assembly? To establish a democratic government? To establish a socialist one? To return confiscated land to the gentry, legitimize the peasants' seizures, work out a compromise? The political problems were so vexed that the career military men tacitly agreed to make winning the war their top priority; only then could they consider political and social matters.

This fatal mistake cost Kolchak his victory, for despite his successful advance, the rear was not secured. There was no structure for administering conquered territory or winning the support of the population, especially the peasants. No attempt was made to counter the insistent Bolshevik propaganda that they were the ones defending the revolution. More than anything else the peasants wanted to keep the land they had taken from the gentry since 1917. Land was what the revolution had given them, and hardened by years of toil and sometimes severe landlords, they were more willing to bear harsh, oppressive treatment from the Bolsheviks than to give up their land. The appearance, attitude, and conduct of the White officers encouraged identification with the old system, and they took no steps to correct this perception.

In the south Denikin was making significant progress on his

own. The Cossacks, in gratitude for his protection, joined forces with him and greatly accelerated his advance toward Tsaritsyn, disastrously late though it was. From there he issued his Moscow Directive on July 3, ordering the three main arms of his White Volunteer Army to advance in a pincer movement converging on Moscow (the capital had been moved there in March 1918): one arm to approach from Tsaritsyn through Saratov and Nizhnyi Novgorod, one from Voronezh, and one from Kharkov through Orel and Tula. Through the summer they advanced steadily toward the assigned targets, easily capturing every one. Often the Reds ran away at the sight of them. In October Denikin was outside Orel and only one hundred miles from Tula, with Moscow just beyond.

His spectacular progress threw the Bolsheviks into a panic as these fresh, well-supplied and well-trained troops advanced to within 250 miles of the capital. Some of the leaders were outright craven: tearing up their party tickets and renewing acquaintance with their erstwhile bourgeois friends, making plans to go underground or escape abroad with getaway cars ready. Panic increased and drastic measures were taken to protect the city, especially when it was learned that a second White army, commanded by General Nikolai Yudenich, was gathering on the outskirts of Petrograd and threatening Moscow from the north. For a few fleeting days in October it seemed that the Bolsheviks might be finished.

It was Trotsky who realized and convinced Lenin that the city of Tula with its huge arsenal was more important to their survival than Moscow, and no-nonsense Dmitry Os'kin was sent to save it. His totally ruthless measures tell a lot about the

Bolshevik methods. He rounded up thousands of workers, peasants, ordinary citizens, and organized them into labor teams. They were driven night and day to build fortifications, chop wood for fuel in the factories, dig trenches, haul carts. Members of their families, meanwhile, were held hostage to be shot if the work slackened or was not done as ordered. The city was literally turned into a fortress. Soldiers patrolled the streets, and every building was turned into a barracks with lookouts on the roof.

Denikin continued his advance, his forces strengthened by British tanks and heavy artillery and by his own superb cavalry. As he approached fortified Tula the chances of victory were good, even with all the city's preparations. Then on the eve of battle, the Red ranks were suddenly swelled by a huge contingent of peasants, hundreds of thousands, who had deserted the Whites, persuaded that the Reds were the ones to side with if they wanted to keep their newly acquired lands. After that, the outcome was never in doubt. Brilliant generalship had been neutralized by failures of administration, support, and propaganda. Hopelessly outnumbered, General Denikin and his two able commanders, Baron Wrangel and General Mia-Maevsky, made their fighting retreat south to the Black Sea. It must be acknowledged that sometimes the Whites could almost, but never quite, match the Reds in cruelty as they sought vengeance for the ruin of their lives, their fortunes, and Russia itself. In these battles they took no prisoners.

Meanwhile, General Yudenich's threat to Petrograd brought Trotsky himself hurrying to defend the cradle of the revolution. He succeeded by using the same brutal methods as Os'kin; he may have even acted on Lenin's suggestion that he raise thirty thousand people, set up machine-guns behind them, and shoot several hundred of them to insure a real forward assault on Yudenich. Horsemanship had always been considered an aristocrat's game, but the revolutionaries had recently learned that it was available to them as well and their cavalry was a surprise weapon.

In November came a mortal blow: the British withdrew their support, and Lloyd George's public statement that the White cause was lost generated a wave of hopeless defeatism that totally demoralized the counter-revolutionaries, military and civilian, and sent them fleeing in all directions, desperate to escape the Terror. Omsk was abandoned on November 14, 1919, and Kolchak set out for his new capital, Irkutsk, in six trains, one of which held the tsarist gold captured at Kazan. Just three hundred miles from his destination, the trains were halted by the Czechs and detained for several weeks. As Kolchak sat helpless on the tracks, Irkutsk was taken over by revolutionaries who declared him an enemy of the people. On January 4, he resigned and was promised safe conduct by the Czechs to Irkutsk, where he would be given into Allied hands. Instead he was turned over to the Bolsheviks, along with the gold, perhaps by the Czechs themselves in return for safe passage home. The death sentence was inevitable. Eliot reported, "He died bravely,—in the words of his executioner, 'straight up, like an Englishman.'"[4]

Five months earlier, in June 1919, as the High Commissioner's train was making its slow, deliberate progress westward through

[4] Charles Eliot, *Japanese Buddhism* (London: Edward Arnold, 1935), p. xxviii, *n.*

Siberia, it had stopped in Ekaterinburg, then still occupied by the Whites. Nikolai Sokolov, a professional investigator, was now in charge of the investigation. He had been appointed by Kolchak after Dieterichs' resignation, and Eliot permitted Gibbes to assist in any way he could while they were there. It was painful enough to revisit the grim reminders in Ipatiev House and rehearse events of the final days there, which he did as he carefully copied the depositions from witnesses and others connected with the crime.

These contained haunting phrases: "The murder was so cruel I had many times to go into the air to recover." "Blood, there was so much blood, they swept it with a broom." "She [Anna Demidova] kept running about and hid herself behind a pillow, on her body were 32 wounds." Syd remembered her vividly: "a tall well-built woman rather inclined to be stout, who in direct contrast to her physical appearance was of a singularly timid and shrinking disposition." He recalled the fear she expressed on her last night at Tobolsk: "I'm so afraid of what the Bolsheviks might do to us." The bloodless bayonet thrusts and bloodless bullet holes had been aimed at this frightened, helpless woman; only an eyewitness could have described the scene.

An even more nightmarish dimension was added when the investigators examined the mine shafts at Four Brothers, where the bodies were thought to have been buried. Gibbes went day after day to watch as Sokolov had the standing water pumped out of the shafts and sifted through the debris brought up from the bottom. He combed meticulously through the remains of a nearby bonfire and found many fragments of gems, bits of clothing, six sets of corset stays, belt buckles, shoe buckles, a pocket case in which the Tsar carried his wife's portrait, clasps and fasteners, an earring of platinum and pearl, the badge from a Lancer regiment worn on a bracelet by the Empress, an assortment of coins, nails, and bits of foil from the boyish collection of useful things Alexei accumulated in his pockets—all bore mute testimony to the horrors of that night. "Most terrible of all was a severed finger clean cut off" that Gibbes first thought might have belonged to Dr. Botkin because it was so swollen. Expert examiners, however, determined that it had belonged to a woman over thirty-five years of age who manicured her hands—the Empress. There were also bits of human skin and fragments of bone in the vicinity of the fire, and near one of the mine shafts a set of false teeth belonging to Dr. Botkin.

For all their excavation in the mines where so many who claimed to be witnesses had said they would be, no bodies were ever found. After days of probing and scrutinizing his evidence, Sokolov theorized that the entire family had been murdered, their bodies hacked into manageable pieces, and then tossed onto the huge fire that had been kept going for two days and nights with barrels of petrol. Sulfuric acid had first been used to disfigure the corpses, but there were no graves. Sokolov spent the rest of his life defending his position, hoarding the evidence he had collected, interviewing émigrés, writing away at a book that appeared only a few months before his death.

His conclusion stood until 1976, when Anthony Summers and Tom Mangold, in their book, *The File on the Tsar,* demonstrated how unlikely it was that eleven human bodies could have been consumed by fire. Even had this somehow been accomplished, their teeth would have remained, and there would

have been more than three hundred. Where were they? These
challenges aroused the scientific community, which began to pay
attention, with results that are well known. The remains of the
Imperial Family were eventually located, exhumed, identified,
and the recovered bodies given Christian burial. Only two bodies were missing, and Yurovsky's official report, as we have noted,
indicates that these were Alexei and Demidova, that they had
been partially burned, and the remains buried beneath the bonfire. It would have pleased Charles Sydney Gibbes to know the
truth behind this great mystery, but it came too late to be part of
his story.

In a letter to his Aunt Kate Gibbes wrote:

While we were at Ekaterinburg the military situation grew
rapidly worse and our officers began to entertain fear for
the safety of the town, which however Russian Headquarters did not confess to sharing but which subsequent
events quickly justified, for we had hardly returned to
Omsk before orders were issued to evacuate the town.
The retreat has been in full progress ever since although
it is proceeding less rapidly. Now all the work which the
Investigation Committee had undertaken has been abandoned, and it is doubtful whether anything will be left
after the Bolsheviks have once more been in power in
that region.

In this letter he also told of a moving memorial service held
for the Imperial Family on July 17, 1919, the anniversary of their
death, which had made him deeply sad. From Omsk the English

company's train headed back toward Irkutsk, fifteen hundred miles to the east.

At this point, Gibbes was more anxious than ever to get home to England; he approached the High Commissioner about being released so that he could return with Professor Pares by way of the Kara Sea. Eliot felt, however, that he still needed Gibbes's services and would not release him, though he did promise to try to arrange free steamer passage at the end of October. This did not materialize either, and Syd stayed on in a state of uncertainty and suspense. The uncertainty was over his own future; the suspense came from intrigues developing around the evidence gathered in the Ekaterinburg investigation and the efforts to remove it to safety.

At times he must have felt like a secret agent, for both Dieterichs and Sokolov entrusted him with information they considered dangerous and material evidence they felt was threatened. Both men were convinced there had been German connivance in the murder of the Romanovs and that enemy agents were anxious to destroy the evidence. The facts of the case were plain enough—all members of the family had been shot—but there were unanswered questions, as Gibbes pointed out in his report on the investigation.

> Evidence relating to the events which preceded the crime was more difficult to obtain than that relating to the tragedy itself. . . . It still remains to be shown for what purpose the Bolsheviks committed the crime and not only denied all knowledge of it but took such elaborate pains to conceal evidence of the deed.

Sokolov was right on track when he concluded from his evidence that the murders were not an irresponsible act of the Ural Soviet, but had been approved in advance from Moscow. The German connection was much harder to get a grip on. Both he and Dieterichs believed Boris Soloviev to be a German agent, and they suspected another duplicitous character, known variously as Markov and also as Popoff. As Markov he had been a member of an imperial regiment at Tsarskoe Selo and had been photographed with the sponsoring Grand Duchess; as Popoff he had connections with Berlin that enabled him to help several prominent people get safely through after the Treaty of Brest-Litovsk. These fellows had been seen in Tobolsk and both had sent covert messages to the imprisoned family, promising to help free them. Several times Sokolov presented his case to Gibbes, urging him to pass the information on to the High Commissioner; Gibbes did this, but they both agreed that the matter was too nebulous to act on.

Behind them in Siberia, all White resistance was melting away. In November 1919, Sir Charles Eliot was appointed Ambassador to Japan, and Miles Lampson took his place as British High Commissioner with headquarters in Irkutsk; but in less than two months they were moving still farther to the east. At this time the delegations from many Allied countries were making plans for departure, and the dismal outlook for the future of Russia made Sokolov and Dieterichs even more desperate to get their papers and physical evidence safely out of the country. In Chita on Russian Christmas, January 7, 1920, they visited Gibbes once more. This time they told him that their lives were now in danger because of the "proof" they had in their possession about the

murders and the German involvement with the Bolsheviks. They
had prepared a comprehensive dossier which they intended to
submit to Lampson, though it was not yet signed and sealed.

Then Dieterichs said, "There is one thing I want you to
take with you now." And going to his room brought
out a small despatch box covered in dark mauve leather
that had once belonged to the Empress. With great
emotion the General said, "This contains all their
earthly relics."

Time was running out, our train was to leave at midnight. If Mr. Lampson consented the American Consul
General would be asked to take the trunk containing the
evidence and Mr. Sokolov on his train the following
day. Carefully packing the small despatch box in my
portmanteau, I bid the General a hasty farewell and returned to the station where I informed Mr. Lampson of
what had passed and with his permission completed the
arrangements.

On this same night the general had given Gibbes a letter addressed to Lampson:

To the last possible moment, I wished to retain in my
own hands and in Russia, in the revival of which I still
continue to trust, the affair of the Imperial Family, i.e.
the substantial evidence in the matter and the Remains
of Their Imperial Majesties, which it has been possible to
find on the place where Their Corpses were burnt.

The turn which events are taking now, however, shows that in order to ensure the safety of these Sacred Relics, it is essential that They should not be connected with my fate.

I cannot leave Russia; the German orientation in Chita may compel me temporarily to seek refuge in the forest. Under such conditions I am of course unable to carry with me the Great National Sacred Relics.

I have decided to entrust you, as the Representative of Great Britain, with the safe-keeping of these Sacred Objects. I think you will understand without my having to explain, why I wish it to be Great Britain: you and we have one common historical foe, and the tortuous murder of the Members of the Imperial Family, a deed unprecedented in history, is the deed of *this foe*, aided by their assistants, the Bolsheviks.

The letter also expressed Dieterichs' wish that if the materials could not be returned to him, they should be handed over to Grand Duke Nicholas Nikolaevich or General Denikin. A separate note explains, "This box, which once belonged to Her Majesty the Empress, now contains all that was recovered at the mine shaft from the remains of the burned bodies," and correctly identifies the persons murdered along with the Imperial Family.

The British High Commission moved on on that midnight train to Harbin, where Lampson made a formal report to Lord Curzon of all that Gibbes had told him and the items conveyed to him. The American Consul General was held up by fighting between American and Red troops at Verkhne-Udinsk, but he finally arrived in Harbin and the precious box was handed over to him as he and Sokolov proceeded to Peking. Several other boxes from Dieterichs were placed with the British Consul there in Harbin when Lampson moved to Peking on January 30. His staff was being reduced, but Gibbes was taken along because of his intimate knowledge of the Imperial Family and of the case.

From Peking in February Lampson did report the entire affair to London, with the request that the box and papers be accepted there for safekeeping, and awaited instructions.

In March the reply came: it was negative. Sokolov and Dieterichs, who were both now in Peking, were crushed, but they had the good fortune to obtain an interview with the French General Janin and begged for his help. Janin said "that he considered the mission we entrusted to him to be a debt of honour to a faithful ally." The box is said to be still in the Janin family vault.

Shortly afterward the British High Commission in Siberia ended, and Gibbes's service there also ended. His future prospects were almost as unsettled as they had been when he arrived in St. Petersburg in 1901.

11

Time for Reflection

At last Gibbes was free to return to England, but when he faced the prospect he discovered that his homesickness had been displaced by heartsickness. He could remember the hurt Tsar Nicholas had felt at the British reaction to his abdication, the cheers in Parliament and their congratulatory telegram to the Provisional Government, the unbridled criticism in the press. Those to whom he had been so faithful and for whom he had made such sacrifices positively rejoiced in his fall. It was Gibbes's own country that had reneged on its offer of asylum to the Imperial Family, a failure that might have been avoided had King George V shown a bit more political courage or a deeper compassion for his own kin. Their final poignant appeal for help Gibbes had written with his own hand, when the Empress addressed through him her veiled cry to Miss Jackson. Now he had seen with his own eyes evidence of the heart-numbing horror of the murders—horror that might have been avoided, if only . . .

This personal anguish was compounded by his experience with

the British High Commission. In November, Prime Minister Lloyd George, after declaring the White cause hopeless, left them to struggle on without further aid and support. Gibbes had translated the official bulletins into Russian for distribution to the beleaguered commanders who had once been their allies, and many of whom he knew personally. Most vivid in his mind was the dramatic midnight meeting with General Dieterichs, as the grief-stricken man reverently handed over to him the box containing "the Remains of Their Imperial Majesties, which it has been possible to find on the place where Their Corpses were burnt," along with the letter entrusting Lampson "as the Representative of Great Britain with the safe-keeping of these Sacred Objects." London had rejected even this modest request. Syd decided not to go home just yet.

To Winifred he wrote only that his affairs were somewhat unsettled and that his return home would be delayed. To say his affairs were unsettled was understating the case; he was in the grips of a spiritual crisis as acute as any he had experienced at Cambridge. The emotional turmoil brought on by the tragedy of the imperial martyrs and their beloved Russian land was a primary factor, but another dimension had been introduced by Sir Charles Eliot himself.

Eliot had spent many years in the Orient and had served as vice chancellor of the University of Hong Kong. He had written a monumental study of Buddhism and Hinduism in India, China, and Japan. The books were not yet published because of the war and Eliot's official duties, but they were ready for publication, and he was carrying the printer's proofs with him on his train. Gibbes's interest in Eastern religion was rekindled, and

Sir Charles, pleased to have an eager reader, supplied fuel for the fire. Eliot was a learned and enthusiastic admirer of Eastern theologies and philosophies, and the two men had long earnest discussions as Gibbes read Eliot's material.

Sir Charles was intrigued by India's endless variety of cults and their vast numbers of adherents, asserting that India led the world in spiritual experience because "the national mind finds its favourite occupation and full expression in religion." His researches led him to conclude that there are "few dogmas known to the theologies of the world which are not held by some of India's multitudinous sects." The only exception he had found was the Christian doctrine of atonement or salvation by the death of the Deity.[1]

However, among all the Eastern theologies, Eliot most admired Buddhism. His assertion that "the fundamental principles of Buddhism are more in harmony with the results of scientific research than are the postulates of Christian theism" laid hold on Gibbes's attention, as did Eliot's sympathetic presentation of the Buddhist doctrine that there is no permanent self in persons:

> You will never be happy unless you realize you can make and remake your own soul. . . . Everything that exists has a cause; the cause of evil is lust and the craving for pleasure, which is removed by purifying the heart. Gotama's teaching was simply that a man can attain before death a blessed state in which he has nothing to fear from either death or rebirth.[2]

---

[1] Charles Eliot, *Hinduism and Buddhism: An Historical Sketch*, 3 vols. (London: Edward Arnold & Co., 1921), v. 1, p. xxii.

[2] Eliot, *Japanese Buddhism*, p. 188; *Hinduism and Buddhism*, v. 1, pp. xvi, xxii.

Gibbes, as we know, had long been attracted to Eastern religion, and now it was being presented in a way that made it seem even more profound and spiritual than he had previously thought. He was enthralled all over again. Gibbes's decision to stay in the East so pleased Sir Charles that he used his influence to secure him a position in the Chinese Maritime Customs. This was a favor that took some doing, since Gibbes's knowledge of Chinese was limited; however, his command of Russian and his experience there would definitely be a help at this particularly tense time, and his gift for languages would see him through.

Gibbes was assigned to Harbin, Manchuria, so off he went. This city was only one of many stations in the Chinese Maritime Customs network, but it was unique. The Russians had converted the primitive fishing village into an important commercial and communications hub after they built the Chinese Eastern Railway at the turn of the century. By 1904, the Chinese-owned system had been connected to the Trans-Siberian Railroad leading straight to Moscow, with another leg extending strategically to Port Arthur. Harbin now enjoyed a lively sea trade as well, since the Sungari River, to which the city had first attached itself, was tributary to a mighty tidal river, the Amur, where international trade flourished. For about six months of the year, after the ice had melted, Harbin also operated as an international port.

When Gibbes arrived in Harbin, it was the largest Russian city outside of Russia, and as such became a natural haven for refugees and tsarist sympathizers. Its magnificent Orthodox churches, its shops, bazaars, amusements, cafés—all the things that a fine Russian city would offer—gave it a prerevolutionary atmosphere, an aura it managed to retain into the 1970s. Gibbes felt at home and settled happily into the neat, modern houseboat provided by the customs service. He must have relished being surrounded by water, where he could splash as much as he liked in his ablutions with no objections from a cross landlady.

Gibbes's first glimpse of this city had come in May, 1919, as the British High Commission headed westward toward Omsk. Their train had stopped at Harbin and Gibbes was sent into the "new town," the Russian part, to obtain kerosene to fuel the train's electrical system. When that assignment had been completed, he set off on his own and spent the entire afternoon wandering about the Chinese town overlooking the river. He described what he saw to Aunt Kate.

They seem to swarm everywhere, like ants, more than human beings, but they are so merry and bright, so smiling and cheerful, so knowing and inquisitive, crowding round you if you ever stop. In their manners they are most unconventional, doing everything in public which most people do in private. I had still a few things to buy and went into a shop where I was immediately beset by the shop boys, a great number of them with apparently nothing to do. They asked me lots of questions, particularly about the Japanese and their intentions as to Shantung. They were extremely distrustful and seemed to nurse a deep grudge against their more successful brethren.

I thoroughly enjoyed my first view of the Far East and its wonderful life. As the sun got low, people stopped work and began their evening meal in the street.

He took great interest in their menu, "a mess of pottage of different kinds, one a sort of macaroni made of rice, while another was a sort of thin gruel; all, of course, drank tea in bowls without any handles." Almost before he realized it the sun was setting.

> The scene was very pretty as it grew dusk and the lights began to show here and there, with the hum of conversation and the ripple of laughter coming from the many groups. The streets are all narrow and full of people and seem to teem with life in the same way as does a hive of bees or an ant hill, the people appearing to walk around and over each other. In the end I had to hurry back to the station as I was afraid to miss the train which was due to pull out at ten o'clock.

Gibbes's first assignment as a customs assistant was to prepare a report on developments in the Chinese Maritime Service over the past ten years. He may have been discouraged at the thought of plowing through page after page of dull bureaucratic detail, but he was in for a surprise. The customs service was not like any other bureau, for though administered by the English, it was the main source of revenue for the Chinese government. The story of how this came about was, as Gibbes discovered for himself, full of adventure and intrigue.

Until the mid-nineteenth century Chinese officials had collected the tariffs on maritime shipment, but the system was disorganized and corrupt, the fees being set at the whim of the official in charge for each particular case. In 1853, a local group

calling itself the Small Sword Society rebelled at this official ban-
ditry, invaded the customs office in Shanghai, and threw the
supervisor out of his office. The city's Western traders immediately stepped in to set up a systematic operation, and the Chinese, being very anxious to maintain friendly relations, left the
bureau in English hands. Since then it had not only grown to be
the chief revenue producer for China, it had also charted the
Chinese coast, managed the port facilities, directed the lighting
of the coastal and inland waterways, and in addition organized
and operated the first national postal service.

Harbin was certainly no sleepy outpost; a good bit of adventure enlivened the everyday operations. Most trade was in fur,
lumber, tea, coal, and such ordinary items, but the civil war had
left many munitions lying in various supply depots, and the war-
lords who flourished along the borders of Manchuria were very
anxious to gain possession of them. No matter how innocent the
label or the carton itself looked, every box and crate had to be
opened and carefully inspected—an operation that could turn
dangerous if the transporter became hostile. Notorious opium
traders also had to be dealt with as they began taking advantage
of the wider markets opened by the railroads and the well-
traveled rivers. They too had eyes on the arms supplies that had
become available.

One particularly hot spot was Manchouli, a city located where
the borders of Manchuria, Russia, and Mongolia meet. It was an
important customs station at the western end of the Chinese
Eastern Railway, just where it joined the Russian rail system.
Gibbes went regularly to inspect this tension-filled place. The
consulate was now manned by the Soviets, while most of the

customs officers were White Russians, and one can imagine the resentment that erupted at every encounter. To make matters worse, the Chinese did not know which faction to trust and ended up trusting neither. According to the records, Gibbes was a very skillful diplomat in these explosive situations and often managed to ease the way for White Russians when they were threatened as they tried to reach the safety of Manchuria.

And there were other perils. Between 1914 and 1920 the Chinese and Mongolians had been battling for control of Manchouli. It was real war, and anyone who got in the way was the enemy. One of Syd's surviving nieces, Doreen Gibbes, told me how she listened wide-eyed and open-mouthed as Syd told of being rescued by a friendly Chinese family, who hid him for several weeks in their double attic while a Mongolian raiding party swept the area looking for him. On another occasion he lost his way in a blizzard and somehow managed to survive for many days by taking shelter at night in caves or crevices in the snow. For food he had only a few mangoes he had purchased in Manchouli, which were now frozen. There was only one way to thaw them—he had to sit on them.

In 1922 a resourceful and adventurous young man entered Gibbes's life. George Paveliev was fifteen when he appeared on the scene, the same age as the Tsarevich had been at his death. He had been born in Moscow and, when his father's work took him to the Far East, had accompanied his parents to Shang-hai, where he was enrolled as a boarding student at St. Xavier's School. With considerable wit and spunk he managed to complete his studies there even after his parents had disappeared in the post-revolutionary chaos with his tuition still to be paid.

The boy was enthralled by boats and the sea and spent most afternoons at the harbor to nose about, learn what he could, and see what he could see. One day he got to talking with the officer of a Russian fishing boat which was loaded with herring and unable to leave the harbor because the duty was not paid. Since George was fluent in Russian and Chinese, the officer asked his help in selling their cargo on the local fish market. The venture was a success, and he received enough money in commission to finish his schooling. After that, he made his way to Harbin, hoping to establish himself in a Russian city.

He first encountered Charles Gibbes in one of those curio shops Gibbes loved to browse. The boy's age and his predicament won Gibbes's sympathy, and he found a place for George with a fur-trading company, a job that offered enough excitement to satisfy his bold spirit. Through the years with the imperial household and after, Gibbes had preferred to live alone whenever possible, but now he made an exception and took George into his floating home on the river. This just suited Paveliev, and before long he had organized a company of Sea Scouts who would soon see action.

Gibbes, with his usual generosity, had lent a considerable sum of money to a man in Harbin who was related to the martyred imperial chef, Kharitonov, so that the fellow could lease a local theater. However, the lease payments had not been kept up, and now the property owner was threatening to repossess the premises, which meant Gibbes would never get his money back. Generous though he was, he had no intention of letting this money go without a struggle. He wrote his brother Arthur, who had managed a bank in India, asking advice, and was dismayed to learn that in their part of the world the best solution would be to seize the building and raise the British flag. George, however, was not dismayed. This was just the enterprise his Sea Scouts were waiting for. They had been at work for quite a while converting a Chinese junk into a schooner, and it was finished in time for them to sail into the dock closest to the theater, scramble ashore, storm the building, and capture the cash box.

Gibbes spent seven interesting years in Harbin, years filled with a stimulating mixture of sometimes risky adventure and pleasant social life. As early as 1924, he began to receive inquiries about possible survivors of the massacre of the Tsar and his family. The law firm of Charles Russel in London wrote asking him to identify the lady in an enclosed photograph. Gibbes sent a cautious reply expressing reluctance to speak of the affairs of the Imperial Family. He did say, however, that there was a very general resemblance to Tatiana, though the eyes, her most memorable feature, were shaded and the hands much too large and broad. However, as friends and relatives began to bombard him with articles featuring one or another person claiming to be a surviving grand duchess and urging him to comment, Gibbes adopted a policy of polite silence on the subject.

Despite his renewed interest in Buddhism, Gibbes frequently attended the Russian church and numbered the clergy and several members of the congregation among his friends, who felt a special respect for him because of his association with the Tsar's family. He was surprised and pleased when he was asked to translate some of the Orthodox service books into English, and agreed to try. Thereafter he spent a great deal of time and effort on the project.

However enjoyable, these years had taken a toll on Gibbes's health. In 1919 he had complained to Winnie, "I have aged very much in these last two years and I do not feel the same as I did four years ago. Doubtless a good rest would do me a lot of good for I have not had any real holiday since the war began when I left England on being recalled to Tsarskoe Selo." Since then, he had endured still more anxieties and disappointments, as well as the physical risks and hardships connected with his present position, and he began to look forward to the full English leave that was his due at the beginning of 1928.

As that time approached, Gibbes made a solemn pilgrimage to Peking to visit the shrine where bodies of several members of the extended Imperial Family had been buried after General Dieterichs, at great personal risk, had brought them from Siberia and entrusted them to the care of the Russian Mission there.

On July 18, 1918, the night after the Ekaterinburg massacre, another group of royal prisoners was taken from their prison in Alapaevsk on the pretense of being removed to safety. Grand Duchess Elizabeth, sister of the Empress and founder of a convent in Moscow, her devoted companion, the nun Barbara, Grand Duke Serge Mikhailovich, Prince John Constantinovich, Prince Constantine Constantinovich, Prince Igor Constantinovich, Prince Vladimir Paley, and several of their attendants were thrown alive into a deep mine shaft, and grenades were tossed in to finish them off.

For decades the only account of this massacre was that given by a peasant who happened to be in the vicinity of the execution site and hid as he heard carts approaching. Though bound and blindfolded, the prisoners were singing hymns, and he watched in fear and horror as they were thrown one by one down the shaft and grenades were tossed in after them. He could hear their groans and still the faint singing rising from below. But for the report of this peasant witness, the bodies of the victims might never have been found.

Three months later, White Russian forces entered the territory and an investigation was launched. When the bodies were brought up, it was seen that Prince John's terrible head wound had been bound with the veil of Grand Duchess Elizabeth. The official report of Ryabov, the chief assassin, details the full horror.

> We led the grand duchess Elizabeth up to the mine. After throwing her down the shaft, we heard her struggling in the water for some time. We pushed the nun lay-sister Varvara down after her. We again heard the splashing of water and the two women's voices. It became clear that, having dragged herself out of the water, the grand duchess had also pulled her lay-sister out. But, having no other alternative, we had to throw in all the men also.
>
> None of them, it seems, drowned, or choked in the water and after a short time we were able to hear almost all their voices again.
>
> Then I threw in a grenade. It exploded and everything was quiet. But not for long.
>
> We decided to wait a little to check whether they had all perished. After a short while we heard talking and a barely audible groan. I threw another grenade.
>
> And what do you think—from beneath the ground

we heard singing! I was seized with horror. They were singing the prayer: "Lord, save your people!"

We had no more grenades, yet it was impossible to leave the deed unfinished. We decided to fill the shaft with dry brushwood and set it alight. Their hymns still rose up through the thick smoke for some time yet.

When the last signs of life beneath the earth had ceased, we posted some of our people by the mine and returned to Alapaevsk by first light and immediately sounded the alarm in the cathedral bell tower. Almost the whole town came running. We told everyone that the grand dukes had been taken away by unknown persons.[3]

The coffins had been placed in a crypt in the cemetery church attached to the Russian Mission, about a fifteen-minute rickshaw ride from the mission itself.[4] After Gibbes arrived in England he described this visit in a touching letter to the Serbian Minister, hoping to win financial help for maintenance of the shrine.

At the time of my visit I had some conversation with the Right Reverend Archbishop Inokenty, the aged and learned prelate who has been head of the Russian

---

[3] Andrei Maylunas and Sergei Mironenko, eds., *A Lifelong Passion*, tr. Darya Galy (London: Weidenfeld and Nicolson, 1999), pp. 638–639, from document in Soviet Archives.

[4] Before the time of Gibbes's visit, in 1921, two of the bodies, those of Grand Duchess Elizabeth and the nun Barbara, had been taken on to Jerusalem for burial at the Church of St. Mary Magdalene, where Elizabeth had expressed a wish to be buried.

Mission in Peking for about thirty years. . . .

He had also desired to attach a priest permanently to the church in order that the offices and prayers for the repose of the souls of the dead might be regularly said, but he had not been able to maintain a priest for this purpose. At my request the Archbishop sent a priest with me to say a "panechida" in the crypt, at which I was present. By the piety of the widow of a rich Russian tea merchant in Hankow, Mrs. Litvinoff, a handsome "lampadka" has been placed in the crypt, but for the same reasons it is not kept continually alight.

When the time came to sail for England, Gibbes invited George to come along and suggested that he might study at Cambridge. But George was now twenty-one and that prospect held no appeal, so Gibbes suggested an alternative. He had relatives in Australia who were sheep-ranchers, and George elected to head for the Outback while Syd proceeded home by way of the Philippines. In Manila he was suddenly struck down by a severe attack of gallstones complicated by infection. He wired George, who came immediately and attended the suffering patient for three long months. When Gibbes was finally well, George returned to Australia, and until the day he died Gibbes credited George with saving his life—a debt he tried to repay by adopting the young man and naming him his heir.

This period of helpless inactivity in a strange country provided the opportunity for Gibbes to look deep inside himself and acknowledge a spiritual thirst, still unquenched in spite of the many experiences in which he had expected to find fulfillment.

He prized his close association with the Imperial Family and truly admired their deep faith, but it still seemed foreign and exotic for one who was, after all, an Englishman. Eliot's lofty presentation of Eastern religion had been stimulating, but as he was heading home Gibbes began to wonder whether or not his youthful disaffection with theology had been too impulsive. Had he been too callow to recognize the worth of what was offered so generously? In this state of uncertainty and self-recrimination, he resolved to try once more that first path from which he had bolted. He would renew his theological education and get himself in shape to take up the vocation his father, in fact his whole family, had expected of him.

The family embraced Syd as joyously as if he had returned from the dead, and for the next few months he basked in their affection, while gently rejecting all their urging to sell his photographs and accounts of his experiences. Winnie and her husband welcomed him warmly into Lea Marston Vicarage, and he took advantage of this opportunity for the first real leisure in years. All his relations were delighted when, in September 1928, he proceeded to Oxford to enroll in the ordination course at St. Stephen's House.

This was the first theological college of its type established within a university, though not the last. It had become obvious that something had to be done to correct the deterioration in theological education that occurred at the end of the nineteenth century, a condition that had helped derail Gibbes's earlier studies, as we have noted. St. Stephen's House had been founded by prominent members of the Tractarian Movement and so was Anglo-Catholic in orientation, and for this reason, "[t]he House has never been viewed with favor by the Establishment."[5]

However, this was precisely the atmosphere Gibbes wanted. He had access to the finest theological library in England and began to read deeply in the Fathers of the Church. Indeed, he was inspired to request help from Anna Alexandrovna, one of his former colleagues, in obtaining copies of these "beautiful books" in Russian. But despite the intellectual and spiritual surroundings, he still felt like a stranger and commented to his friend that he was without influence or support as he considered an ecclesiastical career.

Gibbes was fated to renew his studies at another time of unsettling ferment in the church. At issue was a revision of the Book of Common Prayer. A special Liturgical Commission had been appointed and charged with revising the central service book of the Anglican Church in a way that would eliminate archaisms without disturbing its theological principles or traditional grandeur, and after months of labor and negotiation over disputed points they had produced a version that had the unanimous approval of the commission. However, the finished book had to be presented to Parliament for approval, so that it was disparaged and lobbied against by members of Parliament who were not even Christian, much less Church of England. The revision was defeated in 1928 and again in 1929, but the tone of the public debate did the most damage to the prestige of the church. One of the chief objections had been to prayers for the dead, a matter about which Syd felt deeply. After two terms he realized once

---

[5] Peter G. Cobb, *A Brief History of St. Stephen's House 1876–1976* (Oxford: 1976), p. 19. The Tractarian founders were Edward King, William Bright, Edward Talbot, and Edwin Palmer.

again that ordination in the Church of England was not the direction for him to take.[6]

He was still a member of the Chinese Maritime Service and obligated to return when his leave expired in October 1929, though he confided to Winnie and a few others that he no longer enjoyed living in China because of the political situation there. Still, he returned to Harbin in late 1929, and again in 1931 after another short leave in England. This time he found the troubles had intensified markedly.

Japan was the most industrially advanced of the Far Eastern nations at the time and had embarked on a policy of expansion, gaining a firm foothold in Manchuria. However, China was also on the rise after the Chinese Nationalist Party managed to surge ahead of both the weak Peking regime and the Communists, and the Nationalists very much wanted to regain control of Manchuria. The Japanese had no intention of letting this happen and strengthened their military presence in the region. In mid-September 1931, hostilities erupted between Chinese Nationalists and a Japanese army garrison in Mukden. Though the outbreak appeared to be spontaneous, the Japanese government immediately sent enough support to defeat the weaker Chinese. In 1932 Japan launched a full-scale invasion of Manchuria, and Charles Gibbes, within three months of retirement, found himself once more on the other side of the world and without a job.

He had done a great deal of serious thinking in the past few

---

[6] Many of these details were supplied by the Rev. Edward Barnes, Principal of St. Stephen's House, whom I visited there in 1991. St. Nicholas House had been on the same street (Marston Street) as St. Stephen's.

years about spiritual matters. So when Sir Charles Eliot died in 1931, Gibbes, who never took half-steps, may have felt obliged to honor his mentor's memory by giving his views at least a trial, and here he was in the place where he could do it. Silence hangs over the year he spent in the Shinto shrines of Japan. Shrine Shinto was at this time almost the official religion in Japan—though it was hardly a religion, but rather a system of moral order in matters of government, family, and social behavior. As Eliot had written, the Japanese may be considered a religious people "if religion is taken in the sense of devotion to something beyond individual existence, of readiness to sacrifice to it earthly welfare and life itself, nay, even a passion for such sacrifice as the true end of man."[7]

Gibbes was deeply depressed as that year ended. The order and ceremonial etiquette of the shrines may have been calming and instructive in some ways, but the quiet provided time for him to think more deeply about the nature of the spiritual life he had been struggling so long to cultivate. The only fruit of his fifty-eight years of arduous effort seemed to be ruin. His theological studies, early and late, and the just-completed exercise in Shinto were so much dust in his fingers. Even his happy association with the Imperial Family, his efforts on behalf of the White Russians during the war, and his final work in Chinese customs had ended in destruction and defeat. The object of his questing eluded him; an impenetrable barrier seemed still to stand between him and the transcending reality he longed to know and experience. Was there even the possibility for such a life? Where could one find

---

[7] Eliot, *Japanese Buddhism*, p. 188. This throws light on the spectacular suicidal devotion of Japanese warriors in the Second World War.

it? How could one take part in it? Where would it lead? He told Winnie he felt "very discouraged."

And yet, as he thought ruefully on these things, nothing in all his experience was as exalted and significant as the witness of humble faith, devotion, and courage provided by the Imperial Family he had loved and served. Quite suddenly, he saw the truth manifested in their lives: their reliance on a fountain of strength that kept them radiant even as they were buffeted, humiliated, maligned, and their bodies destroyed by the powerful enemies arrayed against them—enemies they forgave.

He recalled the poetic prayer of Countess Hendrikova, herself a martyr, that the family had often read together as their days grew darker. Grand Duchess Olga undertook to translate it into English and had asked Syd to be sure her grammar was correct and her language appropriate, and he kept a copy among his papers.

> Grant us Thy patience, Lord,
> In these our woeful days,
> The mob's wrath to endure,
> The torturer's ire;
>
> Thy unction to forgive
> Our neighbors' persecution,
> And mild, like Thee, to bear
> A bloodstained Cross.
>
> And when the mob prevails,
> And foes come to despoil us,

To suffer humbly shame,
O Saviour, aid us!

And when the hour comes
To pass the last dread gate,
Breathe strength in us to pray,
"Father, forgive them."

He had been in the presence of a great mystery that he was only now able to recognize. In the light of this revelation, he hurried to Harbin to be accepted into the Orthodox faith.

12

꧁꧂

Home at Last

In April of 1934 Gibbes began instruction in Orthodoxy, and though his education and experience had provided a good deal of ecclesiastical knowledge, all he had learned needed to be transposed into a new dimension. But he was soon ready for chrismation, the solemn rite of initiation into the Orthodox Church. For this he prepared by making confession of all the sins he could recall from his youth up and then publicly acknowledging and renouncing his former errors and false doctrines and declaring his allegiance to the Holy Orthodox Catholic Church, reciting the Nicene Creed on his knees. Only then was he anointed by the priest, who made the sign of the cross with the Holy Chrism on his brow and eyes, nostrils and lips, both ears, breast, hands, and feet, sealing all with the gift of the Holy Spirit.[1] Gibbes

---

[1] *Service Book of the Holy Orthodox-Catholic Apostolic Church,* comp., tr., and arr. Isabel Florence Hapgood from Old Church Slavonic Service Books of the Russian Church, rpt. (Englewood NJ: Antiochian Orthodox Christian Archdiocese, 1975), pp. 453–467. Tsar Nicholas provided money for the first 1906 edition.

took the baptismal name of Alexei, which he had chosen to honor the Tsarevich.

As Gibbes made his way into the fullness of Orthodox life, he was fortunate to have as his mentor a most remarkable man, Archbishop Nestor of Kamchatka and Petropavlovsk. Fr. Nestor had been a pioneering missionary in the icy wasteland of Kamchatka, facing incredible hardships and dangers to bring the gospel to the pagan peoples living there in ignorance and misery. He arrived in Harbin in 1921, one among many White Russians fleeing the Red Terror, and here too he set about using his energy and experience to set up soup kitchens, orphanages, and hospitals for the émigré community. He had been elevated to the rank of Archbishop by the time of Gibbes's chrismation.

Gibbes's experiences in Manchuria and Manchouli, though pale in comparison with the dangers Fr. Nestor had survived, enabled him to appreciate the monk's solitary missionary work in the frozen wastes. The two men became fast friends, and Archbishop Nestor became Gibbes's spiritual father. He even showed the new convert relics from his Kamchatka mission—a note from Archpriest John Sergiev, later to become St. John of Kronstadt:

> Give to the Kamchatka missionary (I don't know his monastic name) this set of vestments. May God help him. Give also this bottle and tell him that I have drunk more than half of it myself in the course of my life. He is to drink the remainder. Only let him endure everything with patience. May our Lord God bless him and grant him salvation.[2]

---

[2] *Orthodox America*, 62 (Sept.—Dec. 1997): 5.

The rose-colored vestments were threadbare, and the sherry bottle now empty.

Gibbes had found at last the solace for his "longing soul" which the Empress had prayed for in her Christmas poem. He entered the Church and found the Living God dwelling there among His people even more tangibly than with the first Israel in the pillar of cloud and fire. The total focus in this holy space was celebration of the Supreme Mystery, the union of God with His people, His coming to communicate to them His own eternal life. The impact of this encounter dealt a knockout blow to Gibbes's old idea that an absolute, supra-personal god was more intellectually satisfying and spiritual. Everything he had been seeking since his disillusionment with the rationalized Christianity of Cambridge and the rarefied yet self-centered mysticism of the Eastern religions was here.

As usual, it was to Winnie that he tried to express his feelings. He was feeling better, "almost like getting home after a long journey." Later he told her that she would find much that is familiar in Orthodox worship and order. "But," he added, "I find it richer."

If Gibbes had dreaded confronting theology again, his fears were allayed as he realized, to his astonishment and joy, that the truth offered by the Church is not a dogmatic system or a body of intellectual propositions to which the mind assents, but rather an offer of relationship, friendship, with the living Person of Jesus Christ, who not only lives but gives His life to those in the fellowship. Moreover, the great themes of the faith were sung in glorious poetry and hymns presented now in a different key, and he found special joy in this music for the rest of his life.

Another surprise was the promise of life, not in a vague after-life in some far-off world, but rather a new life beginning now in God's Kingdom, established and growing here in enemy territory (which is what the world became when our first ancestors defected and let Satan become the Prince of this world).

Citizenship in God's Kingdom is attained by a rebirth, "not of blood, nor of the will of the flesh, nor of the will of man, but of God" (John 1:13). And these children of God, whether infants, children, adolescents, or adults, are welcomed and lovingly nourished in the Church as they begin the naturalization process of growing into the likeness of God. *Theosis,* or deification, the ecclesiastical terms for this ascent to and recovery of our lost heritage, the restoration of our now-blurred image and attainment of the true likeness of God, is a fundamental doctrine in Orthodoxy. This doctrine made real the Buddhist concept, so attractive to Gibbes, of "remaking" the soul.

Gibbes never ceased exulting in the Church's expression of the union between God and man in the Eucharist, or Holy Communion—even in later years when, as a priest, he celebrated the sacrament alone with only a chanter. His first response to the Mystical Supper was wonderment at its elaborate beauty coupled with disarming humility. The worshipers adorned their building richly, the clergy vested themselves sumptuously and conducted the ceremony in stately wise with lights, incense, banners, everything arranged as fittingly as possible to receive the King of All. But the offerings made to this King were homely bread and wine, the ordinary stuff of life. The loaves came from a family or monastery oven, and the wine was produced by sweaty traditional procedures: cultivating, harvesting, treading, fermenting, and so

on. In an inexplicable mystery the lowly gifts offered from the
earth are accepted and changed by the Holy Spirit into the Body
and Blood of Christ, and, just as He did long ago in Jerusalem,
He Himself comes to serve His guests. The beauty of it all capti-
vated Gibbes, and he resolved to spend the rest of his years drawing his strength and being from this fountain. Once again, no
half-steps for him.

Seeing his zeal, Archbishop Nestor began to encourage Gibbes
along the path toward becoming a monk and a priest, and lent
support when he took the first steps. As a postulant, Brother Alexei
submerged himself in the writings of the Fathers, *The Ladder of
Divine Ascent,* and the *Philokalia.* He spent many hours in prayer
and in self-examination, regretting the years he had squandered
following other paths. Gradually he came to see that the spiritual
life is not limited to monastics or clergy or other "specialists."
Nor does it involve only "spiritual" matters, but every aspect of
ordinary life lived in communion with God, so that peeling potatoes can be as spiritual as painting an icon.

However, monastics try to live the heavenly life even more
intensely than lay Christians. Though there are no institutional
orders such as those familiar in the West, there is a universal
pattern followed by all monks and nuns, whether they live in
community or wage a solitary warfare to subdue the passions of
gluttony, lust, sloth, pride, envy, anger, and avarice. Since man
does not live by bread alone, monastics fast strictly and give up
flesh meat entirely. Since there is no marriage in heaven, they
turn their backs on that relationship and its entanglements. Since
they are to seek the Kingdom of heaven first, they embrace material poverty and set out to follow St. Paul's injunction to pray

without ceasing. For the monastic the beloved is God, and every act is offered in a spirit of loving sacrifice.

Breathing this new air, Brother Alexei began to discern a shape for his own mission, one that might prove to be as lonely and challenging as Archbishop Nestor's in Kamchatka. The Russia he had known and loved lay bleeding and in ruins, stripped of its glories, but he had found a treasure he could escape with and plant in his native land.

The task would not be easy. He knew from his experience at Cambridge and Oxford, with intellectuals in St. Petersburg, with Englishmen and other Western Europeans during the war, that the Orthodox faith was derided in these circles as superstitious and naïve. Even friends and retainers as devoted to the Imperial Family as Lili Dehn and Pierre Gilliard expressed this view in their memoirs. Quite devout Christians, particularly in the West, had come to judge religion by the social and political progress it produced, progress depending more on human effort than on God. In contrast, the Orthodox take seriously the admonition to "lay aside all earthly cares" as they receive the King of All, and their emphasis on holiness rather than material well-being often strikes Western Christians as preposterous.

Gibbes also intended to "foster a good memory" of the Imperial Family. These martyrs had opened his eyes and he was in their debt, yet everywhere he heard them denigrated and even ridiculed. A few members of their circle had published reminiscences, but these impassioned apologies and defenses had little impact on unsympathetic public opinion. No amount of argument or sentimental appeal could convince the Romanovs' detractors. But Gibbes had another plan in mind, one that would require his total dedication, and this he was willing to give.

In December of 1935, Archbishop Nestor professed him a monk as he took his great vows, and Gibbes wrote Winnie later in the spring to describe the ceremony. Dressed in the long, white shroud intended as his burial garment, he stood in the middle of the crowded church.[3] Two archimandrites placed him between them and, each laying one hand on his neck and holding him by the hands with the other, covered him in the folds of their mantles, bent him down as low as possible, and led him toward the archbishop seated by the altar. Brother Alexei could feel the crowd swaying and moving aside as they made their way forward, though he could see only the floor.

When they arrived at the steps before the Royal Doors he bowed to the ground, and was then led to the archbishop for tonsure. The ceremonial scissors lay on the open Gospels. The archbishop asked for them three times; each time the postulant handed them to him and kissed his hand. The third time, the hierarch took a tuft of hair and sheared it first in one direction and then the other in the form of a cross. Gibbes was then vested in the monk's cowl and mantle and given the name of Nicholas in honor of the Tsar. There were many tears in the church, and though "I did not cry myself, I was overcome." After the ceremony, he kept vigil in the church all night. Later that year he was ordained deacon and then priest, to become Fr. Nicholas.

All this while he had been discussing with his mentor plans

---

[3] Fr. Nicholas kept this shroud through the years. However, at the time of his death it could not be located. George had come across it in 1991 just before I visited him and showed it to me.

for founding a monastery in England. Gibbes had been at home on short leave in 1931, when George arrived from Australia. After serious discussions with the young man about what he would like to do with his life, Gibbes set him up on a farm in Stourmouth, Kent, not far from Canterbury. The main house was sturdy and picturesque, surrounded by assorted outbuildings; here George cultivated raspberries, gooseberries, apples, and pears, and even kept some hogs. Fr. Nicholas was intending to establish a monastic foundation on the farm, and since a monastery needs an abbot, he was advanced to that rank in another solemn ceremony.

Fr. Nicholas had the archbishop's blessing as he set out for home, with special instructions to stop for a year at the Russian Orthodox Mission in Jerusalem in order to experience organized monastic life in that Holy City. The mission had been established in the late nineteenth century to minister to the stream of pilgrims arriving from Russia every year. For the devout, this arduous journey on foot over hundreds of miles, beset by hardships and privations beyond our imagining, fulfilled a lifelong dream. All their sufferings were forgotten in the presence of the Holy Places of our Lord's Passion, Crucifixion, Resurrection, and Ascension. After 1917 Russian pilgrims no longer came, but there were still enough monks and nuns to maintain the life of the monasteries and churches. Here too the bodies of Grand Duchess Elizabeth and the nun Barbara were buried. Fr. Nicholas immersed himself in this life completely.

None of the uplifting experiences of the last few years had prepared Fr. Nicholas for the situation in Stourmouth when he arrived there in 1937. George was having fair success with his farming, but it was labor-intensive and absorbed most of his attention. The big problem was that he had started his family, and they were upset by the intrusion of the monastic regimen. The routine of kitchen and dining room was disrupted, and the sitting room was converted into a chapel for the full round of daily services. Fr. Nicholas reserved the original oast-house, once used for curing hops, as his cell and retreated there to sleep and for prayer and meditation, but no matter how earnestly the parties tried, the two ways of life were not compatible. Life in the young family was too boisterous and unpredictable, with eruptions now of exuberance and now of conflict. Fr. Nicholas's presence imposed a restrictive atmosphere that put great strain on everyone.

Within a few months he was considering other arrangements, though he reserved that oast-house for himself as long as George worked the farm. The oldest son, Charles, said he loved to go there when Fr. Nicholas visited because the little conical house had a special fragrance and mystery, and there his adoptive grandfather would tell him stories and read the adventures of *Biggles*.

About this time, Fr. Nicholas was invited to pay a visit to Walsingham, where his close friend, the Rev. Alfred Hope Patten, had supervised restoration of the Anglican Shrine Church. Since medieval times the shrine to Our Lady of Walsingham had drawn pilgrims from all over England, and from Europe as well. The pilgrims still come, and in 1931 the Anglicans built a special pilgrimage church, which they enlarged in 1938.

Fr. Hope Patten showed Fr. Nicholas the spot where he planned to include "an icon corner on the landing of the South Aisle stair-well," but as they viewed the space together, Fr. Nicholas persuaded his friend "that there was enough room to make a small Orthodox chapel provided only two doors were inserted into the iconostasis." [4] With encouragement from the Anglican Administrator of the Shrine Church, Fr. Fynes-Clinton, Fr. Nicholas designed a concave icon screen to provide space for the royal doors. There was no room for angelic doors, but the screen was set out far enough from the east wall for the clergy to enter and exit the altar. When the Shrine Church was consecrated in 1938, Archbishop Nestor and Fr. Nicholas were present, and on the following day, celebrated an Orthodox Liturgy in the church.

At this time there was a plan—probably the brainchild of Fr. Nicholas—to erect an Orthodox chapel beside the Shrine Church, but the war intervened and attention was diverted elsewhere. When the icon screen was completed in 1944, Archbishop Savva of Grodno of the Polish Church-in-Exile consecrated the chapel. Until the death of Archimandrite David, there was a small monastic skete to care for it. Brother Leon still tends the chapel, and Fr. Nicholas is commemorated along with Archbishop Savva as a founder whenever a service is held. [5]

But in 1938 Fr. Nicholas was needed in London, and Metropolitan Seraphim (Lukianoff) attached him to the parish of St. Philip's on Buckingham Palace Road, a building the Anglicans had made available. Here some of the confusion that beset the Russian Orthodox Church after the rise of the Bolsheviks was

---

[4] *The Journal of the Anglican and Eastern Churches Association,* NS33 (1991): 5.

[5] Information furnished through the courtesy of Bishop Kallistos of Diokleia and the late Archimandrite David, Monastery of St. Seraphim of Sarov, Dunton near Fakenham, Norfolk, who with Brother Leon comprised the skete.

evident. The Russian Orthodox in England were divided into two groups. One group was the Russian Church in Exile, while the other was under the jurisdiction of Metropolitan Evlogy, Exarch of Western Europe, with headquarters in Paris. At that time relations were amicable enough for the two congregations to arrange worship services on alternate Sundays.

Metropolitan Evlogy was a central figure in the shifting tides on a sea of ecclesiastical uncertainty. The long, sad story is too complicated to go into here, and the motivations behind many of the decisions and disagreements are unclear.[6] Briefly, in 1920 Patriarch Tikhon had issued a decree from Moscow authorizing the Russian Orthodox bishops to make independent arrangements for administering their dioceses, for he knew that in the present circumstances he would not be free to exercise proper supervision. The following year a conference of twelve bishops met at Karlovtzy in Yugoslavia, where a Synod of Bishops was formed to exercise supreme authority and an Administrative Board appointed to do just what the name implies. All parties, including the Patriarch, seemed satisfied.

Suddenly in 1922, Tikhon, who was now a prisoner of the Bolsheviks, dissolved the Administrative Board and commissioned Metropolitan Evlogy to draw up a new plan. This was taken care of at the meeting of the Karlovtzy Synod that same year. Perhaps because he could not, Tikhon made no comment on the plan, and many concluded that he approved it. However, his successors in Moscow emphatically condemned it, and this generated a

---

[6] The following is summarized from *The Orthodox Church* by Timothy Ware, Bishop Kallistos of Diokleia (London: Penguin Books, 1963, rpt.1983), pp. 182–84.

deep division between those exiled bishops who wanted to distance themselves totally from Moscow and those who felt it important to maintain some contact (without being subservient) while there was still hope that the Bolshevik regime might soon collapse. Evlogy was of the latter persuasion, and when the dissension became too acrimonious he established a separate Paris Jurisdiction in 1926.

His efforts at maintaining some relation with the Patriarch, who was now Sergius, were repaid with censure. Sergius condemned him for praying for persecuted Christians in Russia, contending that there were none. Since he was still at odds with the Synod, Evlogy placed himself and his flock under the care of the Ecumenical Patriarch in Constantinople. He made an attempt at reconciliation with the Karlovtzy Synod in 1934, but it was short-lived.

This is how matters stood when Fr. Nicholas arrived in London in 1938, but any animosities were overshadowed by the presence of Archbishop Nestor, his mentor from Harbin. Nestor had been in Europe for the All-Emigration Church Sobor (Council) summoned by the Council of Bishops. He now came to London to present the new priest to his people, to raise him to the rank of archimandrite, and to confer on him the miter and staff. Fr. Nicholas was the first Englishman to receive this honor. The beginning of his London ministry was auspicious.

Close by St. Philip's was the Church House, owned by the Exile Church, in which the parish priest resided and where Fr. Nicholas had a basement flat. A small monastic community flourished there in which he could participate as his other duties allowed.

Fr. Nicholas's primary responsibility was a community of English-speaking Orthodox on Bayswater Road. He was immensely pleased, for this was just the sort of opportunity he had been wanting. He had already made English translations of many of the services. However, he urgently needed a choir, for without the music his congregation would not be able to savor the full splendor of Orthodox worship. As he looked about, he happened to hear of a young women's vocal group in Yugoslavia who were anxious to get to England. They needed an English teacher and he needed a choir, so he set about making the necessary arrangements for their passage and lodging in exchange for their singing in his choir. They knew the hymns in Church Slavonic, and Fr. Nicholas made English translations that would exactly fit the music they were familiar with. The arrangement was a happy one, and the young women gained some measure of fame as the "Belgrade Nightingales."[7] After World War II broke out, the young women were unable to return home, and most of them settled permanently in London.

The war also brought a change for Fr. Nicholas. When the Germans began their blitz on London in 1941, he was called away from London, where relations at St. Philip's were no longer cordial, to Oxford to organize a community of émigrés who had fled to the university town—translators, BBC commentators, scholars. This congenial assignment, however, became part of the widening breach between the different Russian jurisdictions, another tragic twentieth-century upheaval in which

---

[7] Much of the information here and above on the London situation was furnished through the courtesy of Protodeacon Christopher Birchall from his as yet unpublished history of the Orthodox Church in London.

Fr. Nicholas found himself involved.

In 1943 Stalin issued his policy of religious toleration, a thoroughly hypocritical act of political expediency aimed at improving morale and stimulating patriotism as the Russian people faced invasion by the powerful German war machine. Stalin's deceit was not then apparent, and in a swell of patriotic fervor for their suffering homeland and oppressed Church, many Russian émigrés wanted to believe in it. Metropolitan Evlogy was swept up in the same enthusiasm, though he did not actually submit to the Moscow Patriarch until 1945, a short time before he died. Though Fr. Nicholas could not have known it during these vexed years because of the strict Russian censorship, his beloved friend Archbishop Nestor had also submitted to the Patriarchate, and was persuaded in 1948 to come to Moscow—only to be sent immediately to the gulag.

Meanwhile, Fr. Nicholas went to work with his new congregation. They met in a borrowed chapel that had once been attached to a medieval hospital for lepers, St. Bartelmas, bordering the playing fields of Oriel College. The interesting mix of people made for a lively parish life, and they were thriving vigorously when the war ended. As students streamed back to college, Oriel needed the chapel once more, and Fr. Nicholas set out to find permanent quarters.

He located three very suitable cottages on Marston Street, just off Cowley Road in East Oxford, and invested most of his life savings to purchase them. One of the buildings had once housed a charity dispensing medicines to poor patients and during the war had served as the central telephone office for all of Oxfordshire. In this sturdy building, Fr. Nicholas took up residence on the second floor and established a chapel on the ground floor.

It was 1946, the year of Metropolitan Evlogy's death, when Fr. Nicholas established St. Nicholas House as a personal declaration of his veneration for the Tsar who was sacred to him. (The house was formally dedicated to St. Nicholas of Myra, a Father of the Church.) As soon as Fr. Nicholas had repaired the building, he brought out from the trunks and boxes he had been guarding for almost thirty years and had carried halfway round the world an astonishing collection of relics of the Imperial Family and reminders of the terrible regicide. Most of the relics had been gathered from the ruins of Ipatiev House in 1918 with the permission of General Dieterichs.

In the center of the chapel Fr. Nicholas hung a chandelier of pink blown-glass lilies suspended among metallic green leaves and a spray of violets; this had once adorned a bedroom in their last prison house. Within the altar area he placed a pair of the Tsar's felt boots that he had packed in his own luggage the day he and the family remnant left Tobolsk for Ekaterinburg, thinking the Tsar might need them; but he never saw the Tsar again. Along the walls he mounted his collection of icons, some given to him by members of the Imperial Family and some salvaged from the fireplaces and dustbins in Ipatiev House. In that chapel the Tsar, Tsaritsa, Tsarevich, and Grand Duchesses were commemorated at every service.

This purchase and renovation were very costly and used up the savings Gibbes had accumulated during the months of exile with the Imperial Family and in the service of the High Commissioner, when living expenses were minimal. During this time Gibbes had regularly sent most of his salary to his brother Percy to bank as advantageously as possible. He also had a civil service pension from his years in the Chinese Maritime Customs. The extent of his personal sacrifice can be seen from a letter written in 1949 to Prof. de Schmidt, a man of shared sympathies who had established a Russian Orthodox Center in New York City.

> At the end of 1946 I bought this House for 2,500-0-0 [pounds] of which I paid 750-0-0 and raised the rest by mortgage. I have spent a good deal of money in modernizing the House, which was used for war purposes during the last War and was in very poor shape.
>
> The Orthodox colony in Oxford is not more than 50 or 60 church-goers and there are no people who are really well off. Contributions about cover the current expenses, so instead of using the House as a museum and cultural center for meetings and lectures, we must let nearly all the accommodations in order to pay off the mortgage. I myself receive no salary from the congregation and live on my own savings, not an easy task now-a-days.

At the professor's request he enclosed a short article on his life with the Imperial Family that ended with a clear statement of his intentions.

> St. Nicholas House in Oxford is an endeavour to carry the light of this faith to the chief intellectual and cultural center of the British Empire. The House contains several

relics of the last days of the Imperial Family and is in a way a memorial for the repose of their souls in that heavenly kingdom, where is neither strife, nor sorrow but life everlasting.

Though Fr. Nicholas was reluctant to speak or write about the family, when he did he never failed to mention their piety and saintliness as well as their nobility in suffering. He had hoped to use the three Oxford houses to create a museum, using his own store of memorabilia to attract exhibits from others, and as a Russian cultural center for lectures, readings, and retreats; but the financial situation never permitted this. However, he did turn the library-study just behind the chapel into a miniature museum. Here he displayed many of the photographs he had made in Tsarskoe Selo, Tobolsk, and Ekaterinburg, along with the exercise books of Marie and Anastasia, some pieces of porcelain dinnerware from Tobolsk bearing the imperial crest, a pencil case that had once belonged to the Tsarevich, a bell he had played with, a brass coat-of-arms from the yacht *Standart*, a collection of sleigh bells, and numerous other items he had saved.

Fr. Nicholas served the community in St. Nicholas House faithfully and became well known both in Orthodox circles, where he was an impressive figure—tall and slim with a fine white beard—and in Oxford, where he appeared more eccentric. A tribute published in the *Cardiff Western Mail* on March 27, 1963, shortly after his death, gives an idea of his unconventional and far-reaching efforts to spread "the light of this faith" and the impression he made on those who met him.

The death in London of Archimandrite Nicholas Gibbes means the abandonment of the plan to establish a branch of the Russian Orthodox Church in Wales.

"Having started a small church in Oxford . . . he was anxious to have one in Wales," Miss Jennie Williams, the authority on folk music—she is vice-president of the Folk Song Society—said yesterday at her Hampstead home.

"He believed that the people of Wales would be most sympathetic to the Russian Orthodox type of service because it is not only very beautiful in form but entirely unaccompanied and therefore ideal for a nation like the Welsh. Although a member of the Welsh Presbyterian Church I was so impressed by his enthusiasm for Wales that I promised to rally all possible support for what seemed a most exciting prospect.

"In view of his death, however, it would be pointless to pursue the matter."

With his easy affability Gibbes made many friends in Oxford. Especially close was George Katkov, a Russian scholar who happened to be a specialist on German influences during World War I. Here was a man with whom Fr. Nicholas felt free to discuss his experiences with the Imperial Family. In examining many of the secret German documents available after World War II, Katkov had discovered how deeply Germany was involved in subsidizing subversive forces to undermine Nicholas II and supply ammunition for his political enemies during the first war. The two men often talked deep into the dawn hours, and then Fr. Nicholas would make the long walk home as the sun was rising.[8]

≈ ≈

World War II had also brought change for George. As a resident alien he was forced to leave the farm on the coast, and the family moved into Camden Town. At this time he gave up his Russian name, Paveliev, took the name Gibbes, and joined the RAF. After the war George went to work as a salesman for several book publishers. Whenever he could manage it, Fr. Nicholas visited the family, and grandson Charles confided that the visits were not very eagerly awaited—chiefly because the radio was turned off, and he in his adolescence was embarrassed when he had to go shopping with this strange figure in black robes and white beard. As the boys, Charles and Andrew, grew older these matters resolved themselves, and they often accompanied George to Oxford to make repairs on the houses there, houses that would one day be their inheritance.

Fr. Nicholas was sixty-five when he arrived in Oxford in 1941, and by 1952 he felt the need of some assistance. He described the situation to his old friend Baroness Buxhoeveden in 1956, after failing health had forced at least semi-retirement.

> Your letter reached me here where I have a little flatlet near to Regents Park and in the orbit of the Academic center round the University of London from whence the other tenants of this house also come.

---

[8] George Katkov, *Revolution 1917: The February Revolution* (New York: Harper & Row, 1967) gives the full story of the German involvement and a sympathetic treatment of Tsar Nicholas II.

Here I spend most of my time when duty does not detain me in Oxford, where the Orthodox Institution I have founded appears to be taking root. It is now 4 years past since I invited a son of Stolypin's Minister of Agriculture [Krivochein] to come to me from Mt. Athos where he had spent 25 years as a monk since taking his degree at the Sorbonne. These years were passed in the study of MSS of the Patristic Fathers and Father Basil is now a scholar of some eminence still pursuing the same course. In the second year of his arrival I arranged for his ordination and appointed him as Chaplain. Since when he has taken on all the duties of the chapel, which has set me free to come and go as necessary.

He does not mention the illnesses that plagued him with pain so severe that he tried extreme measures to get some relief, using almost half his tiny flatlet to install a sauna bath, in which he would spend hours.

Nor does he mention another deliberate decision he had made in 1945, a decision which would affect his Oxford ministry in ways he did not anticipate. In that year he submitted to the Moscow Patriarchate, convinced that its reinstatement would mean a wholesome alteration in the Russian Orthodox Church polity by restoring the church's autonomy. The Patriarchate had been abolished by Peter the Great, who established in its place a Synod of Bishops over which he had total control, and in the serious attempts at reform just before the Great War and the Revolution, restoration of the Patriarchate had been a primary aim.

Fr. Nicholas's decision caused shock and dismay among his

friends in the Russian Church in Exile, and resulted in a painful isolation. He could no longer concelebrate or take communion in the parish where he had been so deeply involved and was sincerely loved. Even so, according to his friend, John Harwood, he always seemed more at home at the Cathedral of the Dormition Emperor's Gate than in the Patriarchal church.

There were also unsettling repercussions in the Oxford community. After the war, most of the émigrés departed, and it became clear to the church leaders that if Orthodoxy was to flourish in Oxford it could not be at Marston Street. In 1959 the Russian Parish Council decided to move to Canterbury Road, where Dr. Nicholas Zernov had established the House of St. Basil and St. Macrina, site of the present Holy Trinity and Annunciation Church in Oxford. Fr. Basil Krivochein, who would later become Archbishop, moved as well. Fr. Nicholas was deeply hurt, but there was little he could do.[9]

But these last years were brightened by several young friends. One, a staunch young Anglo-Catholic, Peter Lascelles, was well known in London church circles because of his attendance at Anglican, Roman Catholic, and Orthodox churches in turn. He had studied theology at Halki in Istanbul and knew the Orthodox services and music. He became greatly attached to Fr. Nicholas and helped him in many ways, driving him around and chanting for him when he served the Liturgy, sometimes alone in Oxford or in small chapels like the one in Walsingham. While Fr. Nicholas sang the service in English and Slavonic, Lascelles

---

[9] Information through the courtesy and assistance of Bishop Kallistos of Diokleia, who shares the church on Canterbury Road with Bishop Basil of Sergievo.

chanted in a very nasal Byzantine Greek style, but this curious mix produced no dissonance. The friendship must have had a lasting influence on Lascelles because, two weeks before his death in the 1990s, he was received into the Orthodox faith and is buried at Fr. Sophrony's monastic foundation in Essex.[10]

The trips back and forth from London to Oxford continued even after Fr. Nicholas's strength had begun to ebb. When David Beattie came to study classics and then Russian at Lincoln College in Oxford, he heard intriguing stories of Fr. Nicholas, and began to note with interest a black-robed figure he thought might be the man. Quite unexpectedly in 1961, only two years before Fr. Nicholas died, they met while Beattie was attending a festival occasion at an Anglican church in London. While having tea and sherry in the vicarage, he saw through the window an unexpected guest coming up the garden path. It was none other than Fr. Nicholas, who often called on the vicar when in London. He was introduced to Beattie, who had just returned from Moscow, where he had been interpreter at the first British Trade and Industry Fair, and the two fell into conversation.

Sensing Beattie's sympathy toward the Imperial Family, Fr. Nicholas spent an hour telling of his life with them, extolling the solid virtues of the Tsar and Tsaritsa and expressing his affection for the Tsarevich, so brave and high-spirited in his suffering. Only as the party was ending did Beattie learn that he "had been greatly honored," for the former tutor rarely spoke of the family.[11]

---

[10] I am indebted to John Harwood, who supplied this information.

[11] I am indebted to David Beattie, Ambassador in the British Diplomatic Service, for sharing the notes he made on his encounters with Fr. Nicholas.

During these last two years, in which they had only three meetings, Beattie took notes that provide many engaging vignettes. In May 1962, during traditional Ascension Day celebrations at Lincoln College, he happened to spot Fr. Nicholas and went over to greet him. The archimandrite was in Oxford trying to sell two of his cottages, since he was prohibited by law from raising the rents, though he still had mortgage payments to make and prices for necessities were inflated.

Later in the day, after the festivities were over, the priest came to call on Beattie on the chance that his new friend might be lonely. Beattie could see that Fr. Nicholas was rapidly losing strength and this might well be their last meeting. The man was thinner and more hunched than before, but,

> his face was delightful; very rosy cheeks, twinkling bright blue eyes and a snow-white beard, rather straggly and not thick, coming roughly to a point at the middle of his chest. He was a lucid and witty talker, his mind perfectly clear. He struck me as being at once simple but practical. He was no mystic. In spite of his history and appearance he was entirely English in his practical approach to mundane matters and in his sense of humour. . . . He had plenty of natural authority; he was a man to be appreciated and not argued with.

Beattie's description of his attire comes as a shock. After all the years of meticulous attention to his appearance and grooming, he was now very humbly dressed.

Indeed, he wore what looked rather like a collection of

rags. His main garment was a threadbare old cassock. His right hand held a stick [his staff] and on his left arm there hung a disreputable large black shopping bag.

Despite his appearance, Fr. Nicholas was not altogether penniless. He still owned property, though he gained nothing from it. The Oxford cottages were mortgaged and dedicated to the chapel. A house in Broadstairs seems to have been a kind of rescue mission for Russians, and perhaps others, who had fallen upon hard times; the Regent's Park flat he reserved for himself was minuscule. He invited Beattie to stop at Broadstairs whenever he was in London, and should the house be full he could have the hayloft.

At that last meeting a bit of Gibbes's wry humor came out. All who saw him noted his remarkably clear skin even at age eighty-six, and he offered to let Beattie in on his secret.

Have you ever observed the ways of the **serpent**? He sheds his skin regularly, and that's just what I do. In my flat in London I have a very strong electric fire and a very small cubicle. I turn on the fire and wait until the cubicle is very hot. Then I take off all my clothes, pour water all over myself, and go and sit in the cubicle. Very soon all my skin falls off and I come out young again. But do you know (this with an amused and quizzical glance), I can't find any pupils to follow my example.

After this, Fr. Nicholas's health continued to deteriorate rapidly, and he died on March 24, 1963, in St. Pancras Hospital.

According to John Harwood, who visited him several times with Lascelles during those last months, though he was old, frail, and poor he was still smiling. And well he might, for he had done what he set out to do: he spent himself and his resources to witness to the sanctity and nobility of the royal martyrs and to the truth and beauty of their Orthodox faith.

After his death, David Beattie and a friend called on George Gibbes at the London flat to inquire whether there was any danger that Fr. Nicholas's papers and the imperial relics might be dispersed. George assured them that this would not happen, and then conducted them into the priest's small bedroom to see the icon hanging over the bed. It was one given him by the Imperial Family and, according to George, over the years its colors had become dull and faded. Then, during the three days before Fr. Nicholas's death, the colors gradually came back to their original brightness. It was as if the Imperial Family had sent a gift from heaven to reward Fr. Nicholas for his long and devoted service and friendship, both during their lifetime and after their death.

Appendix

On the Tsar and Sainthood

The Russian Church Abroad canonized the imperial martyrs in 1981, while Moscow Patriarch Alexey II has hesitated to grant such recognition. In 1997, when controversy arose about the burial of the remains of the Imperial Family finally unearthed in Ekaterinburg, the hierarch was quoted in the *Orthodox Observer* (Sept. 1997) as saying "that Czar Nicholas II and his family did not deserve that honor because of the way they ruled the country and led the church before being executed in 1918. 'His life, his actions . . . the first Russian revolution, abdication—all of this is regarded by the church and society in an ambivalent way.'" He went on to express doubts about the identification of the skeletal remains which had been determined by DNA testing, referring to them as "the Yekaterinburg remains."[1] When their burial took place in St. Petersburg, the Patriarch did not attend, though he did conduct a private memorial service in Moscow.

Fr. Nicholas had declared his belief in their sanctity decades earlier, but as was his custom he did it with deeds rather than words. So it might be well to spend a few words on the subject of the Tsar and sainthood.

Nicholas II has been widely dismissed as a weak, inept ruler who led his country to disaster, a disaster that could have been avoided by granting a constitution and initiating a more democratic government. But those charges will not stand, for his difficulties were too intractable. His fate was to be caught in the collision between two worlds locked in mortal combat, combat that destroyed him and the older world he loved and had sworn to defend. Had he had a tougher, more confrontational temperament and had he been capable of political maneuvering and intrigue, he might have

---

[1] *Time Magazine* (July 27, 1998), p. 34.

sustained the defense a while longer, but it is hard to see how he could ultimately have triumphed. The forces set loose against him were too huge, too ruthless, too pervasive, and had insinuated themselves into his own stronghold.

The battle lines had been formed long before Nicholas came to the throne, when the Western world embraced in varying degrees a socialist democratic ideology, putting its trust in enlightened social legislation and economic prosperity to transform the human race into unselfish, conscientious citizens fit for a new order. Faith in this enticing secular-humanist vision was rapidly displacing traditional religion. In the anticipated new world where man would be able to control not only himself but nature as well, the Kingdom of Heaven was becoming obsolete, and any attention spent trying to achieve it diverted energy from the urgently exciting prospect of a commonwealth in which man himself would call the shots. The concept of deification would give way to sensitive socialization, and government's role would be to respond to the will of an empowered people—but a people who had turned their backs on God.

This surging tide of aroused expectations had burst full force against Russia several decades before Nicholas became emperor, but his upbringing, his heart, and his deepest instincts bound him to the old order that "did not glorify the individual or believe in one's right to choose one's own path in life." Though he did not, perhaps could not, articulate the theological and political implications of the onslaught, Nicholas understood them in his bones, and his response was thoroughly Russian, thoroughly Orthodox. He saw catastrophe ahead and assumed the role fate had assigned him in fear and trembling, knowing it might cost him everything; but he fully believed in the role of the tsar for Russia and dedicated himself to fulfilling it. His coronation was "a religious service of communion, binding together God, the Tsar, and the Orthodox people." Nicholas asked God "to direct, counsel and guide him in his service as Tsar and Judge of the Russian Empire, to keep his heart in the will of God, to help him so to order all to the good of his people and the glory of God, that at the day of Judgment he may answer without shame." He privately renewed this vow almost daily.[2]

The traditionalists were too aware of mankind's corrupted nature to trust in legislation to refashion it. As for the democratic process, it seemed to open the door to anarchy, as individuals demanded that the government serve their personal interests, even base and selfish ones, and ambitious politicians pandered to the mythical "will of the people." The Russia the traditionalists knew needed a tsar.

A dauntingly complex situation faced Nicholas. The anti-establishment forces anxious to eliminate the autocracy and join the secular-humanist wave were concentrated in the cities—St. Petersburg, Moscow, Kiev. They comprised intellectuals who had drunk from the wells of French and German political theory, as well as aristocrats who had traveled abroad and were now impatient at what they saw as their homeland's backwardness.

Out beyond the cities were the peasants, who made up four-fifths of the population and were a separate and distinct cultural group—but not the downtrodden, dispirited folk who peopled the dreams of the socialist democrats. In fact, the peasants were hostile to the revolutionaries who came out to indoctrinate them. "There is no indication that the peasant regarded serfdom, which so appalled the intellectuals, as an intolerable burden."[3] The peasants' grievances were not political; they wanted the land, and since the emancipation of the serfs in 1865 and the reforms begun by Stolypin, they expected the Tsar to be granting it any day. After that they would go on living as before in their village communes.

These villages were actually small, nearly autonomous units governed by patriarchal codes of conduct, where individual rights counted for nothing and the will of the communal family prevailed. The arm of the tsarist government reached in only to collect taxes and recruits for the army. The peasants' way of life may have seemed grueling, harsh, and squalid to outsiders, but not to the sturdy, resilient peasant, whose misfortunes and blessings came from nature and were accepted with a certain resignation and grace. Their colorful,

---

[2] Lieven, *Nicholas II*, pp. 43, 64.
[3] Pipes, *Revolution*, p. 116.

elaborately embroidered costumes, the exuberant carvings hewn during winter's lull, the lusty folk songs and dances witness to their rough but vibrant spirit.

Their labor itself had a ritual.

> Boris and Gleb must be invoked before the autumn sowing, which must be completed for their feast-day. . . . Basil is the protector of pigs, Cosmas and Damian cure the ailments of poultry, Zosimus is associated with bees, Jeremiah looks after tools, Florus and Laurus are guardians of horses. Anastasius keeps a favourable eye on sheep; and there are many more such. . . . If there is superstition here, it is no more marked than the sort we meet in other lands. But is this not rather an embellishment of the patterns of life—every action tied to some ceremony, so many days lifted out of the general monotony, every job devoutly allocated its patron saint and so enriched with significance?[4]

Nicholas put great faith in these sturdy folk he considered "the true Russians." The problem was that they were apolitical, and though they deeply reverenced the God-anointed Tsar, they had no concept of patriotism, no sense of commitment to the country beyond their village, and so were incapable of any concerted support for him.

The intellectuals in the cities were much more militant. After the manifesto of 1905 granting freedom of the press, newspapers and periodicals set about systematically destroying the authority and dignity of the autocracy with a campaign of false rumors. These rumor-mongers specialized in tales of Rasputin's influence on the Tsar and his relations with the Tsaritsa, Alexandra's German connections, and during the war when things were going badly, accusations of treason against the Emperor and the Empress. When the Provisional Government conducted extensive investigations of the charges after the abdication, not a shred of proof could be found, but the terrible

---

[4] Pierre Pascal, *The Religion of the Russian People* (Crestwood, NY: St. Vladimir's Seminary Press, 1976), pp. 19–20.

damage had been done. The press also provided a medium for the Tsar's political opponents to keep up an incessant stream of criticism to show how behind the times and out of step he was.

The Western world had no intention of tolerating a Tsar who was an autocrat, and even as he fought as their ally in the Great War, they despised him. When the Duma was instituted and a limited constitution drawn up in 1905, the British Labor Party sent a delegation to St. Petersburg to congratulate and encourage them to press on. This event prompted Nicholas to comment to his mother, "How angry they would be if a deputation went from us to the Irish to wish them success in their struggle against their Government."[5]

The French Ambassador, Paléologue, reflecting archly on "so much that is archaic and backward, primitive and out-of-date in the social and political institutions of Russia," concluded that Europe would be in the same state if they had had "no Renaissance, no Reformation, no French Revolution"![6] He was correct, the Orthodox world had been fortunate enough to escape such upheavals. A U.S. commentator in *The Nation* described the autocracy as "a concrete and visible danger to the free and peaceful development of the entire world."[7]

For all this calumny, Nicholas II was no power-hungry despot; he deeply loved his people and earnestly desired their welfare. He was constantly bombarded with advice to achieve it by opening the door to progressive forces, but he saw this as the way to spiritual ruin; he dismayed some of his friends and all of his foes by standing immovable in the entryway. He knew his people were still deeply Christian and not yet the mass of politically awakened people demanding liberation imagined by the Western liberals and romantically dramatized by the revolutionaries; and he truly believed they were not ready for constitutional government. He had had grave misgivings when he signed the manifesto of 1905, for his coronation oath prevented his transferring personal responsibility into other hands, and the Fundamental Laws of

---

[5] Bing, *The Secret Letters,* p. 15.

[6] Paléologue, *Memoirs,* p. 156.

[7] *Nation,* 104 (March 29, 1917): 361.

the land had no provision for making the sovereign subject to legislative authority.

Moreover, Russia had serious problems not faced by the Western democratic states. The emerging middle class was too new and too small to lead the way into participatory democracy, and the population consisted of so many diverse ethnic and cultural groups that it was impossible to discover "a Russian people" or "a Russian culture." The symbolic, sacred power of the tsar provided the single unifying factor.

Nicholas's fate placed him in that role in a season of fury, but for him fate represented God's will. He was ready to submit to its agonies as well as its glories—he fully expected its agonies. He often reminded his friends and his ministers that he had been born on the day of Job the Much-Suffering, adding that he felt some severe trial awaited him and that he would not receive his reward in this life. As Pares explains, his "strong and fatalistic conception of his anointed mission took the direction that he was before all things the victim, the sufferer for his people."[8]

The Tsar expressed this same understanding of his role in the hearing of Paléologue—possibly on the same occasion—as he explained the decision to take command of the army. " 'Perhaps a scapegoat is needed to save Russia. I mean to be the victim. May the will of God be done.' He was very pale when he said this, but on his face was an expression of utter resignation."[9]

One of the knottiest problems on the docket was land reform. Everyone knew it had to be addressed, but how? The peasants were clamoring for land, but they could not be allowed to seize it. The landowners had to be compensated, and the difficult, delicate transition handled in an orderly fashion.

These thorny issues simmered in an atmosphere of tension created by hostile political challengers and revolutionary terrorists who never let up in their campaign of violence and assassination. When war erupted in 1914, requiring all the nation's attention and resources, Nicholas declared his

---

[8] Pares, *Russian Monarchy*, p. 240.

[9] Paléologue, *Memoirs*, p. 65. Paléologue often embellished remarks made to him in order to maintain his own engaging style, but the substance of this recollection rings true.

intention to grant a constitution and proceed with land reform, but insisted that these matters had to be carefully worked out after the Germans had been defeated. Since the Tsar was betrayed before this could be achieved, we will never know what Russia's future might have been.

Many historians have concluded that Nicholas was the wrong ruler at the wrong time, but such an assessment does not take into account the true stature of the man. His failings as a leader were not the ones for which he is usually maligned. Some dismiss him as a simpleton when he was actually very intelligent, able to grasp at once matters that were presented to him. He was fluent in French, German, English, and Russian and had an exceptional memory. He was not a master politician, having been trained more as a soldier than a statesman, but he worked diligently to understand the bewildering challenges facing him, reading every report sent by his ministers and struggling with his conscience over the decisions required. His refusal to pursue progressive political policies was perceived as retarded political understanding, which put him at odds with hostile forces rapidly gaining strength.

Nicholas's astonishing self-control, so often remarked, had not been easily won, for he was subject to what we call panic attacks. In August 1896 he wrote his mother, "I had one of my fits of nerves, which reminded me of the old days when I got them before every review. I felt green and trembled all over. When four battalions and the Artillery had drunk my health, I felt better and tried to look cheerful, especially when talking to the officers after lunch." He reports the same problem on his arrival in Paris for his state visit.[10] And yet the steady calm he finally achieved was often interpreted as weakness or indecision by those who expected flamboyance, self-assertion, even anger from the Tsar. As Alexandra wrote ruefully to her sister, "He has learnt the hard lesson of self-control, only to be called weak; people forget that the greatest conqueror is he who conquers himself."[11] This composure served him well during the hard years of war and the heartbreak of the abdication; it steadied his family during the dark days of their captivity.

---

[10] Bing, *Secret Letters*, pp. 108, 113.
[11] Lieven, *Nicholas II*, p. 108.

"To be happy at home," said Samuel Johnson, "is the end of all human endeavor," but even Nicholas's domestic happiness was mocked in the sophisticated social circles of the capital. And yet the strength of the family's love and faith shines in every account of their steady good humor during the months when they were confined in close quarters, facing day after monotonous day, each one with twenty-four hours to be got through.

Even the Tsar's piety and that of his family were derided, though it was deep and genuine and the source of all their other virtues. Nicholas may have placed too much confidence in the power of good to triumph in the world and been too slow to see evil even in his enemies, but as he often explained, he was so little troubled because he placed himself and his people in God's hands and trusted that his efforts would be blessed and his nation would prosper. What a test then, when in spite of all his prayers and his trust in God's mercy, the forces of evil were winning, spoiling the costly victories of the war and ravaging his country, and he and his dearest ones were prisoners. Even in the face of such contradiction the family's faith never wavered, and as we have seen, they were able to forgive their tormentors. Do they get no credit for that?

St. Silouan the Athonite held that love for one's enemies is the sole authentic criterion of truth.

> The bidding, 'Love your enemies,' is the 'fire on the earth' that the Lord brought by His coming (cf. Luke 12:49). It is the uncreated Divine Light which shone down on the Apostles on Mt. Tabor. . . . It is the Kingdom of God in us 'come with power' (Mark 9:1). It is the fulfillment of the human being and the perfection of likeness to God (cf. Matt. 5:44-48.)[12]

In 988 Prince Vladimir led his Russia into the Orthodox faith. At his death two of his sons, Boris and Gleb, learned that their elder brother Sviatopolk, unwilling to share power, intended to eliminate them and their

---

[12] Quoted by Archimandrite Sophrony in selections from *St. Silouan the Athonite* in *Divine Ascent: A Journal of Orthodox Faith*, No. 5. 1999, p. 24.

eight brothers. Instead of rallying their troops and fighting Sviatopolk, they decided to follow Christ's example and give themselves up to his henchmen in order to spare the lives of their followers. Their example captured the hearts of the people, and Boris and Gleb became the first Russian saints.

As a dark shadow passed over the Russian land in 1917, eclipsing for a season the Christian faith, the last Tsar followed in the footsteps of those first passion-bearers and relinquished his throne to preserve unity among the people and rally the support necessary for victory over Germany. "During these decisive days for the life of Russia, WE considered it a duty of conscience to facilitate OUR people's close unity and the rallying of all popular forces in order to achieve victory as quickly as possible, and, in agreement with the State Duma, WE consider it to be for the good to abdicate from the Throne of the Russian State and to surrender supreme command."[13] His loyal, courageous family followed him to imprisonment and death. Now they are praying together for Russia.

---

[13] Steinberg and Khrustalev, *Fall,* pp. 100–101.

Index

K

Kaledin, General Alexei 211
Karlovtzy Synod 263–264
Kate, Aunt 205, 208, 226–227, 237–238
Katkov, George 103n., 270–271
Kerensky, Alexander 155, 156, 163, 168, 169, 175
   becomes leader of Provisional Government 142–143
   decides to send Imperial Family to Tobolsk 149–150
Khabalov, General Sergei 114–115
Kharitonov, Ivan 191, 192, 197, 198, 241
Knox, General Alfred 83–85, 210, 216
Kobilinsky, Colonel Yevgeny 134, 156, 158, 160, 163, 174, 187
Kolchak, Admiral Alexander 207, 215–216, 217, 219–220, 223, 224
Kornilov, General Lavr 132–133, 134, 168, 211, 213
Krivoshein, Fr. Basil 272, 273

L

Lampson, Miles 228, 231
Lascelles, Peter 273, 274, 277
Lenin, Vladimir Ilyich 161n., 168, 176–177, 221, 222–223
Lewes, G. Henry 16
Lloyd George, David 149, 223

M

Maria (Rasputina). *See* Solovieva (Rasputina) Maria
Marie, Dowager Empress 45, 122, 283, 285
Marie, Grand Duchess 39, 52, 53, 80, 112, 127, 140, 150, 165–167, 178, 180, 186, 193
Medvedev, Pavel 197
Michael, Grand Duke 79–80, 120, 121, 150
Miliukov, Pavel 107
Myasoedov, Colonel S. N. 103

N

Nagorny, Klementy G. 155, 189, 190
Nestor, Archbishop 254, 257, 258, 259–260, 262, 265, 266
Nicholas (Nicholai), Grand Duke 87–88, 90–91, 104–105, 230
Nicholas II, Tsar 193, 198
   response to Bloody Sunday 34–35
   approves creation of Duma 64–65
   orders full mobilization against Austria and Germany 78–79
   assumes military command in World War I 90–92, 104–105
   abdication of planned by Guchkov 107
   accusations of treason against 107
   abdication of 116–123
   arrest of 122–123
   assessment of his reign and character 279–287
   See also Imperial Family
Nikolsky, Alexander 163, 175

About the Author

Christine Benagh makes her home in Nashville, Tennessee. After earning her degree from Vanderbilt University, she began serious writing while overseeing the household for her husband and four lively children. As their demands on her time and attention diminished, she took up a career in editing and continued writing, publishing two books, several journal articles, and numerous book reviews.

Her interest in Fr. Nicholas Gibbes was aroused by his spiritual journey from the Anglican Church to Orthodoxy, since she had made a similar journey, though without as many exciting adventures along the way. Tracking Gibbes from England, through Russia, and beyond provided ample satisfaction for her interest in matters historical and theological.

CPSIA information can be obtained
at www.ICGtesting.com
Printed in the USA
FFOW01n0135220216
21708FF